D1381305

Josceline Dimbleby's Complete Cookbook

Josceline Dimbleby's Complete Cookbook

HarperCollins*Publishers*

First published in 1997 by
HarperCollins*Publishers* London

Text © Josceline Dimbleby 1997
Photographs © HarperCollins*Publishers* 1997
All rights reserved

Josceline Dimbleby asserts the moral right to
be identified as the author of this work

Editor: Jane Middleton
Designer: Graeme Andrew
Food photographs: Simon Smith
Assistant: Howard Shooter
Home Economists: Lucy Knox, Sarah Lowman
Stylist: Clare Hunt
All other photographs: Michelle Garrett
Indexer: Susan Bosanko

For HarperCollins*Publishers*
Commissioning Editor: Barbara Dixon

A catalogue record for this book is available
from the British Library

ISBN 0 00 414012 5

Typeset in Stone sans
Colour reproductions by Saxon Photolitho Ltd
Printed and bound in Italy

contents

introduction

To me, food means sensual, visual and oral pleasure, creativity and discovery, fun and adventure, conviviality and friendship – and, most importantly, the enjoyment of life. This book spans a large part of my adult life and much of my children's childhood. Choosing and revising the recipes I created for my column in *The Sunday Telegraph* has brought back memories, encapsulated moments and revived emotions – all in the way that the tastes and smells of food can do so evocatively. The result is, I feel, a veritable orgy of all the things I like best and which I think have made others happy too.

Not only my children were brought up on culinary experiments while I conceived these recipes; constantly at my side as I cooked for 12 of the last 15 years, my cats, Olive and Hilda, have been treated to many scraps, even apparently enjoying some quite spicy morsels. And, of course, my husband and many friends gave their seal of approval to all sorts of newly tried-out ideas. I find that my recipes nearly always work out better if I am cooking specifically for people, rather than just testing.

At school I failed dismally in the cookery lessons that formed part of our 'domestic science' class. Miss Gregson, our teacher, threw up her hands in horror at the sight of my rock buns, and gave me a look of despair when she saw the half-hearted way I washed the floor. But the cause of my failure was lack of inspiration: when I tasted food abroad, and realized, too, what my mother and grandmother could produce in the kitchen, I saw that cooking could be a way of being creative, and of giving pleasure both to oneself and to others.

I also link food with music. Since my student days, when I studied singing, I have come across many musicians who seem

deeply interested in food and eating. Perhaps the mixture of creativity, sensitivity and sensuality that is needed to produce good music can also be applied to being able to cook an exceptional meal. However, as my mother and grandmother were both painters, I think this theory can encompass artists too.

The last 15 years could hardly have been a more exciting time to be involved in the world of food. The interest in food and the urge to eat well and adventurously have blossomed at an astonishing rate. Newspapers used to have one small cookery column; now they often have several pages devoted to all aspects of food and wine. Magazines have ever more beautiful and mouthwatering photographs of food to go with their features. Food-orientated television series have increased steadily and are popular with wide and diverse audiences.

Vast food shows and exhibitions are crammed to bursting with thousands of enthusiastic visitors. Chefs have emerged from their subterranean kitchens to achieve the status of film stars.

All this has been extraordinary in a country which was certainly not renowned – and often even derided – for its gastronomy. We can now boast some of the best innovative cooks and restaurants in the world, and have at last become aware that food provides some of the greatest pleasures in life.

The best thing for the home cook has been the ever-growing availability of wide-ranging ingredients, both exotic and familiar, of every type and variety. Now even organically produced vegetables, fruit, cereal, meat and poultry are becoming more widespread and affordable. The fact that almost every time I have gone shopping over the years I have found something different to inspire me has helped enormously when trying to think up and try out new recipes. This book is for the home cook (though perhaps not exclusively, as I have quite often been delighted to find my recipes used in restaurants); it demands no special skill but enough enthusiasm to be prepared to discover the satisfaction of a little time spent in the kitchen. The recipes

are for those who do not want to spend the earth on luxury ingredients, who may not have time for long or elaborate preparation, but who do want to offer their family and friends something a bit special, and less usual. Above all, the book represents my constant and irrepressible urge to share with others something I think tastes good.

Josceline Dimbleby

first impressions

The first impression of a meal is all-important. If you are entertaining, an interesting first course can stimulate both appetite and conversation; it can impress, flatter, inspire eager anticipation, and provide much visual pleasure. But tastebuds are at their keenest at the beginning of the meal so you must also offer flavours that will be noticed and appreciated even if the talk is riveting.

Asparagus and Cherry Tomatoes with Orange Pepper and Dill Eggless Mayonnaise

In mayonnaise-type sauces, all sorts of things other than egg can be used to form the base with which to amalgamate the oil. In this recipe sweet peppers add a specially good flavour. If you like, you can grill the asparagus instead of steaming it. Serve with good bread, which can be torn up and dipped into the delicious sauce.

SERVES 6

675g/1½lb asparagus

225g/8oz cherry tomatoes

For the sauce:

225–275g/8–10oz orange peppers

4 large cloves garlic

175–225ml/6–8fl oz extra virgin olive oil

1 teaspoon green peppercorns in brine

1 tablespoon wine vinegar

generous bunch fresh dill, finely chopped

salt

black pepper

To make the sauce, cut the peppers in half, discard the seeds and stem and chop the flesh roughly. Peel the garlic and chop roughly. Put 2 tablespoons of the olive oil in a heavy saucepan over a medium heat. Add the chopped peppers and garlic, put on the lid and cook fairly gently for 10–15 minutes, until the peppers are completely soft. Leave to cool.

Empty the contents of the saucepan into a food processor with the green peppercorns. Whizz to a purée and then, with the motor running, add the remaining olive oil a little at a time, until the sauce has thickened slightly. Next whizz in the vinegar and season to taste with salt and black pepper. Lastly, turn the sauce into a bowl, stir in the chopped dill and refrigerate.

Shortly before your meal, cut off and discard the tough part of the asparagus stalks, then steam the asparagus until just tender and still bright green. Drain and rinse with cold water to cool quickly. Lay the asparagus on absorbent paper to dry.

To assemble the dish, lay out 6 individual plates and spoon the orange pepper mayonnaise evenly on to each one. Divide the asparagus into 6 and lay it on one side of each plate. Cut the tomatoes in half crossways – this makes a pretty pattern of pips – and place cut-side upwards on the mayonnaise, next to the asparagus.

When the countryside becomes covered with lacy drifts of cow parsley, one of the greatest vegetable luxuries can be enjoyed at its best. A well-established asparagus bed is perhaps the most enviable thing in any kitchen garden. Each time the asparagus season starts I think of a friend's garden in Norfolk which I used to visit frequently as a young girl. A wonderful cook, Billa grew all sorts of good things in her garden, from purple Brussels sprouts to white cherries and raspberries, and a profusion of fresh herbs which were an early inspiration to me in the kitchen. But the best times of all were her so-called 'asparagus weekends', when we literally gorged on an unlimited amount of delectable asparagus, thin stemmed and dark green with purple tips.

Celeriac and Garlic Mousse with Fresh Coriander Sauce

SERVES 5-6

450g/1lb celeriac

8–10 large cloves garlic

a little olive oil

1 rounded teaspoon paprika

1 large egg white

300ml/½ pint double cream

1 teaspoon honey

1 teaspoon ground mace

salt

black pepper

For the sauce:

300ml/½ pint Greek-style yoghurt

3 teaspoons white wine vinegar

generous handful fresh coriander leaves, chopped

cayenne pepper

No one seems sure of its origins but from the earliest records garlic has been reputed to have both curative and preventative powers. In Ancient Egypt it was regarded as a deity, while in Classical Greece athletes used to eat garlic before games in the stadium, and fighting cocks were fed it before being put in the ring.

But to me the main bonus is the flavour, which combines so well with countless ingredients. Although this recipe uses a large amount of garlic the taste is smooth, mild and sweet, which is what happens when the garlic has been cooked long and gently.

Peel the celeriac and chop it up roughly. Put it into a pan of cold water with the whole unpeeled garlic cloves and bring to the boil. Simmer until soft and then drain. Smear a 1.2 litre/2 pint mould or loaf tin generously with olive oil and sprinkle the paprika over the bottom. Put a roasting tin of hot water in the centre of the oven and heat the oven to 170°C/325°F/gas mark 3.

Pop the boiled garlic cloves out of their skins and put them into a food processor with the celeriac, egg white, cream, honey and mace. Whizz until very smooth, then season to taste with salt and black pepper. Pour slowly into the prepared mould or tin and put into the roasting tin of water in the oven. Cook for 30–40 minutes, until firm to a light touch in the centre. Remove from the oven and leave until almost cold, then loosen the sides carefully, using a round-bladed knife if necessary, and turn out on to a serving plate.

To make the sauce, simply mix the yoghurt, vinegar and chopped coriander together and season to taste with salt and cayenne pepper.

Serve the mousse at room temperature. Cut it into thick slices and place on individual plates, with the sauce on the side of each plate.

The first time I tasted green peppercorns was in a creamy sauce served with steak and pommes frites in a little bistro in Paris. It was a revelation. Even more fragrant than black peppercorns, but less hot, the green kind are in fact from the same vine-like tropical plant, Piper nigrum, grown most famously along the Malabar coast in Southwest India. But for green peppercorns, the berries are picked unripe and then freeze-dried or bottled in brine (which allows them to remain soft).

Green peppercorns can enhance sweet dishes as well as savoury; they really improve fresh fruit salads, stewed fruit, creamy puddings and ice cream. The combination of green peppercorns and mango is particularly good. For long-cooked dishes such as meat, poultry and game stews, and also to grind on to cooked eggs, grilled fish and chicken, the dried green peppercorns are the best.

Broad Beans and Quail's Eggs with Prosciutto

SERVES 4

12 quail's eggs
_____
450g/1lb frozen baby broad beans or
1.35kg/3lb really fresh small
broad beans
_____
75g/3oz prosciutto (Parma ham) or
Serrano ham, thinly sliced
_____
2 handfuls fresh flat-leafed parsley
_____
1 small clove garlic
_____
1 teaspoon bottled green
peppercorns
_____
2 tablespoons sherry vinegar
_____
125ml/4fl oz extra virgin olive oil
_____
sea salt
_____
black pepper

A simple but delicious cold starter that can be made at any time of year, as frozen broad beans are excellent. However, if you or a friend grow broad beans in the garden, this is a dish for the first picking of the season. Dill can be used instead of parsley and you can scatter shavings of Parmesan cheese on top if you like. Serve with warm crusty bread.

Put the quail's eggs into a pan of warm water and bring to the boil. Boil for 2 minutes, then drain, cool under cold water and drain again. Cook the broad beans in boiling salted water for 3–6 minutes, until tender. Drain and leave to cool. Pull the ham apart into small pieces. Roughly chop the parsley, reserving a few sprigs for garnish.

Peel the garlic, chop finely and put it into an empty jar. Add the green peppercorns, vinegar, olive oil and a sprinkling of sea salt and black pepper. Put the lid on the jar and shake vigorously to make a dressing.

Put the broad beans and ham into a bowl. Peel the quail's eggs and cut them in half lengthways. Stir the chopped parsley into the broad bean mixture and then very gently mix in the quail's eggs and the dressing.

Just before serving, spoon the mixture on to individual plates and garnish each with a sprig of parsley.

Cheese-capped Yellow Peppers Filled with Tomatoes

SERVES 6

25g/1oz butter
_____
1 heaped tablespoon plain flour
_____
150ml/¼ pint milk
_____
100g/4oz red Leicester cheese,
grated
_____
freshly grated Parmesan cheese
_____
900g/2lb plum tomatoes
_____
3 cloves garlic
_____
about 12 fresh sage leaves
_____
3 medium to large yellow or
orange peppers
_____
a little butter
_____
salt
_____
black pepper

These golden yellow pepper boats with their surprise red tomato filling are a treat for a winter first course. They can be kept warm for an hour or more in a really low oven before eating.

To make the topping, melt the butter in a pan, remove from the heat and stir in the flour. Gradually stir in the milk. Return to the heat and bring to the boil, stirring all the time. Let the sauce bubble, still stirring, for 2–3 minutes until very thick. Then add the red Leicester and remove from the heat. Stir until the cheese has melted and the sauce is smooth. Stir in a generous sprinkling of Parmesan, then season.

Preheat the oven to 180°C/350°F/gas mark 4. Put the tomatoes into a bowl, pour boiling water over them and leave for 2 minutes, then drain, peel and cut up fairly small. Peel the garlic and slice thinly. Roughly chop the sage. Mix the tomatoes, garlic and sage together and season.

Cut the peppers in half lengthways and discard the seeds and stems. Arrange the peppers fairly close together in a large, shallow ovenproof dish. Spoon the tomato mixture into them and then spoon over the cheese sauce on top, completely covering the tomatoes. Sprinkle with more Parmesan, dot with butter and cook in the oven for 1–1¾ hours, until the peppers feel soft when you insert a knife. Serve hot or warm.

Aubergine and Chicory Tart

This easily made upside-down tart is both sweet and slightly bitter, with a melting softness that contrasts beautifully with the thin, crisp filo pastry.

2 large aubergines

3 plump chicory

65g/2½oz butter

1 rounded tablespoon caster sugar

finely grated rind of ½ orange and 2 lemons

2 level teaspoons cumin seeds

6 sheets filo pastry

salt

black pepper

Bring a pan of salted water to the boil. Slice the unpeeled aubergines in thin rounds and drop immediately into the boiling water. Boil for 4–5 minutes, until the slices have just softened. Drain and lay the slices in a single layer between 2 towels to dry them thoroughly.

Cut the ends off the chicory and slice thinly lengthways. Spread 40g/1½oz of the butter over the bottom of a 24cm/9½in glass or earthenware flan dish and sprinkle evenly with the sugar. Then sprinkle with the citrus rind, cumin seeds and some salt and black pepper. Lay the long slices of chicory evenly on this mixture. Then lay on top of this a layer of aubergine slices, packed closely together. Continue laying on the rest of the aubergine slices, pressing them down evenly.

Melt the remaining 25g/1 oz of butter and put on one side. Lay one sheet of filo pastry over the aubergines, turning in the edges to fit the dish. Brush all over thinly with melted butter. Then lay on another sheet of filo at a different angle so the edges even up. Brush again with butter. Continue like this with the other sheets of filo. Finally, prick the pastry all over with a fork. If not ready to cook, refrigerate the tart.

To cook, preheat the oven to 220°C/425°F/gas mark 7 and put the tart in just above the centre. Bake for 20–30 minutes, until the pastry is a rich golden brown. Turn down the heat to 170°C/325°F/gas mark 3 and bake for a further 25–30 minutes.

Remove from the oven, leave for 5 minutes, then loosen the sides carefully with a knife. Put a large, flat serving plate on top of the flan dish and turn them both upside down. Give a shake and turn the tart on to the serving dish. Serve warm.

A Good Asparagus Tart

The freshest English asparagus is such a treat that it seems a pity to serve it in any other than the simplest way. However, if you haven't enough to satisfy everyone, or if the asparagus is imported or slightly less fresh, an asparagus tart is always appreciated. This one uses my hot butter method for the pastry, which gives a more biscuit-like texture, ideal for tarts. Since it is just a question of stirring the dough together you don't have to worry that you haven't the right touch for pastry making. The tart can be made ahead and reheated gently.

To make the pastry, sift the flour and salt into a bowl. Melt the butter gently with the water in a saucepan and then add to the flour a little at a time, stirring with a wooden spoon to form a soft dough. Press the warm dough evenly over the base and up the sides of a 24–25cm/9½–10in loose-based fluted aluminium flan tin. Prick lightly all over and then refrigerate for half an hour or more. Meanwhile, prepare the filling.

Cut any woody-looking stems off the asparagus. Boil or steam the asparagus until just tender – don't overcook it. Rinse with cold water and drain well on paper towels. Then whisk the cream with the egg yolks and the whole egg until well mixed. Whisk in the lemon rind and season with the nutmeg and some sea salt and black pepper.

Preheat the oven to 220°C/425°F/gas mark 7. Put the chilled pastry case, unfilled, in the centre of the oven for 10–15 minutes. Then remove from the oven and lower the heat to 190°C/375°F/gas mark 5. Arrange the cooked asparagus in a fanned-out pattern in the pastry case. Slowly pour on the cream mixture and then sprinkle the Parmesan over the top. Put back in the centre of the oven for about 25 minutes, until the filling is only just set to a light touch in the centre. Push the tart up out of the flan tin and on to a serving plate. Serve warm.

SERVES 6

450g/1lb asparagus

300ml/½ pint double cream

2 egg yolks

1 medium or large egg

finely grated rind of 1 lemon

¼ whole nutmeg, grated

25g/1oz Parmesan cheese, freshly grated

sea salt

black pepper

For the pastry crust:

225g/8oz strong plain flour

1 teaspoon salt

150g/5oz butter

2 teaspoons water

Poached Eggs in Tomato Shells with a Tomato, Sweet Garlic and Basil Sauce

5 large cloves garlic

2 extra-large, firm tomatoes

1 teaspoon caster sugar

2 teaspoons tomato purée

1 tablespoon lemon juice

8–10 fresh basil leaves

2–3 tablespoons white wine vinegar or dill-flavoured vinegar

4 medium or large eggs

75ml/3fl oz whipping cream

cayenne pepper

decorative salad leaves, to garnish

salt

The fresher they are, the better poached eggs will be, with a creamy, textured white and a compact shape. If possible, use eggs that you know were only laid in the last day or so. This way of serving them is a wonderful mingling of gentle flavours; the garlic is cooked until it is soft and mild.

Boil the unpeeled cloves of garlic in water for 10–15 minutes until soft. Put the tomatoes in a bowl, pour boiling water over them and leave for about 2 minutes, then drain, cut them in half crossways and peel. Using a curved grapefruit knife or a small, sharp-sided spoon, carefully scoop out the tomato flesh.

Put the tomato shells on a large serving plate or 4 individual ones. Pop the soft cloves of garlic out of their skins into a food processor, add the scooped-out tomato flesh, caster sugar, tomato purée and lemon juice and whizz until very smooth. Then sieve the mixture into a bowl, pressing it through with a wooden spoon. Using a small, sharp knife, cut the basil leaves across in thin strips and stir them into the sauce. Put in the fridge to chill well.

Meanwhile, poach the eggs: bring a large, deep-sided frying pan of water to the boil, adding the vinegar to it. When it is boiling fiercely, break one of the eggs into a cup and then slide it into the boiling water. Spoon any white that is spreading back towards the yolk. Poach for 3–5 minutes; the white should be just set and the yolk still soft – test by gently pressing the centre with your finger. Remove the egg with a slotted spatula and leave on some absorbent paper to drain. Repeat with the remaining eggs. Carefully transfer an egg into each tomato shell.

When the tomato mixture is well chilled and you are almost ready to eat, whisk the cream until it holds soft peaks and then fold the tomato mixture into it. Season to taste with cayenne pepper and salt; be generous, as the sauce has to season both the egg and the tomato shell. Just before serving, spoon the sauce over the top of the eggs and add a tiny sprinkling of cayenne pepper over the centre of each. Garnish the serving plates with a few pretty leaves.

Marinated Scallops Set in Saffron Wine

8 large fresh scallops

lemon juice

8 small florets broccoli

300ml/½ pint dry white wine

1 rounded teaspoon caster sugar

good pinch saffron strands

2–3 pinches cayenne pepper

2 teaspoons gelatine

somewhat less than 300ml/½ pint creamed smatana or soured cream

salt

A truly glamorous first course for a dinner party. The scallops are in effect 'cooked' by the lemon juice, as in the South American dish ceviche. Much the prettiest thing is to set the scallops in their shells (available from good kitchen shops and some fishmongers) but otherwise use wide cocotte dishes.

Cut the orange coral from the scallops and keep whole. Slice the white part of the scallops across thinly. Put the slices and coral closely together in a shallow dish and pour over enough lemon juice to cover them completely. Leave on one side for 30–45 minutes, until opaque. Divide the broccoli florets into small sprigs, cutting off any stems. Steam or boil the broccoli for about 3 seconds, just until bright green. Rinse immediately in cold water to cool and then leave on one side.

Put the white wine in a saucepan and bring to the boil. Remove from the heat and stir in the caster sugar, saffron strands, cayenne pepper and salt to taste. Sprinkle in the gelatine and stir well until completely dissolved.

Put the scallops into a sieve to drain off the liquid, then rinse with cold water and drain again. Put a heaped dessertspoon of smatana or soured cream into the centre of each scallop shell or cocotte dish. Place the corals of the scallops on top and arrange the slices all round. Dot the broccoli among the slices and around the edge of the shells.

Place the shells in patty tins to keep them level, then very slowly spoon the wine and saffron mixture into each shell. Leave until cold, then carefully transfer, still in the patty tins, to the fridge to set.

*In the first year of my marriage I was lucky to be part of a historic journey: the last voyage of the **Queen Mary** from New York to Southampton. It was the end of an era. Everything on that lovely boat seemed to be left over from another generation – the gym with its mahogany exercise machines, the opulent 1930s decor, the spacious cabins and bathrooms with both hot and cold sea and fresh water, the age and character of the staff themselves, the printed invitations to shipboard parties pushed under the door each morning, the fancy dress party where members of the ship's Midland Bank dressed as the Seven Deadly Sins, evening clothes for dinner every night, and the food itself.*

As they spooned an astonishing pile of glistening caviare on to my plate, the cheerful Cockney waiters would say, 'Have some more raspberry jam, love.' Those few days were also when I realized what artistry could be achieved by working with aspic. Almost everything cold seemed to be set in crystal-clear aspic or in a creamy chaudfroid sauce, almost as much as the boat was set in time.

550g/1¼lb skinless salmon fillet

300ml/½ pint full cream milk

2 cloves garlic

75g/3oz butter

50g/2oz plain flour

3–4 pinches cayenne pepper

leaves from 1 bunch watercress

50g/2oz fresh white breadcrumbs

groundnut oil for frying

salt

Salmon Fish Balls

These are like very light fishcakes. Their lightness is a result of being made with a thick béchamel sauce instead of potato. If you can use finely chopped fresh red chilli instead of cayenne pepper I think it is a bonus. Although a sauce is not strictly necessary, you could serve them with mayonnaise, tartare sauce or a fresh tomato sauce.

Lay the salmon fillet in a wide saucepan, then add the milk. Cover the pan and put over a fairly low heat. Let the milk just bubble for about 5 minutes, until the fish flakes easily. Remove from the heat and pour off the milk into a jug.

Peel the garlic and chop finely. Melt the butter in a saucepan and add the garlic. Remove from the heat, sift in the flour and stir thoroughly. Gradually stir in the fish poaching milk. Put the pan back on the heat and bring to the boil, stirring all the time with a wooden spoon. Bubble gently, still stirring, for about 4 minutes, until very thick. Remove the pan from the heat and flake in the poached salmon. Season well with cayenne pepper and salt. Chop the watercress leaves fairly small and stir them in. Turn the mixture into a shallow dish and leave until cold, then cover with cling film and chill for at least an hour.

Put the breadcrumbs into a bowl and flour your hands. Take small amounts of the chilled mixture and roll lightly into round shapes, a little bigger than pingpong balls. Dip the balls in the breadcrumbs one by one and set aside.

To cook, heat about 1.25cm/½in groundnut oil in a deep, heavy-based frying pan until very hot. Fry the balls over a fairly high heat for a few minutes on each side until golden brown. Remove carefully with a slotted spatula and drain on absorbent paper. Arrange on a serving dish or on individual plates. You can keep the fish balls warm in the lowest possible oven for up to an hour until ready to eat. Before serving, garnish with a pretty leaf or two.

Grilled Oysters Topped with a Crust of Fresh Chilli, Ginger and Coriander

SERVES 4

16 fresh oysters

4 rounded tablespoons fresh white breadcrumbs

1–2 fresh red chillies

2.5cm/1in piece fresh ginger

handful fresh coriander leaves

40g/1½oz butter

I first ate grilled oysters in a restaurant in Mexico, where they were served with a variety of toppings. The most delicious had a slight bite of fresh chilli; it inspired me to try out this version when I came home. Serve on a bed of pretty salad leaves.

Open the oysters either by putting them on a tray in a moderate oven for a minute or two or in the normal way, with a short-bladed knife or special oyster knife. Throw away the top shell and pour any juices surrounding the oysters into a mixing bowl. Cut the oysters free from the shells but leave them in their half shells.

Put the breadcrumbs into the bowl with the oyster juices. Cut the chilli open lengthways under running water and discard the seeds and stem. Peel the ginger. Finely chop the chilli and ginger. Roughly chop the coriander leaves. Mix the chopped ingredients into the breadcrumbs. Gently melt the butter and pour it into the breadcrumb mixture, stirring it in thoroughly.

Heat the grill to its highest. Put a piece of crumpled foil in the grill pan so the oysters won't tip over. Arrange the oysters on it and spoon the breadcrumb mixture on top of each one, covering them completely. Put them under the grill for 2 minutes, until the breadcrumbs are browned.

Purée of Grilled Courgettes Topped With Goat's Cheese and Hazelnuts

SERVES 4

675g/1½lb similar-sized courgettes

a little olive oil

40g/1½oz butter

¼ nutmeg, grated

75g/3oz wide-diameter goat's cheese log

40g/1½oz slivered hazelnuts (available in healthfood shops)

salt

black pepper

Courgette purée tastes lovely but can be quite wet. Grilling the courgettes before puréeing instead of steaming them dries them out a bit and also adds a pleasant smoky taste. Serve with crusty bread.

Top and tail the courgettes, cut them in half lengthways and smear all over with olive oil. Heat the grill to its highest and grill the courgettes on both sides until blackened in patches. Then put them into a food processor with the butter, grated nutmeg and some salt and black pepper. Whizz until smooth and scrape out into a gratin dish.

Cut or crumble the goat's cheese into small pieces and sprinkle it over the top of the purée. Sprinkle on black pepper and lastly scatter on the hazelnuts. Drizzle a little olive oil over and put under a hot grill again until the cheese is bubbling. The dish can be kept warm in a low oven for up to half an hour.

Puffballs with Plum Tomatoes and Olive Oil

SERVES 6

675g/1½lb ripe plum tomatoes

3 large cloves garlic

about 350–450g/12oz–1lb puffballs

125ml/4fl oz extra virgin olive oil

1 rounded teaspoon dried oregano

2 teaspoons caster sugar

1 dessertspoon sherry vinegar

salt

black pepper

During the autumn, in a good mushroom year, young puffballs are a treat which can easily be found on walks through the fields. They have a fine, smooth texture and a special affinity with tomatoes, garlic and olive oil. For this recipe use puffballs that are completely fresh, firm and white.

Put the tomatoes into a bowl, pour boiling water over them and leave for about 2 minutes, then drain, peel and cut into smallish cubes. Peel the garlic and chop finely. Slice the puffballs across in pieces 1.25cm/½in thick and then roughly into 1.25cm/½in cubes. Put 75ml/3fl oz of the oil into a large, deep frying pan or saucepan over a fairly low heat. Add the garlic and stir around, then add the tomatoes and oregano and stir for about 3 minutes, until the juices run into the oil. Now add the pieces of puffball and stir gently for 3–4 minutes. Stir in the sugar and vinegar and remove from the heat. Add the remaining oil and season with salt and plenty of freshly ground black pepper. Turn into a dish and serve warm or cold, with good bread to mop up the juices.

Stuffed Courgette Flowers and Sage Leaves in a Light Beer Batter

SERVES 4–5

100g/4oz plain flour

1 egg

200ml/7fl oz lager

65–75g/2½–3oz Gruyère cheese

8–10 courgette flowers

groundnut oil for deep-frying

about 15 large sage leaves
(pick the largest you can find)

salt

black pepper

One of the bonuses of growing your own courgettes is that you can also use their flowers, which have a lovely tender sweetness. To me, the most delectable way of eating them is deep-fried in batter, as they do in Italy. The courgette flowers should be picked shortly before cooking and should be closed rather than open. If the flowers are still closed you can insert a piece of cheese into the centre, which melts as they cook.

As this recipe means cooking at the last moment it is ideal for a few friends sitting informally in the kitchen. The batter is beautifully light and crisp.

Put a large, shallow serving dish in a low oven to keep warm. Whizz the flour and egg in a food processor to mix. Then add the lager gradually – the batter is better if it isn't too smooth so don't whizz for long after each addition. Season with salt and plenty of pepper and pour into a bowl.

Cut the cheese into small cubes and insert 1–3 cubes between the petals and into the centre of each courgette flower. Heat plenty of groundnut oil in a large, deep pan until smoking hot. Dip a few of the stuffed flowers into the batter, then put them immediately into the hot oil and fry until light golden brown all over – you may have to turn them over in the oil once. Lift out the fried flowers with a slotted spatula and leave on kitchen paper to drain while you continue with another batch. When you have finished the flowers, put the sage leaves into the batter all at once, then pick them out and put them into the oil separately, frying them just until slightly brown and crisp. Drain on kitchen paper. Then put the flowers into the warmed serving dish, pile the fried sage leaves on top and serve at once.

450g/1lb small cleaned squid

1 small raw beetroot

1 medium onion

1 litre/1¾ pints water

1 rounded teaspoon salt

2 level teaspoons caster sugar

2–3 pinches cayenne pepper

juice of 1 lemon

4 level teaspoons gelatine

300ml/½ pint creamed smatana or soured cream

3 tablespoons milk

sprigs of fresh dill, to garnish

Scarlet Hearts

A jewel of a first course for a Valentine's Eve party, these transparent ruby hearts are the ultimate in romance. However, if you feel squid is unromantic, substitute prawns or just feathery herbs. If you have no individual moulds you could use one large heart-shaped cake tin.

Slice the squid across thinly into rings, including the tendrils but discarding the goggly black eyes if they are still there. Then cut the squid rings in half. Steam over boiling water for 1 minute only, until just opaque. Rinse through with cold water to cool quickly and leave on one side.

Peel the beetroot and chop up into very small pieces. Peel the onion and chop up fairly small. Put the beetroot and onion into a saucepan with the water, salt, sugar, cayenne pepper and lemon juice. Cover the pan, bring to the boil and simmer for 20–25 minutes. Strain the liquid through a fine sieve into a saucepan. Sprinkle in the gelatine and put over a gentle heat for a few minutes, stirring until the gelatine has dissolved. Remove from the heat.

Distribute the steamed squid evenly between 10 individual moulds or deep patty tins. Gently pour in the beetroot juices. Leave until cold and then chill until set.

To turn out, dip the moulds very briefly in hot water and then hold them upside down against a board, giving a good shake. Using a wide spatula, carefully transfer the jellies from the board on to individual plates. Mix the smatana or soured cream and milk together in a bowl and spoon this white sauce carefully all round each heart on its plate. Garnish with sprigs of dill.

To me, early February means both St Valentine's Day and my birthday. In my teens I was frequently disappointed on Valentine's Day because if I received any cards they were always from the wrong boys. But I looked forward to my birthday tremendously because I knew that it was a time when I could be sure of being the centre of attention. Nowadays I don't mind if no one remembers my birthday yet I am thrilled if anyone at all sends me a Valentine's card.

The heart is a pretty and evocative shape which inspires many culinary treats. Since cooking and eating seem undeniably associated with love, it can be especially appropriate to present delicious creations in the shape of a heart. Heart-shaped moulds come in all sizes; I have several sizes of cake tin, smaller patty tins, and different heart-shaped cutters to make biscuits or even little pies in the shape of the symbol of love.

Roasted Onions Stuffed with Sun-dried Tomatoes, Pine Kernels and Goat's Cheese

SERVES 6

3 very large onions

3 large cloves garlic

8–10 sun-dried tomatoes in oil

3 tablespoons olive oil, plus extra for smearing on the onions

50g/2oz pine kernels

2 teaspoons dried oregano

a little caster sugar

225g/8oz wide-diameter goat's cheese log

salt

black pepper

These luscious onion cups make an excellent hot first course during cold weather. Conveniently, they can also be made ahead and reheated.

Preheat the oven to 200°C/400°F/gas mark 6. Put the whole, unpeeled onions in a roasting pan and cook in the centre of the oven for 45 minutes. Leave until cool enough to handle, then, using a sharp knife, cut off the tops and bottoms of the onions and peel off the hard skin. Cut the onions in half crossways and remove the inner layers, leaving just the outer shells. Arrange the half onion shells like cups in a shallow ovenproof dish. Chop the insides of the onions into small pieces. Peel the garlic and chop finely. Slice the sun-dried tomatoes into small pieces.

Heat the olive oil in a frying pan over a medium heat. Add the chopped onion, garlic, sun-dried tomatoes, pine kernels and oregano. Stir around over the heat for 4–5 minutes, then season with salt and plenty of freshly ground black pepper and spoon into the onion cups. Smear the outside of the onions with olive oil and a very little caster sugar.

Preheat the oven to 230°C/450°F/gas mark 8. Slice the goat's cheese into 6 rounds and place a piece on top of each stuffed half onion. Sprinkle with black pepper and bake just above the centre shelf of the oven for about 20 minutes, until the cheese is bubbling and browned.

Shallots Cooked in Extra Virgin Olive Oil and Balsamic Vinegar

SERVES 4-6

450g/1lb shallots

6–7 tablespoons extra virgin olive oil

2½–3 tablespoons balsamic vinegar

1 level tablespoon caster sugar

handful fresh flat-leafed parsley

sea salt

black pepper

ROASTED ONIONS STUFFED WITH SUN-DRIED TOMATOES, PINE KERNELS AND GOAT'S CHEESE

In Italy this is a famous and excellent way of using their syrupy, fragrant balsamic vinegar. It makes a lovely first course, either on its own or served with slices of mozzarella or soft goat's cheese. Have warmed ciabatta bread on the side.

Top, tail and peel the shallots. Put the olive oil into a heavy sauté pan over a low heat, add the shallots and stir to coat with the oil. Then cover the pan with a lid or foil and cook very gently for about an hour, stirring now and then, until the shallots are almost soft right through. Add the balsamic vinegar, cover the pan again and cook gently for another half an hour or so, until the shallots are completely tender. Finally stir in the caster sugar, a sprinkling of sea salt and plenty of freshly ground black pepper. Cook in the uncovered pan, still over the lowest possible heat, for 12–15 minutes, stirring until the shallots are a rich, glossy brown. Then turn the shallots and juices into a bowl to cool. Before serving, chop the parsley roughly and mix it into the shallots. Spoon out either on to individual plates or into a shallow serving dish.

simply soups

Soup is so easy to make, convenient, versatile, inexpensive and nutritious that it hasn't lapsed in popularity since ancient times, playing a similar role to bread. In some countries, such as France, every family meal must start with a *potage*. A good soup rarely fails to make you feel, as it slips easily down your throat, that this is exactly what you wanted.

SERVES 6

2 large heads garlic

1 large Spanish onion

1.2 litres/2 pints milk

2 rounded teaspoons caster sugar

100g/4oz ground almonds

1 level tablespoon tomato purée

3 tablespoons lemon juice

2 teaspoons paprika

3–4 good pinches cayenne pepper

60ml/2fl oz extra virgin olive oil

salt

SERVES 6

450g/1lb ripe plum tomatoes

3 large cloves garlic

225g/8oz chestnut mushrooms

2 fresh green chillies

5 tablespoons olive oil

1 rounded teaspoon paprika

1 teaspoon ground cinnamon

juice of 1 lemon

juice of 1 orange

1 rounded tablespoon tomato purée

600ml/1 pint water

6 tablespoons plain yoghurt (optional)

fresh lovage or mint leaves, to
      garnish

TOP: CHILLED ALMOND
AND GARLIC SOUP

BELOW: CHILLED
MUSHROOM AND
TOMATO SOUP WITH
◀ GREEN CHILLI

Chilled Almond and Garlic Soup

This soup was inspired by the garlic soups of Spain, which are usually served hot. The garlic is cooked until it has become irresistibly sweet.

Peel the cloves of garlic but keep them whole. Peel the onion and chop roughly. Put the garlic cloves and onion into a large saucepan and add 300ml/½ pint of the milk. Bring to bubbling, then cover and simmer as gently as you can for about 25 minutes, until the garlic and onion are very soft. Stir in the sugar and ground almonds, then whizz the mixture in a food processor to a smooth paste. Turn the paste back into the pan and stir in the remaining milk. Season generously with salt. Bring to the boil, stirring all the time, and then simmer gently, still stirring constantly, for 8–10 minutes. Pour into a bowl and leave to cool, then chill.

Meanwhile, put the tomato purée, lemon juice, paprika and cayenne pepper into a small saucepan. Heat until almost bubbling and keep it like that, stirring all the time, for about 3 minutes. Remove from the heat and leave until cold. Just before serving, spoon the chilled soup into individual bowls. Stir the olive oil vigorously into the cold tomato and paprika mixture and then spoon it in a whirl in each bowl.

Chilled Mushroom and Tomato Soup with Green Chilli

Cold tomato and vegetable soups can be wonderfully refreshing, like the Spanish gazpacho. Unlike gazpacho, the ingredients for this recipe are cooked rather than raw, which I think brings out the flavours more fully.

Put the tomatoes in a bowl, pour boiling water over them and leave for about 2 minutes, then drain, peel and cut into cubes. Peel the garlic and slice thinly. Slice the mushrooms fairly thinly. Cut the chillies lengthways under running water, discard the seeds and stem and then slice the chilli halves across very thinly. Put the olive oil and garlic in a large saucepan over a medium heat. Let it sizzle for a minute or two until the garlic is just beginning to brown. Don't let it burn. Add the paprika and cinnamon, stir for a moment or two and remove from the heat. Add the tomatoes, lemon and orange juice, mushrooms and chillies. Stir the tomato purée into the water and pour into the pan. Cover, put the pan over a high heat and bring to the boil. Lower the heat and simmer very gently for 30 minutes. Transfer the soup to a bowl, leave to become cold and then chill.

Just before serving, spoon the soup into individual bowls and add a large blob of yoghurt to the centre of each, if using. Finally, slice a few lovage or mint leaves and sprinkle on top of each bowl of soup.

Clear Beetroot Soup with Broad Bean Kernels and Petits Pois

1.7 litres/3 pints chicken or vegetable stock (home-made if possible)

strained juice of 1 lemon

1 medium-sized raw beetroot

450g/1lb frozen broad beans

good handful fresh mint leaves

good handful fresh flat-leafed parsley

2 teaspoons caraway seeds

225g/8oz frozen petits pois

salt

black pepper

A simple, pretty and delicate soup. Serve with some good crusty bread. To make it more substantial you can add thin rings of 4–5 small squid at the same moment as the petits pois – delicious.

Pour the stock and strained lemon juice into a large saucepan. Peel the beetroot, chop it up into small pieces and put it into the stock. Bring to the boil, then cover the pan and simmer gently for about half an hour. Meanwhile, put the frozen broad beans into a bowl and pour boiling water over them. Leave them for a few minutes, then drain. Pop the beans out of their skins back into the empty bowl again and leave them on one side.

When the beetroot has been cooking for about half an hour, strain the stock through a fine sieve into another saucepan, discarding the beetroot. Check for seasoning and add salt and black pepper if needed. Chop the mint leaves quite finely and the flat-leafed parsley only very roughly.

Just before serving, add the caraway seeds to the soup and bring up to boiling. Add the petits pois and boil for about 2 minutes, then add the skinless broad beans and boil for only 1 minute more. Finally stir in the chopped mint and parsley, pour into a soup tureen or spoon into bowls, and serve at once.

Cauliflower and Cheese Soup

1 small cauliflower

65g/2½oz butter

1 teaspoon caraway seeds

2 teaspoons dried or bottled green peppercorns

2 rounded tablespoons plain flour

1.2 litres/2 pints full cream milk

1 small to medium red pepper

100g/4oz full-flavoured cheese, grated

150ml/¼ pint creamed smatana or soured cream

salt

black pepper

Many people say they don't like cauliflower but even they should realize it is wonderful for soup. This is rich and warming, suitable for cold nights. If you can get them, sprinkle chopped fresh chives on to each bowl of soup.

Cut the cauliflower in half, pull off the florets and chop them roughly. Melt the butter in a large, heavy-based saucepan over a fairly low heat and add the caraway seeds, cauliflower and green peppercorns. Stir to coat the cauliflower in butter, then stir in the flour, followed by the milk, a little at a time. Bring to the boil, still stirring, then cover the pan and simmer for 30 minutes.

While the soup is cooking, cut the pepper in half, discard the seeds and stem and chop the flesh finely into tiny cubes. Add the chopped pepper to the soup after 30 minutes and cook for another 10 minutes. Then add the cheese and stir until it melts into the soup. Remove from the heat, stir in the creamed smatana or soured cream and serve.

CLEAR BEETROOT SOUP WITH BROAD BEAN KERNELS AND PETITS POIS ▶

Mussel, Red Pepper and Tomato Soup with Pesto

SERVES 4-6

1.35kg/3lb mussels

150ml/¼ pint red wine

675g/1½lb ripe tomatoes

1 small red pepper

2 large cloves garlic

75g/3oz butter

1 heaped teaspoon paprika

40g/1½oz plain flour

450ml/¾ pint fish or chicken stock

150ml/¼ pint double cream

4–5 teaspoons pesto sauce

salt

black pepper

Mussels are perfect for soups because of the wonderful juices that run from them. Being quite rich and substantial, this soup can be served on its own with hot crusty bread as a light meal for four people.

Scrape any barnacles off the mussels with a knife and wash them very thoroughly. Put them into a large saucepan with the red wine, cover the pan and put them over a high heat. Shake the pan for about 2–3 minutes, just until the mussels have opened, then remove from the heat and set aside.

Put the tomatoes in a bowl, pour boiling water over them and leave for 2 minutes, then drain and peel. Cut the pepper in half and remove the seeds and stem. Put the tomatoes and pepper into a food processor and whizz until smooth.

Peel the garlic and chop finely. Melt the butter in a large saucepan over a medium heat, stir in the garlic and paprika, then remove from the heat and stir in the flour with a wooden spoon. Gradually stir in the stock, followed by the puréed tomatoes and red pepper. Using a fine sieve, strain in the liquid from the mussel pan. Put back over a high heat and bring to the boil, stirring, until you can see that the soup has thickened. Then cover the saucepan and simmer very gently for at least half an hour.

Meanwhile, take half the shell off each mussel, emptying the trapped juices back into the pan, pulling off any beards and leaving the mussels in the half shell; if some of the mussels fall out of the shell simply discard the shell. Stir the extra juices into the saucepan of soup. Before serving, stir in the cream and pesto sauce and season to taste with salt and black pepper. Add the mussels in their half shells and reheat gently. Then either serve from the pan or transfer to a large soup tureen.

TOP: MUSSEL, RED PEPPER AND TOMATO SOUP WITH PESTO

BELOW: COD AND MUSSEL SOUP WITH SAFFRON (PAGE 36)

Cod and Mussel Soup with Saffron

SERVES 4

900g/2lb fresh mussels

300ml/½ pint white wine

2 large cloves garlic

600ml/1 pint fish or chicken stock

generous pinch saffron strands

1 teaspoon paprika

300ml/½ pint double cream

50g/2oz butter

25g/1oz plain flour

450g/1lb skinned thick cod fillet

generous bunch fresh flat-leafed parsley

juice of 1 small lemon

cayenne pepper

salt

Often a good soup accompanied by warm French bread seems the most desirable meal there could be. Main-course soups should be nutritious, sustaining and a fusion of flavours; this is just such a soup.

Rinse the mussels in cold water, then scrub them thoroughly, pulling off any beards, and rinse again. Discard any open mussels that do not close when tapped lightly. Pour the wine into a large saucepan and bring to the boil. Add the mussels, then cover and boil for about 2 minutes, until the shells have opened. Using a slotted spoon, transfer the mussels to a bowl and remove them from their shells, discarding any that have not opened and leaving 8–10 unshelled for garnish. Keep the mussels on one side in the bowl, tipping any juices back into the saucepan with the wine. Then pour the wine and juices through a fine sieve into a clean saucepan.

Peel and finely chop the garlic, then add it to the wine and mussel juices with the stock, saffron and paprika. Bring to the boil and boil for 1 minute, then remove from the heat, cover the pan and leave for 20–30 minutes. Finally stir in the cream.

Melt the butter in a large, heavy pan, remove from the heat and stir in the flour. Put back on the heat and gradually add the stock and cream mixture. Bring to the boil, stirring, then simmer gently, stirring constantly, for 4–5 minutes. Remove from the heat, season with cayenne pepper and salt and cover the pan.

Shortly before serving, slice the cod into 2.5–4cm/1–1½in pieces. Roughly chop the parsley leaves. Bring the soup to a rolling boil, stirring, then drop in the pieces of cod and simmer gently for 4–5 minutes, until just cooked through. Add the shelled mussels, then pour in the lemon juice through a strainer, stir gently and remove from the heat. Taste again for seasoning. Scatter the chopped parsley on to the soup, garnish with the unshelled mussels and serve at once.

4–5 medium tomatoes, the plum variety if available

2.5cm/1in piece fresh ginger

2 large cloves garlic

2 fresh red chillies (use only 1 if adding sour shrimp paste)

900ml/1½ pints fish or chicken stock

juice of 2 lemons

100g/4oz shiitake or chestnut mushrooms

450g/1lb skinned cod fillet

1 bunch spring onions

generous handful fresh coriander leaves

2 rounded tablespoons coconut milk powder

150ml/¼ pint boiling water

salt

Far Eastern Fish and Mushroom Soup

If you have ever travelled in the East, or even just been to a Thai restaurant, you will find the flavours of this soup evocative. If you live near an oriental grocer's, buy a jar of Thai sour shrimp paste (sometimes called tom yum) – a teaspoon or two will make the soup even more authentic. And if you can find fresh kaffir lime leaves, add three or four to the stock.

Put the tomatoes into a bowl, pour over boiling water to cover and leave for 2 minutes, then peel and cut into small cubes. Peel the ginger and garlic and slice across very thinly. Cut the chillies open under running water, discard the seeds and stem and slice the chillies across very finely. Pour the stock into a large, heavy-based saucepan and add the lemon juice, tomatoes, ginger, garlic and chillies. Bring to the boil (adding the shrimp paste now, if used), then cover the pan and simmer gently for about 20 minutes.

Meanwhile, slice the mushrooms finely across. Slice the cod fillet across at 1.25cm/½in intervals. Trim the spring onions and cut them across fairly thinly, using as much of the green part as possible. Roughly chop the coriander leaves.

Put the coconut milk powder into a measuring jug, pour in the boiling water and stir until smooth. Stir this into the stock and tomato mixture and bring to the boil. Then add the sliced mushrooms, cover and simmer for another 15 minutes.

Shortly before serving, drop in the slices of cod, bring up to bubbling again, then remove from the heat immediately. Add the spring onions, then leave the pan covered on top of the stove for 5–8 minutes, until the fish is lightly cooked through. Taste the liquid and add salt if necessary, then pour into a heated soup tureen and very roughly stir in the chopped coriander leaves.

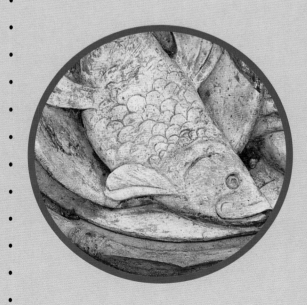

Sweetcorn and Coconut Milk Soup with Red Chilli and Fresh Coriander

SERVES 8

2 fresh red chillies

3 large cloves garlic

1.7 litres/3 pints chicken stock

juice of 2 lemons

675g/1½lb frozen sweetcorn

4 rounded tablespoons coconut milk powder

300ml/½ pint very hot water

generous handful fresh coriander leaves

salt

This sunny yellow soup combines a soothing sweetness with the lovely bite of fresh chilli. It can be served either hot or cold, according to the weather.

Cut the chillies in half lengthways under running water, discard the seeds and stems and cut across in very thin strips. Peel the garlic and slice across as thinly as possible. Put 1.2 litres/2 pints of the stock in a large saucepan, then put the remaining stock in a smaller one with the sliced chillies, garlic and lemon juice. Bring the first pan to the boil, add 450g/1lb of the sweetcorn and boil for a few minutes, until tender. Remove from the heat.

Now bring the saucepan of stock containing the chillies and garlic to the boil and simmer gently for 8 minutes. Pour the contents of the large saucepan into a food processor, whizz until the sweetcorn is puréed and return to the large saucepan. Add the contents of the smaller saucepan to the puréed mixture. Then bring to the boil, add the remaining sweetcorn and simmer for 2–3 minutes, until the sweetcorn is just cooked. Remove from the heat.

Put the coconut milk powder into a bowl with 1 level teaspoon of salt, pour in the hot water and stir until smooth. Then stir the coconut milk into the soup. Before serving, roughly chop the coriander leaves. Reheat the soup if necessary but don't let it boil, then throw in the coriander leaves.

Chicken Quenelles and Watercress Soup

SERVES 6

275g/10oz skinless chicken breast fillets

7.5–10cm/3–4in sprig fresh tarragon

finely grated rind and juice of 1 lemon

1 medium egg white

1 bunch watercress

1.7 litres/3 pints chicken stock

salt

black pepper

SWEETCORN AND COCONUT MILK SOUP WITH RED CHILLI AND ◀ FRESH CORIANDER

I love the delicacy of clear soups and the way they leave you feeling somehow cleansed. If possible, use good home-made stock.

Chop the chicken breasts finely in a food processor and then turn them into a bowl. Take the leaves off the tarragon stalk and chop finely. Add the chopped tarragon and lemon rind to the chicken. Season well with salt and then beat in the egg white thoroughly with a wooden spoon. Using wet hands, form the mixture into small balls or ovals; these are your quenelles.

Pick just the leaves off the watercress stems and keep on one side. Line a sieve with 2 layers of muslin or a linen cloth and then strain the chicken stock slowly through it into a saucepan. Strain in the lemon juice, check for seasoning, and then bring to a rapid boil. Drop in the chicken quenelles and simmer for 4–5 minutes. Add the watercress leaves and remove from the heat after a second. Serve immediately.

Green Pea and Chicory Soup with Grilled Pepper and Crispy Bacon

SERVES 4

1 large red pepper

225g/8oz chicory

50g/2oz butter

2 level teaspoons caster sugar

600ml/1 pint vegetable or chicken stock

225g/8oz frozen peas

large handful fresh flat-leafed parsley

225g/8oz rindless smoked streaky bacon

1 tablespoon olive oil

150ml/¼ pint soured cream

sea salt

black pepper

In this homely soup, perfect for lunch with bread and cheese, the sweetness of the peas complements the unique and pleasurable bitterness of chicory. Vegetarians can simply omit the bacon.

Cut the pepper in half, discard the seeds and stem and put the halves skin-side up under a very hot grill until blackened all over. Then put them into a plastic or paper bag and leave to cool. Slice the chicory roughly. Melt the butter in a pan, stir in the chicory, cover and cook gently for 10–15 minutes, until soft. Stir in the sugar, add the stock and bring to the boil. Add the peas and boil for 3 minutes. Remove from the heat, put a sieve over a saucepan and pour the mixture into it, keeping the solids in the sieve. Whizz the contents of the sieve and 2 tablespoons of the liquid in a food processor until smooth. Then stir the purée back into the stock in the saucepan. Season to taste.

Skin and finely slice the red pepper. Chop the parsley. Cut the bacon into 1.25cm/½in pieces. Heat the oil in a frying pan and fry the bacon until crisp, then remove from the heat. Just before serving, reheat the soup and stir in the red pepper and most of the parsley. Add the bacon and spoon the soup into bowls. Swirl in the soured cream and sprinkle with the remaining parsley.

Fresh Cream of Tomato Soup with Courgette Cubes

SERVES 6

675g/1½lb ripe tomatoes

300ml/½ pint freshly squeezed orange juice

350g/12oz courgettes

450ml/¾ pint water

2 teaspoons caster sugar

1 tablespoon tomato purée

4–5 pinches cayenne pepper

300ml/½ pint double cream

salt

Fresh tomato soup is one of the best, and is especially worth making at the end of the summer when there is a glut of properly ripe tomatoes.

Put the tomatoes into a bowl, pour boiling water over them and leave for 2 minutes, then drain, peel and chop finely. Put them into a large pan with all their juice and the orange juice. Add a little salt and cook over a fairly low heat, stirring now and then, for about 15 minutes or until mushy.

Cut the courgettes into small cubes. Stir the water, sugar, tomato purée and cayenne into the tomatoes. Bring to the boil, add the courgettes and bubble, stirring now and then, for 4–5 minutes, until the courgettes are just cooked but still slightly crunchy and bright green. Finally, stir in the cream, bring to the boil, bubble for half a minute and remove from the heat. Season with more salt and cayenne if needed and then serve.

TOP: GREEN PEA AND CHICORY SOUP WITH GRILLED PEPPER AND CRISPY BACON

BELOW: FRESH CREAM OF TOMATO SOUP WITH COURGETTE CUBES ▶

Red Cabbage Soup with Crusted Top

SERVES 6

225–350g/8–12oz red cabbage

225g/8oz thick smoked streaky bacon rashers

2 medium onions

25g/1oz butter

2 teaspoons dill seeds (optional)

1.5 litres/2½ pints chicken stock

juice of 1 lemon

2 teaspoons sugar

3 rounded tablespoons fresh white breadcrumbs

generous handful fresh parsley, finely chopped

25g/1oz Parmesan cheese, freshly grated

salt

black pepper

I always think of Portugal when I make green cabbage soup; there you are surrounded by the incongruous sight of hundreds of cabbages growing between the vines. But red cabbage too, cooked long and gently, makes a wonderful soup.

Cut the cabbage in quarters, cut out any core part and slice the rest up very finely. Cut the rind off the bacon and slice into 2.5cm/1in pieces. Peel the onions, cut in half and slice thinly.

Melt the butter in a large, heavy-based saucepan and add the dill seeds, bacon and onions. Stir over a low heat for a few minutes until the onions have softened. Then stir in the sliced cabbage and add the stock, lemon juice and sugar. Bring to the boil, then cover the pan, lower the heat and simmer gently for about 2 hours.

Shortly before the soup is ready, preheat the oven to 180°C/350°F/gas mark 4. Spread the breadcrumbs in a roasting pan and put on a high shelf in the oven for 10–20 minutes, until golden. Turn out into a bowl and mix in the chopped parsley and grated Parmesan. Taste the soup and add salt if necessary and plenty of black pepper. Pour into a tureen and sprinkle the toasted breadcrumb mixture evenly over the top just before serving.

Pumpkin and Sweet Potato Soup

SERVES 6

2 medium onions

50g/2oz butter

1.1kg/2½lb pumpkin

450g/1lb sweet potatoes

5cm/2in piece fresh ginger

2 rounded teaspoons caraway seeds

1.8 litres/3 pints chicken stock

2 teaspoons clear honey

300ml/½ pint double cream

¼ nutmeg, grated

2 handfuls fresh coriander or parsley

salt

black pepper

This is one of my favourite soups: sweet, smooth, soothing and golden – perfect for cold weather. Pumpkins are always orange-fleshed; sweet potatoes are exasperatingly not. Scrape off a bit of the skin when buying them to make sure you get the orange-fleshed kind.

Peel and slice the onions. Melt the butter over a medium heat in a large, heavy-based saucepan, add the onions and fry until golden brown. Remove from the heat.

Cut the skin off the pumpkin, scrape away any seeds and the stringy part and cut the flesh up roughly. Peel the sweet potatoes and cut them into smallish cubes. Peel the ginger and chop roughly. Add the pumpkin and sweet potatoes to the onions in the saucepan together with the ginger, caraway seeds and chicken stock. Sprinkle with salt, bring to the boil, then cover the pan and simmer for 15–20 minutes, until the pumpkin and sweet potatoes are very soft.

Purée the mixture in batches in a food processor, putting the purée into a clean saucepan. Add the honey, cream and nutmeg, bring to the boil again and bubble for 4–5 minutes. Remove from the heat and season if necessary. Chop the coriander or parsley leaves roughly, stir into the soup and serve.

RED CABBAGE SOUP WITH CRUSTED TOP

Sweet Potato, Fennel and Leek Soup

SERVES 4

225g/8oz sweet potatoes

1.2 litres/2 pints good chicken or game stock

450g/1lb leeks

2 medium to large bulbs fennel

2 large cloves garlic

75g/3oz butter

1 teaspoon caraway seeds

sea salt

black pepper

Sweet potatoes are, as their name suggests, sweet, but they are also deliciously nutty. They make a smooth and wonderful soup. Be sure to buy the orange-fleshed kind; scrape the skin of the sweet potatoes in the shop with your nail – if the flesh underneath is a pale peach colour, they are the ones you want. If, however, they have white flesh it will go a rather unappetizing grey colour when cooked. This sustaining soup, accompanied by crusty bread, makes a lovely light lunch or supper.

Peel the sweet potatoes and chop them up roughly. Put them into a saucepan with the stock, bring to the boil, then cover and simmer for 20–30 minutes until the potatoes are very soft.

Meanwhile, wash and trim the leeks and cut across in roughly 2.5cm/1in pieces. Cut the bases and tough stalks off the fennel bulbs and remove any scarred outer layers. Reserve any green leaves for garnish. Slice the fennel in half and then cut across in thin slices. Peel the garlic and slice across thinly.

Melt the butter in a large, deep frying pan over a medium heat and add the sliced leeks and fennel. Cook, stirring around fairly often, for about 8 minutes. Then add the sliced garlic and the caraway seeds and cook for 5 more minutes or until both leeks and fennel are soft and slightly browned.

When the sweet potatoes are soft, put them into a food processor, using a slotted spoon and making sure you leave no bits of potato in the stock. Pour a little of the stock into the food processor and whizz until the sweet potatoes have turned to a smooth purée. Return the purée to the pan of stock and stir thoroughly. Add sea salt and black pepper to taste. Add the sautéed leeks and fennel to the soup and reheat if necessary before serving. Chop up any reserved fennel leaves and sprinkle some on to each bowl of soup as you serve it.

Three-part Asparagus Soup

SERVES 4

450g/1lb green asparagus

1 medium onion

600ml/1 pint chicken stock

50g/2oz butter

1 level tablespoon plain flour

juice of ½ lemon

300ml/½ pint double cream

chopped fresh chives, to garnish

salt

black pepper

Ever since my student days I have hated wasting food, so I devised this asparagus recipe in order to use even the toughest part of the stalk. The result is a well-flavoured, smooth, creamy soup dotted with asparagus tips.

Cut the asparagus spears into three pieces: the heads, the centre tender green part and the tougher base of the stalk. Peel the onion and chop roughly. Put the base pieces of the asparagus into a saucepan with the chicken stock, cover and bring to the boil, then lower the heat and simmer gently for 20–30 minutes. Pour the stock through a fine sieve into a jug and discard the asparagus stalks.

Now melt the butter in a heavy-based saucepan and add the chopped onion. Stir for a minute and then mix in the flour. Gradually add the chicken stock and lemon juice. Bring to the boil, stirring, and then allow to bubble for 3–4 minutes before adding the centre pieces of asparagus.

Simmer for 8–10 minutes, until the asparagus is completely soft but has not lost its bright green colour. Pour the mixture into a food processor and whizz until smooth. Then return it to the saucepan, stir in the cream and season to taste with salt and black pepper.

Shortly before serving, bring the soup up to the boil, add the asparagus heads and simmer for 3–4 minutes, until they have softened but still have a slight bite. Sprinkle with chopped chives and serve.

Walnut and Onion Soup with Chilli

SERVES 6

1 large onion
2 tablespoons olive oil
25g/1oz butter
2 fresh red chillies
100g/4oz walnut pieces
1 level tablespoon caster sugar
1 teaspoon ground mace
25g/1oz plain flour
600ml/1 pint chicken or vegetable stock
750ml/1¼ pints milk
1 bunch spring onions
300ml/½ pint creamed smatana or soured cream
sea salt

In this creamy, sweet soup the emphatic flavour of walnuts is tempered beautifully with a dash of fire. It is excellent for a light lunch or supper, accompanied by fresh crusty bread.

Peel the onion, cut it in half and slice as thinly as possible. Put the olive oil and butter into a large, heavy-based saucepan and melt over a medium heat. Add the sliced onion and cook, stirring frequently, for about 10 minutes, until the onion is soft and slightly brown. Remove from the heat.

Cut the chillies open lengthways under running water, discard the seeds and stem and slice the halves across as thinly as you can. Put the walnut pieces into a food processor and whizz briefly to grind finely – don't leave the machine on too long or the nuts will become sticky and oily.

Stir the caster sugar, ground mace, sliced chillies and ground walnuts into the onion and then stir in the flour. Gradually stir in the stock and milk. Put the saucepan back on the heat and bring to the boil, stirring frequently. Allow to bubble for 2–3 minutes, stirring all the time, then cover the pan, lower the heat and simmer very gently for 20 minutes.

While the soup is cooking, trim the spring onions and slice across at 5mm/¼in intervals, using as much of the green part as possible. When the soup is ready, add salt to taste and stir in the spring onions. Ladle the soup into bowls and spoon a dollop of creamed smatana or soured cream on to each.

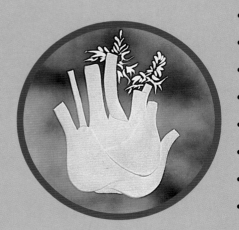

fish feasts

Fish is exciting to buy because it is so beautiful to look at. I find it almost impossible to pass the fish counter without buying something, even if I have not planned to eat fish that day. Fish is quick and interesting to cook, adapting itself to all sorts of wonderful sauces.

Green Pasta with Mussels and Bacon

2.25 litres (4 pints) mussels

2 large cloves garlic

225g/8oz rindless smoked streaky bacon

2 large handfuls fresh parsley

50g/2oz butter

1 tablespoon olive oil

150ml/¼ pint double cream

350g/12oz fresh or dried green tagliatelle or tagliolini

freshly grated Parmesan cheese, to serve

salt

black pepper

Mussels are one of the most richly flavoured, nutritious and yet inexpensive shellfish. Since they are so often served in their shells as moules marinière it is nice to make the most of them in a different way, as in this recipe.

Wash and scrub the mussels but don't bother about scraping off any barnacles. Pour about 1.25cm/½in of water into a large saucepan and put over the heat. Add the mussels, cover the pan and bring to the boil. Cook for about 2 minutes or a little more, shaking the pan until all the mussel shells are open. Then drain off the water and leave the mussels until they are cool enough to handle.

Peel the garlic and chop finely. Cut the bacon into small pieces. Remove the large stalks from the parsley, then put the parsley in a food processor and whizz to chop as finely as possible. Take the mussels out of their shells, discarding any that have not opened, and keep them on one side.

Bring a large saucepan of water to the boil. Meanwhile, melt the butter with the olive oil in a heavy-based saucepan over a medium heat, then add the bacon and toss about for a few minutes until slightly crisp. Add the chopped garlic and stir for another minute. Now add the cream and finely chopped parsley and bring up to bubbling, stirring all the time. Season to taste with salt and plenty of black pepper. Lastly, stir in the mussels, remove from the heat and cover the pan.

When the water in the large saucepan is boiling, stir in the pasta and cook for 3–10 minutes (depending on whether the pasta is fresh or dried), until just tender but still with a bite to it. Drain and put into a large heated serving dish. Pour the mussel and bacon mixture over the noodles, stirring it in only slightly, and serve immediately. Put a bowl of grated Parmesan on the table for people to sprinkle on to their individual helpings.

Casserole of Mussels and Aubergines

450–550g/1–1¼lb aubergines

white wine vinegar for sprinkling

225g/8oz smallish onions (red ones if possible)

2 large cloves garlic

900g/2lb fresh mussels

300ml/½ pint white wine or cider

400g/14oz tin tomatoes

2 tablespoons tomato purée

2 teaspoons sugar

3 tablespoons olive oil

15g/½oz pine kernels

handful fresh dill

salt

black pepper

I made this dish after a visit to Istanbul, where large, deep-orange mussels are found in the Bosphorus. Aubergines and pine kernels are the epitomy of Middle Eastern cooking but in Turkey I was surprised to find so much dill, which I had always thought of as a northern European herb.

Slice the aubergines across, then cut the slices in half, sprinkling them with vinegar as you do so. Rub the slices all over with salt and put them in a colander in the sink to drain while you prepare the other ingredients.

Peel the onions and slice into rings. Peel the garlic and slice across finely. Wash the mussels and scrub them thoroughly, discarding any open ones that do not close when tapped on a work surface. Pour the wine or cider into a large saucepan and bring to the boil. Add the mussels, cover the pan and boil for about 2 minutes, shaking the pan round a bit, until all the shells have opened. Pour the liquid from the mussels through a fine sieve into a fairly large flameproof casserole. Extract the mussels from their shells and put them into a bowl on one side.

Rinse the salt from the aubergines. Bring the mussel liquid in the casserole to the boil and add the aubergines, onions, garlic, tinned tomatoes, tomato purée and sugar. Stir in the olive oil and season generously with black pepper. Cover and simmer very gently on top of the stove for 45 minutes. Check for seasoning – it probably won't need salt. Add the mussels to the mixture just to warm through.

Heat a small dry frying pan and toss the pine kernels in it for a minute or so to brown them. Just before serving, stir the roughly chopped dill into the mussels and aubergines and scatter the pine kernels on top.

Mussels in a Bay- and Saffron-flavoured Gratinée with Goat's Cheese

SERVES 6

2.5–2.75kg/5–6lb mussels

150ml/¼ pint white wine

600ml/1 pint milk

4–5 bay leaves

good pinch saffron strands

2 cloves garlic

50g/2oz butter

2 heaped tablespoons plain flour

75g/3oz Cheddar cheese, grated

75g/3oz goat's cheese, crumbled

cayenne pepper

salt

I love the sweetness and fleshy plumpness of mussels. This is a wonderful dish, best served with a crisp green vegetable such as broccoli and a bowl of buttered noodles or new potatoes.

Wash the mussels and scrub them thoroughly, discarding any open ones that do not close when tapped on a work surface. Put them into a very large saucepan with the wine. Cover the pan and put over a high heat. Shake the pan around for 2–4 minutes, just until the mussels have opened, then remove the lid and leave the pan on one side.

Put the milk, bay leaves and saffron into a saucepan and bring just up to the boil, stirring now and then. When it reaches boiling point, remove from the heat and leave on one side for at least 15 minutes, stirring occasionally to help the bay and saffron flavours infuse the milk. Meanwhile, remove the mussels from their shells over the pan in which they were cooked, so the juices pour back in. Put the mussels into a large, shallow heatproof dish. Strain the mussel liquid through a fine sieve into the pan of milk. Remove the bay leaves from the pan.

Peel and finely chop the garlic. Melt the butter in a saucepan over a medium heat, add the garlic and stir for a minute or two. Remove the pan from the heat and stir in the flour until smooth. Gradually stir in the milk and mussel liquid and put back over a fairly high heat. Bring to the boil, stirring all the time until the sauce has thickened. Stir in the grated Cheddar and all but 25g/1oz of the goat's cheese. Continue stirring until the cheese has melted. Finally add cayenne pepper and salt to taste.

Pour the sauce over the mussels and sprinkle the remaining goat's cheese on top. Put the dish under a hot grill until speckled brown and then either serve immediately or keep warm in a very low oven until ready to eat.

Fish Steaks and Avocado with Tomatoes, Lime, Chilli and Angostura Bitters

SERVES 4

4 white fish steaks, 200–225g/ 7–8oz each

enough milk to cover the fish

225g/8oz shallots or small onions

3 large cloves garlic

1 fresh red chilli

450g/1lb ripe tomatoes

3 tablespoons olive oil

3 bay leaves

juice of 2 limes

1 large, ripe avocado

lemon juice for sprinkling

1 rounded teaspoon caster sugar

2–3 teaspoons Angostura bitters

salt

I created this recipe from the memory of a dish I once tasted in Trinidad. There I also learnt how much Angostura bitters (whose recipe is still kept secret, locked in a bank) can enhance both savoury and sweet dishes. You can use any white fish that produces good steaks, such as cod or swordfish. A Trinidadian told me that marinating fish in milk makes it more tender.

Put the fish steaks into a dish in which they fit fairly closely and pour enough milk over them to cover. Cover the dish with cling film and leave in the fridge for 2 hours or more. Then remove the fish and discard the milk. Pat the fish dry with absorbent paper.

Peel the shallots or onions and slice across thinly. Peel and finely chop the garlic, keeping 1 level teaspoon of it to one side. Cut open the chilli under running water, discard the seeds and stem and chop the flesh finely. Put the tomatoes into a bowl, pour boiling water over them and leave for 2 minutes, then peel and chop.

Put the olive oil in a heavy-based saucepan over a medium heat, add the shallots or onions and stir around for a few minutes until soft and golden. Add the chilli and garlic, leaving the reserved teaspoonful of garlic to one side. Stir for a minute and then remove from the heat. Add the chopped tomatoes and their juice, together with the bay leaves, lime juice and some salt. Cover the pan and cook gently for about 10 minutes, until the tomatoes are mushy. Add the drained fish steaks, baste with the tomato sauce and cover the pan once more. Continue cooking over a low heat for 10–15 minutes or until the fish feels just firm when lightly pressed. Remove from the heat.

Using a slotted spatula, transfer the fish to a heated serving dish. Cut the avocado in half, remove the stone, peel the skin off carefully and slice the flesh thinly crossways. Arrange the slices between the fish steaks and sprinkle with lemon juice. Add the reserved garlic to the sauce and bring to the boil, stirring constantly for 2–3 minutes. Then remove from the heat and add the sugar and Angostura bitters to taste. Pour the sauce over the fish and avocado and serve at once.

Fish Pie with Sweet Potato and Parsnip Top

450g/1lb orange-fleshed sweet potatoes

350g/12oz parsnips

75g/3oz butter

800g/1¾lb skinned thick cod fillets

750ml/1¼ pints full cream milk, plus 2 tablespoons

3–4 pinches cayenne pepper

bunch spring onions

2 rounded tablespoons cornflour

2 rounded teaspoons whole grain mustard

salt

black pepper

If you can find really fresh, thick fillets of cod, this is a dream of a fish pie. Serve with a green vegetable such as broccoli or a salad. To make sure the sweet potatoes are the orange-fleshed kind, scrape off a little skin before buying.

Peel the sweet potatoes and parsnips, then cut them up roughly. Steam or boil until very soft, then drain and mash with 50g/2oz of the butter. Cut the cod fillet into 2.5–5cm/1–2in chunks. Spread them over the base of a wide saucepan and pour over 150ml/¼ pint of the milk. Cover the pan, put over a medium heat and bubble very gently for 3–4 minutes, until the fish is opaque. Pour the poaching milk into the mashed potatoes and parsnips and mix in thoroughly. Season with the cayenne pepper and some salt.

Trim the spring onions and chop them across fairly thinly, using as much of the green part as possible. Preheat the grill to high and put a shallow heatproof serving dish in a low oven to warm.

Put the cornflour and 2 tablespoons of milk into a saucepan and stir until smooth. Gradually stir in the remaining milk. Bring to the boil, stirring, and bubble, still stirring, for about 3 minutes, until thickened. Add the spring onions and bubble for another minute. Remove from the heat and stir in the mustard, with salt and black pepper to taste. Put the pieces of poached cod in the warm serving dish and pour the spring onion sauce over them.

Spoon the sweet potato and parsnip mixture over the fish and spread it in rough flicks. Dot with the remaining butter and put under the grill for 5–8 minutes or until the surface is very darkly speckled all over. If necessary, keep in a very low oven for up to 20 minutes before serving.

The sweet potato is not a potato at all, nor, as is often supposed, is it a yam. It is a tropical root vegetable, the tuberous root of a member of the convolvulus family, a native of South America but grown and eaten all over the tropics and in the southern states of America.

I love sweet potatoes both for their versatility and their taste, which is nutty and rather chestnut like. They are excellent peeled, cut into pieces and roasted with a sprinkling of brown sugar and cinnamon as an accompaniment to a Sunday joint of meat or chicken. As with pumpkin, their subtle sweetness responds beautifully to spices. They can be cooked in the same ways as potatoes but don't take quite as long. They are arguably better for soups than potatoes and can be used in puddings as well. You can grate them raw and add them to a sponge or carrot cake mixture.

Sweet potatoes also make wonderful toppings for shepherd's or fish pie, either on their own or mashed together with floury potatoes or parsnips. They are excellent in lamb stews and other casseroles, and delicious fried as chips or baked in their skins, served with butter or soured cream and sprinkled with crispy bacon.

Cod with Peanut, Ginger and Avocado Sauce

SERVES 4-5

5cm/2in piece fresh ginger

3 medium to large cloves garlic

1 medium red pepper

3 tablespoons groundnut oil

1 rounded teaspoon ground coriander

juice of 1 lemon and 1 orange

3 tablespoons water

2 rounded tablespoons crunchy peanut butter

½ level teaspoon cayenne pepper

675g/1½lb skinned cod fillet

1 medium avocado

salt

I made this dish after a trip to look at the peanut industry in Georgia, in America's Deep South. On our first evening our hosts, the peanut farmers, welcomed us with an unusual grace: 'Dear God, we thank you for our British friends and for the interest in peanuts which has brought them here.' I left Georgia not much more enamoured with peanuts than I had been before, yet in some savoury dishes and sauces I really could see their point for the first time.

Peel the ginger and garlic and chop together finely. Cut the red pepper in half, remove the seeds and stem and chop the flesh finely. Gently heat the oil in a medium saucepan and stir in the coriander, followed by the ginger, garlic and red pepper. Put the lid on the saucepan and cook over a very low heat, stirring now and then, for 15–20 minutes. Remove from the heat and add the lemon and orange juice and the water. Then stir in the peanut butter, add the cayenne pepper and salt to taste and put on one side.

Steam the fish for 8–14 minutes according to thickness – it should be just opaque in the centre. Halve and stone the avocado, peel off the skin and slice across thinly. Reheat the peanut sauce gently, stir in the avocado and keep over the heat for a minute or so, just to warm the avocado.

Drain the steamed fish on absorbent paper, then transfer it to a shallow serving dish. Spoon the sauce over the top and try to leave plenty of white fish showing. Serve at once.

Herring Fillets Rolled with Capers, Yellow Pepper and Mace

SERVES 4

1 medium yellow pepper

3 teaspoons capers

1 rounded teaspoon ground mace

¼ teaspoon cayenne pepper

4 large or 8 small herring fillets

2 teaspoons dried green peppercorns

strained juice of 1 lemon and 1 orange

5 tablespoons extra virgin olive oil

fresh flat-leafed parsley, to garnish

sea salt

Herrings are especially good eaten cold, and if you have them filleted you do not have to worry about the bones. If you like, you could use other white fish; John Dory is especially delicious. Serve with a salad and good bread to mop up the lovely juices.

Preheat the oven to 140°C/275°F/gas mark 1. Cut open the pepper, discard the seeds and stem and then chop the flesh very finely. Chop the capers very small and mix in a bowl with the yellow pepper, mace and cayenne pepper. Add a sprinkling of salt and stir to mix all together. Lay out the herring fillets flesh-side up and spoon the yellow pepper mixture evenly all over each one, patting it down. Loosely roll up the fillets and place them in a single layer in a shallow ovenproof dish. Sprinkle with the green peppercorns and a little more salt. Pour on the strained lemon and orange juice and then the olive oil. Cover the dish with foil. Cook in the centre of the oven for 1½ hours. Take out of the oven, remove the foil from the dish and leave to cool. Before serving, roughly chop the parsley and scatter it over the herrings.

Cod and Spring Greens with a Goat's Cheese Gratinée

SERVES 4

2 large, thick slices white bread

75g/3oz medium-firm goat's cheese

500g/1lb 2oz skinned thick cod fillet

about 550g/1lb 4oz spring greens

2 rounded teaspoons dried pink peppercorns (optional)

2 level teaspoons coriander seeds

2 tablespoons extra virgin olive oil

sea salt

black pepper

Both cod and spring greens are excellent ingredients which are often underrated. As long as you don't overcook either of them they are better than many grander fish and vegetables. For ease, ask your fishmonger to skin the cod fillets for you. Serve with new potatoes and a tomato salad.

Cut the crusts from the bread, put it in a food processor and whizz to make breadcrumbs, them turn them into a bowl. Cut the goat's cheese into very small pieces, cutting off any rind, add to the breadcrumbs and mix together. Season with salt and black pepper and leave on one side. Put the cod in the top of a steamer over boiling water and steam for 8–14 minutes, until just cooked to the centre but still succulent. Remove from the heat but keep covered.

Put a large saucepan of salted water over a high heat and warm up a shallow ovenproof dish. Discard any large, marked outer leaves of the spring greens and slice the rest across into 1.25cm/½in strips. When the water in the saucepan is boiling, add the sliced spring greens and boil for 2–5 minutes, until just tender and bright green. Drain and put into a mixing bowl. Crush the pink peppercorns, if using, and coriander seeds in a pestle and mortar and stir into the spring greens, together with the olive oil and a sprinkling of sea salt and black pepper. Flake in the steamed cod and mix gently with the greens. Turn into the warmed ovenproof dish and spread level.

Turn on the grill to a medium heat, sprinkle the breadcrumbs and goat's cheese mixture all over the top of the greens and cod and put under the grill until lightly browned. Serve immediately.

Kinsale is an ancient port in County Cork, Ireland. Now a small harbour town, it is reputed to be the 'Gastronomic Capital of Ireland', and hosts an annual food forum when gastronomes from all over the world gather to discuss food and enjoy the many restaurants.

I found it the most convivial conference imaginable and relished the local ingredients: an orgy of oysters, fish and shellfish, rosy spring lamb, and butter-tender beef. But one delicacy stood out above everything else – the freshest, most succulent cod, which made me realize that this oft-derided fish is certainly a prince, if not a king, of the sea.

Red Rice and Smoked Haddock Pudding

2 medium onions

75g/3oz butter

2 rounded teaspoons coriander seeds, roughly crushed

300ml/½ pint chicken stock

200g/7oz Camargue red rice

400g/14oz smoked haddock fillet

3–4 pinches cayenne pepper

225g/8oz puff pastry

salt

Red rice is a unique, rosy-coloured whole rice which grows in the Camargue area of Southern France. Its nutty flavour goes especially well with smoked fish. This impressive golden dome of crisp pastry encloses an excellent combination, and it can be prepared in advance and cooked just before your meal. Serve simply with a green salad.

Peel the onions and cut them into smallish pieces. Melt 50g/2oz of the butter in a saucepan over a fairly low heat, add the onions and crushed coriander and stir around until the onions have just softened. Then pour in the stock and bring to the boil. Add the rice, cover the pan and simmer gently for 25 minutes. Meanwhile, bring a little water to the boil in a deep frying pan which has a lid, add the smoked haddock, cover the pan and simmer very gently for 5–8 minutes, until the fish is just cooked. Pour away the water, discard the skin of the fish and flake the flesh.

When the rice is ready, remove from the heat and turn it into a bowl. Stir in the flaked fish and season with the cayenne pepper, and salt if necessary. Leave to cool.

If cooking immediately, preheat the oven to 190°C/375°F/gas mark 5. Gently melt the remaining butter and use some of it to grease a 600ml/1 pint pudding basin. Cut off three-quarters of the puff pastry, form into a ball and roll out thinly, shaping it into a circle large enough to line the pudding basin and to generously overlap the edges.

Line the buttered basin with the pastry circle and brush with butter. Then roll out the last quarter of pastry very thinly into a piece big enough to line the basin with a second layer but this time not to overlap the edges. Brush the pastry lining with more melted butter and place the second piece of rolled-out pastry on top of the first layer. Now spoon in the cooled rice and fish mixture and fold the pastry edges in over the filling to cover it, brushing with melted butter where the pastry overlaps. Cook in the centre of the oven for 45 minutes, then turn out on to an ovenproof serving plate and return to the oven for 10–15 minutes, until golden brown.

Salmon and Spinach Curry with Mango and Lime Pickle

SERVES 4

450g/1lb fresh spinach

3 medium-sized ripe tomatoes

1 tablespoon groundnut or sunflower oil

50g/2oz butter

1 level tablespoon green masala paste

150ml/¼ pint freshly squeezed orange juice

1 tablespoon mango and lime pickle

4 salmon steaks

salt

Farmed salmon is now relatively inexpensive and it is a fish that takes well to spices. This simple but unusual salmon dish goes very well with boiled potatoes.

Wash the spinach and pick off any thick stalks. Bring a saucepan of water to the boil, add the spinach leaves and cook for 1–2 minutes, just until limp. Then turn them into a colander, run under cold water, drain well and chop finely.

Put the tomatoes into a bowl, cover with boiling water, then drain, peel and chop up small. Put the oil and butter into a fairly wide cast-iron casserole dish over a medium heat until the butter has melted, then add the tomatoes and green masala paste. Stir around for a few minutes until the tomatoes are mushy, then add the orange juice and the chopped spinach. Cover the casserole dish, lower the heat and simmer very gently for 10–15 minutes, until the spinach is really soft. Stir in the mango and lime pickle and add salt to taste.

Place the salmon steaks on top of the mixture in the casserole and cover again. Cook very gently for 5–10 minutes (the time will depend on the thickness of your steaks), until the fish is just cooked but still a slightly darker pink in the centre when you insert a small knife. Serve at once.

Salmon Fillet in a Bay Leaf Cream

SERVES 4

50g/2oz butter

50g/2oz plain flour

300ml/½ pint white wine

300ml/½ pint double cream

2 teaspoons dried or bottled green peppercorns

4 fresh bay leaves

about 675g/1½lb tail piece of salmon, filleted and skinned

good handful fresh dill

sea salt

black pepper

This is a delicate summer dish. New potatoes make a perfect accompaniment, together with either really freshly picked peas or broad beans or frozen petits pois. Ask your fishmonger to fillet and skin the salmon for you.

Melt the butter gently in a heatproof casserole on top of the stove. Then remove from the heat and stir in the flour until smooth. Gradually stir in the white wine, followed by the cream. Season with salt and a little black pepper. Return to the heat and bring up to bubbling point, stirring all the time. Continue stirring the bubbling mixture for 2–3 minutes until thickened. Then stir in the green peppercorns and bay leaves, cover and barely simmer over the lowest possible heat for 15–20 minutes. Meanwhile slice the salmon evenly across at 5mm–1.25cm/¼–½in intervals.

Add the sliced salmon to the sauce, cover again and continue to simmer very gently for 5–10 minutes, until the salmon is lightly cooked through but still a darker pink in the centre – the time will depend on how thickly the fish has been sliced. Check the sauce for seasoning, chop the dill roughly and add it to the dish just before serving.

Saffron Blanquette of Salmon

450ml/¾ pint fish or chicken stock

2 generous pinches saffron strands

300ml/½ pint double cream

50g/2oz butter

2 teaspoons pink peppercorns, roughly crushed

40g/1½oz plain flour

1.1–1.25kg/2½–2¾lb tail piece of salmon, filleted and skinned

good bunch fresh dill

2 tablespoons lemon juice

salt

black pepper

This rich and quickly made dish is perfect served with new potatoes and either just a green salad or some early summer green vegetables such as broad beans, peas or French beans. Ask your fishmonger to fillet and skin the salmon for you.

Put the stock into a saucepan, add the saffron strands and bring up to bubbling. Remove from the heat and leave for 10 minutes, then stir in the double cream.

Put the butter and pink peppercorns in a fairly large heatproof casserole over a gentle heat until the butter has melted. Remove from the heat and stir in the flour until smooth. Return the pan to the heat, gradually stir in the stock and cream mixture and bring to the boil, stirring all the time. Bubble, still stirring, for 2–3 minutes, until thickened and smooth. Cover and simmer very gently for 10 minutes. Meanwhile, cut the salmon into 4cm/1½in chunks and chop the dill.

Stir the lemon juice slowly into the simmering sauce and season to taste with salt and black pepper. Drop in the pieces of salmon, cover with the lid again and simmer gently for another 5–8 minutes or until the salmon is just cooked through but still slightly dark pink in the centre. Stir in the chopped dill and serve as soon as possible.

Salmon Sausages with a Goat's Cheese and Sorrel Sauce

450g/1lb skinned salmon fillet

2 large egg whites

15g/½oz cornflour

1 teaspoon baking powder

2–3 pinches chilli powder or cayenne pepper

grated rind and juice of 1 orange

1 large handful sorrel leaves

50g/2oz butter

1 teaspoon paprika

25g/1oz plain flour

450ml/¾ pint milk

100g/4oz goat's cheese log

2 large egg yolks

salt

black pepper

These are delicate and tender little poached fish sausages in a gratinée sauce. The sausages contain orange zest which has an inexplicable affinity with fish. Broccoli or courgettes and new potatoes make ideal accompaniments.

Cut up the salmon fillet roughly and put into a food processor with the egg whites, cornflour, baking powder, chilli powder or cayenne and some salt. Whizz until smoothly blended. Then stir in the grated orange rind. Using wet hands, form the mixture into small, fat sausages. Bring a large saucepan of water to a rolling boil, then drop in the fish sausages and simmer for 7 minutes. Drain the sausages in a colander and put them into a shallow ovenproof dish. Preheat the oven to 150°C/300°F/gas mark 2.

To make the sauce, chop up the sorrel finely. Melt the butter in a saucepan with the paprika. Remove from the heat and stir in the flour with a wooden spoon until smooth. Stir in the milk and orange juice, put back on the heat and bring to the boil, stirring. Bubble, still stirring, for about 3 minutes. Crumble the goat's cheese into the sauce and stir until it has melted, then stir in the chopped sorrel and, lastly, the egg yolks. Stir thoroughly for a minute or two, then remove from the heat and season to taste with salt and black pepper. Pour the sauce over the fish sausages. Heat the grill to its highest and put the dish under it for 2–4 minutes, until the topping is speckled dark brown. Then put the dish on the centre shelf of the oven and cook for 15–20 minutes before serving.

Salmon and Fennel Cooked in a Pumpkin

SERVES 8

7.5cm/3in piece fresh ginger

6 cloves garlic

6 cardamom pods

2 teaspoons fennel seeds

2 fresh green chillies

900g/2lb skinned salmon fillet

2 medium bulbs fennel

675g/1½lb onions

100g/4oz butter

50g/2oz plain flour

juice and finely grated rind of
    1 lemon

300ml/½ pint milk

1 large pumpkin, about 3.25–3.5kg/
    7½–8lb

a little sunflower oil

sea salt

I love using pumpkins as a cooking pot. People are always staggered when I put the whole pumpkin on the table, take off the top and reveal the steaming, aromatic contents. Choose an evenly round pumpkin which stands steadily on its base.

Peel the ginger and garlic and cut into thin slices. Extract the seeds from the cardamom pods and put with the fennel seeds into a wiped-out coffee grinder or a pestle and mortar. Grind fairly finely. Cut open the chillies under running water, discard the seeds and stem and chop the flesh finely. Cut the salmon into 2.5–5cm/1–2in chunks. Cut off the base of the fennel bulbs, remove any marked outer parts, cut in half lengthways and then into thick slices. Peel the onions and slice thinly.

Melt 75g/3oz of the butter in a large, heavy-based saucepan, add the onions and cook over a low heat, stirring now and then, until the onions are soft. Add the ginger, garlic, ground spices and chillies. Add the remaining butter and, when melted, add the sliced fennel. Stir around to coat with the butter. Then stir in the flour and gradually add first the lemon juice and grated rind and then the milk. Bring to the boil, stirring all the time, and bubble, still stirring, until the sauce is very thick. Season to taste with sea salt. Remove from the heat, leave until cool, then fold in the salmon pieces.

Preheat the oven to 240°C/475°F/gas mark 9. Cut the top off the pumpkin with a very sharp knife and reserve. Use a big spoon with sharp edges to scoop out the seeds and the stringy interior, leaving only the firm, orange flesh. Spoon the salmon mixture into the pumpkin, put into a roasting pan and put the top back on the pumpkin. Smear the pumpkin skin all over with sunflower oil and put into the oven. Bake for 25–30 minutes, then reduce the heat to 180°C/350°F/gas mark 4 and cook for another 45 minutes–1 hour, until the pumpkin flesh feels very soft right through when you insert a sharp knife. Using a wide spatula and holding the pumpkin with a cloth, carefully lift it from the roasting pan on to a large, round serving plate. To serve, scoop out the salmon filling and the pumpkin flesh.

One of the most unusual invitations resulting from my life as a food writer was to be a guest of honour at 'The Vessel Forum'. I could not imagine why I had been invited to a nautical event, but soon learned that it was a gathering of 200 potters, glassblowers and metalworkers – all creators of vessels. My own presence was thought appropriate, since in my work I was a constant user of them.

The invitation included instructions that everyone should bring their vessel with them. By chance I had just developed a recipe in which I cooked some spiced chicken in a beautiful pumpkin, so during my short speech I was able to apologize for not bringing my vessel with me as a result of having eaten it the night before.

Salmon Pie with Capers, Black Olives and Toasted Pine Kernels

SERVES 4

400g/14oz skinned salmon fillet

125g/4½oz black olives

1 bunch spring onions

25g/1oz pine kernels

75g/3oz butter

1 tablespoon capers

finely grated rind of 1 lemon and 1 orange

4–5 pinches cayenne pepper

350–400g/12–14oz puff pastry

1 egg yolk

1 tablespoon milk

salt

The contrasting flavours of capers, olives and pine kernels add a lot of interest to the salmon in this simply made but attractive-looking pie. Serve with new potatoes and a green salad, fresh peas or beans.

Cut the salmon into 1.25cm/½in pieces and put them into a mixing bowl. Roughly cut the flesh from the olives and discard the stones. Trim the spring onions and cut them across fairly thinly, using some of the green part too. Heat a dry frying pan over a fairly high heat, add the pine kernels and stir around for a minute or two until just browned. Remove from the heat and add the butter to the pan so it melts slowly.

Add the olives, spring onions, capers and lemon and orange rind to the bowl of salmon pieces and stir to mix, adding the melted butter and pine kernels too. Season with the cayenne pepper and some salt.

Preheat the oven to 220°C/425°F/gas mark 7. Divide the pastry in half and form each piece into a ball. Roll out the balls into very thin circles. Butter a 25cm/10in round flan tin or a baking sheet. Lay one circle of pastry on the flan tin and pile the salmon mixture on top of it, leaving 2.5cm/1in around the edge uncovered. Moisten this edge with water and lay the second circle of pastry on the salmon. Press the edges to seal and then trim them neatly. Roll out the trimmings to make decorations. Moisten these underneath before placing them on top of the pie. Pierce 2 holes in the pastry to let the steam escape.

Whisk together the egg yolk and milk and brush over the pie to glaze. Cook in the centre of the oven for 25–35 minutes or until the pastry is a rich golden brown. Serve immediately.

Star Anise Fragrant Mackerel with Apricots and Fresh Lime

SERVES 4

4 small mackerel, gutted, with heads left on

4 whole star anise

225g/8oz fresh apricots

2 cloves garlic

juice of 2 limes

3 tablespoons sherry

4–5 spring onions

soy sauce

salt

black pepper

This healthy dish is really quick to prepare. It also tastes excellent. Serve with steamed new potatoes and briefly cooked sliced spring greens.

Preheat the oven to 190°C/375°F/gas mark 5. Lay the mackerel in a shallow ovenproof dish and insert a whole star anise inside each fish. Cut the apricots in half, remove the stones and chop the flesh finely. Peel the garlic and chop finely. Spoon the chopped apricots and garlic between the fish in the dish. Pour the lime juice and sherry all over and sprinkle with a little salt and plenty of black pepper. Cover the dish tightly with foil and cook the fish on the centre shelf of the oven for 30–35 minutes.

Meanwhile, trim the spring onions and chop finely across. When the fish is cooked, remove the foil. Just before serving, sprinkle with the chopped spring onions and trickle a little soy sauce over each fish.

Squid with Tomatoes, Red Pepper and Chillies

SERVES 4

450–675g/1–1½lb prepared squid

675g/1½lb tomatoes

1 large red pepper

2 fresh green chillies

3 large cloves garlic

good handful fresh mint leaves

3 tablespoons olive oil

50g/2oz butter

1 rounded tablespoon tomato purée

juice of ½ orange

sugar

salt

black pepper

One of the best fish buys is squid, which is never expensive. I use it for stir-frying, steaming or poaching. It takes well to oriental, Mediterranean or Indian flavourings and it makes all the difference to a fish stew, dropped in at the last minute. If you are put off by having eaten rubbery squid it is almost bound to have been the result of prolonged or fierce cooking.

Serve this dish with basmati rice and a crisp green vegetable or, if you want to eat it cold, simply accompany it with a green salad and crusty bread.

Unless the squid are very small, cut them into thin rings. Leave on one side. Put the tomatoes into a large bowl, pour over boiling water and leave for about 2 minutes, then drain, peel and chop up roughly. Slice the red pepper in half lengthways, discard the seeds and stem and slice the flesh across fairly thinly. Cut the chillies open under running water and discard the seeds and stem. Peel the garlic and chop both chillies and garlic up finely. Chop up the mint leaves roughly.

Heat the olive oil and butter in a flameproof casserole or deep sauté pan over a medium heat. Add the red pepper, garlic, chillies and tomatoes. Then stir in the tomato purée, orange juice and a sprinkling of salt. Cover and cook very gently, stirring often, for 15–25 minutes, until the peppers are completely soft and the tomatoes have turned to a thick sauce. Taste and add more salt and a little black pepper if necessary.

Just before serving, bring the tomato mixture almost to bubbling, add the squid and cook, stirring, for 2–4 minutes only, just until the squid is opaque. Stir in the mint leaves and remove from the heat. Serve at once.

STAR ANISE FRAGRANT MACKEREL WITH APRICOTS AND ◄ FRESH LIME

Baked Mackerel with Pernod, Pine Kernel and Dill Sauce

SERVES 4-5

2 teaspoons ground coriander

1 teaspoon paprika

3–4 pinches cayenne pepper

handful fresh dill, finely chopped

2 large mackerel, 450–675g/1–1½lb
    each, cleaned and gutted

2 small lemons

1 small red onion

125ml/4fl oz Pernod

15g/½oz pine kernels

150ml/¼ pint double cream

salt

black pepper

With its shimmering midnight-blue and deep-green skin, striped in waves of velvet black, the mackerel is a beautiful fish. It is also very nutritious, smooth and melting in consistency, rich in flavour and inexpensive – a word that applies to few fish nowadays.

Mackerel should be absolutely fresh; avoid any with dull, sunken eyes or less than shiny skin. Ask the fishmonger to clean and gut the fish but to leave the heads on.

Preheat the oven to 200°C/400°F/gas mark 6. Generously butter a large piece of foil – large enough to wrap the fish in – and place it in a large roasting pan. In a bowl, mix together the coriander, paprika, cayenne pepper, 1 tablespoon of the dill and a sprinkling of salt. Sprinkle some of this mixture inside the gutted fish and rub the rest over the skin. Lay the fish on the buttered foil.

Slice the lemons across very thinly. Peel the onion and slice it as thinly as possible into rings; use a food processor if you have one. Arrange the lemon and onion slices alternately underneath and on top of the fish. Bring the foil up a little and pour the Pernod gently over the fish. Then wrap it up completely in the foil and bake in the centre of the oven for 30–40 minutes. Meanwhile, toast the pine kernels over a high heat in a dry frying pan for a minute or two until browned. Keep on one side.

To check whether the fish is cooked, insert a small knife to see if the flesh is opaque to the bone. Unwrap one end of the foil and pour the juices out into a saucepan. Then unwrap the foil completely and push the mackerel gently on to a large warmed serving dish. Arrange the lemon and onion slices on and around the fish. Pour the cream into the saucepan with the juices and add the toasted pine kernels and the remaining chopped dill. Bring to the boil and bubble for a minute. Season to taste with black pepper and more salt if necessary. Pour the sauce into a jug to serve with the fish.

Fish Curry with Ginger and Kaffir Lime Leaves

SERVES 6

450ml/¾ pint hot water

4 rounded tablespoons coconut milk powder

1 level teaspoon salt

1 kg/2¼ lb skinned thick cod fillet

5cm/2in piece fresh ginger

2 large cloves garlic

1 fresh red chilli

4 fresh or dried kaffir lime leaves

225g/8oz tomatoes

3 tablespoons groundnut oil

1 tablespoon oyster sauce

juice of 1 lemon

Since my travels in Vietnam I have become almost addicted to the unique flavour of kaffir lime leaves. You can buy them in oriental food shops and sometimes in supermarkets. Serve this curry with fragrant rice or Chinese noodles.

Pour the hot water into a measuring jug, stir in the coconut milk powder until dissolved, then add the salt and leave on one side. Slice the cod into large chunks. Peel the ginger and garlic. Cut the chilli open under running water and discard the seeds and stem. Chop the ginger, garlic and chilli together finely. Tear the lime leaves in half. Put the tomatoes into a bowl, pour boiling water over them and leave for about 2 minutes, then drain, peel and chop finely.

Pour the groundnut oil into a large heatproof casserole dish over a medium heat. Add the chopped ginger, garlic and chilli and stir around for a minute. Add the lime leaves and tomatoes and stir for another 2 minutes. Pour in the coconut milk and then stir in the oyster sauce and lemon juice. Bring just up to bubbling, then gently add the pieces of cod, cover the casserole and barely simmer for 20 minutes, until the fish is cooked through.

Monkfish and Fennel Cooked in Saffron Yoghurt Cream

SERVES 6

2 large bulbs fennel

1 large Spanish onion

500g/1lb 2oz plain yoghurt

2 rounded teaspoons cornflour

2 tablespoons milk

10–14 saffron strands

300ml/½ pint double cream

3–4 pinches cayenne pepper

900g/2lb monkfish fillet

chopped fresh fennel leaves or chives

salt

In this dish the yoghurt is stabilized so that it won't curdle and then combined with saffron and cream. It forms a lovely base in which to poach the fennel and fish. Serve with new potatoes and a green vegetable.

Cut the stalks and ends off the fennel bulbs and discard any marked outer pieces. Cut the bulbs lengthways into 6–8 pieces each. Peel the onion and slice across into rings.

Pour the yoghurt into a fairly large flameproof casserole. Mix the cornflour with the milk in a cup until smooth and then mix into the yoghurt. Put the casserole over a medium heat and bring to bubbling, stirring all the time in one direction only. Bubble, still stirring, for about 2 minutes. Then add the saffron, stir in the cream, cayenne pepper and some salt and put in the sliced fennel and onion. Bring to bubbling again, cover the pan and simmer gently over the lowest possible heat for about 30 minutes, stirring now and then, until the fennel and onion are very soft.

Meanwhile, slice the fish into large chunks. When the vegetables are soft, add the fish, cover again and continue barely simmering for 10–15 minutes, just until the fish is cooked through. Stir in some chopped fennel leaves or chives and serve at once.

family
favourites

Family meals can be the most enjoyable of all. They can put an end to bad moods and arguments and emphasize affection. A favourite family dish sometimes conjures up pleasures and fond memories for a lifetime; I still think of my grandmother's special roast chicken with a feeling of intense nostalgia. Family food must please both young and old; it must have the reassuring qualities of nursery food plus the flavour and interest of more exotic dishes. It must be practical and suitable for either preparing ahead and keeping warm, or cooking very quickly after a day out. This chapter contains some of my family's favourites, which they have eaten up enthusiastically, remembered, and asked for again.

Autumn Leaf Chicken and Spinach Pie

SERVES 6-8

450g/1lb spinach

800g/1¾lb skinless boneless chicken thighs

2–3 large cloves garlic

350g/12oz onions

1 tablespoon sunflower or groundnut oil

90g/3½oz butter

2 teaspoons ground coriander

2 teaspoons ground cinnamon

1 heaped tablespoon thick-cut marmalade

350g/12oz filo pastry

salt

black pepper

A pie is convenient for family life as it can be prepared ahead and simply reheated when required. This deliciously flavoured, crispy pie goes best with a mixed green salad instead of vegetables. The unusual combination of spinach and orange marmalade works especially well, and the filo pastry makes the pie look like a rich, golden pile of curling autumn leaves, so it always causes a sensation.

Boneless chicken thighs are more succulent than breast meat and are available in all supermarkets.

Wash the spinach well and remove the stalks. Bring a large pan of salted water to the boil and plunge in the spinach leaves for just a minute, until limp. Drain well, pressing out all the liquid you can, then chop up small. Cut up the chicken into small pieces, removing any skin. Peel the garlic and chop finely. Peel the onions and chop into fairly small pieces.

Heat the oil and 15g/½oz of the butter in a large frying pan. Add the chicken and stir around over a high heat for about 5 minutes, until lightly browned. Then add the garlic, onions and spices and stir for another minute. Cover the pan tightly with foil and leave just bubbling over a low heat for 30 minutes, stirring round now and then, especially towards the end when the juices evaporate. If the juices don't evaporate completely, remove the foil, increase the heat and bubble until they do. Remove the pan from the heat and season with salt and black pepper. Stir in the marmalade. Lastly, stir in the chopped spinach and leave until cold.

Preheat the oven to 180°C/350°F/gas mark 4. Melt the remaining butter in a saucepan. Brush a deep, loose-based, 19cm/7½in round cake tin thinly with melted butter. Lay a whole sheet of filo pastry in it, press it down in the tin and let the ends hang right over the sides. Brush the pastry thinly with butter. Lay another sheet across the other way so that the tin is completely lined. Continue like this in layers, buttering each sheet and letting the pastry hang out all round the edges of the tin. Spoon in the cooled chicken mixture. Bring in the overlapping pastry sheet by sheet, loosely over the top, lightly buttering each piece. The top 2–3 layers should be completely crumpled, sticking up towards the centre.

Cook the pie in the centre of the oven for 30 minutes, until the top is well browned. Then put the tin on a narrower, round object (such as a tin of tomatoes) and push the pie up and out of the tin. Using a wide spatula, lever it carefully off the base on to an ovenproof serving plate and put it back in the oven for another 20–30 minutes to brown the sides and crisp up the base.

Chicken and Fennel Pie with a Double Herb and Cheese Crust

1 large bulb fennel

450–550g/1–1¼lb skinless chicken breast fillets

2 cloves garlic

3 tablespoons olive oil

2 level teaspoons paprika

finely grated rind of 1 lemon

1 rounded tablespoon tomato purée

salt

black pepper

For the pastry:

175g/6oz plain flour

1 teaspoon baking powder

½ teaspoon salt

50g/2oz fresh white breadcrumbs

3 teaspoons dried oregano

50g/2oz mature Cheddar cheese, grated

100g/4oz vegetable suet

juice of 1 lemon

a little milk for brushing

This pie has a light crust made with vegetable suet, which is a nice change from normal pastry. It is also very easy to prepare. The pie only needs a green salad as an accompaniment, though frozen petits pois or broad beans also go well.

Cut off the base and stalks of the fennel bulb and, if necessary, remove any marked outer parts. Chop the bulb into small pieces. Cut the chicken breasts into very thin slices crossways. Peel and finely chop the garlic. Put the oil into a large, heavy frying pan over a medium heat. Add the chopped fennel and the paprika and stir around for 6–8 minutes, until the fennel has just softened. Then add the chicken, garlic and lemon rind and stir for another 3–4 minutes, until the chicken is opaque right through. Stir in the tomato purée and season to taste with salt and plenty of black pepper. Remove from the heat, turn into a bowl and leave to cool.

To make the pastry, sift the flour, baking powder and salt into a bowl and, using a fork, stir in the breadcrumbs, oregano, grated cheese and suet. Add the lemon juice and enough cold water to form a stiff dough.

When the filling is cold, butter a pie plate 23–25cm/9–10in in diameter. Divide the pastry in half, form into 2 balls and roll each one out on a floured board into a circle big enough for the pie plate. Line the plate with one circle and spoon in the chicken filling. Dampen the edges and cover with the other circle. Trim the edges and use the trimmings to decorate the top. Refrigerate the pie until ready to cook.

To cook, preheat the oven to 200°C/400°F/gas mark 6. Brush the pastry all over with milk, and bake the pie in the centre of the oven for 25–30 minutes, until golden brown.

Chicken and Anchovy Marbles with a Rosemary, Tomato and Crème Fraîche Sauce

SERVES 4

50g/2oz crustless white bread

350g/12oz skinless chicken breast fillets

50g/2oz tin anchovies

½ medium-sized red-skinned onion

handful fresh flat-leafed parsley

1 medium egg, lightly whisked

15g/½oz butter

2 tablespoons olive oil

1 sprig fresh rosemary

3–4 tomatoes, the plum variety if available

200ml/7fl oz carton crème fraîche

1 level teaspoon caster sugar

salt

black pepper

Chicken balls are more unusual than meatballs and in this recipe the anchovy works wonders for adding flavour.

Tear up the bread, put it in a food processor and whizz to make breadcrumbs. Put the breadcrumbs into a large bowl. Cut up the chicken breasts roughly, put into the food processor and whizz until finely chopped. Stir the chopped chicken into the breadcrumbs.

Open the tin of anchovies and pour the oil into the bowl of chicken and breadcrumbs. Slice the anchovy fillets across thinly. Chop the onion finely. Reserve a few whole leaves of parsley for garnish and chop the rest roughly. Add the anchovies, onion, parsley and egg to the chicken and breadcrumb mixture, together with salt and plenty of black pepper. Mix together very thoroughly with a wooden spoon. Using wet hands, form the mixture into small balls the size of large marbles.

Put the butter and olive oil into a large, heavy-based frying pan over a fairly gentle heat. Add the chicken marbles and fry for about 15 minutes, turning around several times to cook evenly. Then transfer them to a warm serving plate and keep warm in a low oven.

Take the spikes of rosemary off their stalks and chop finely. Put the tomatoes into a bowl, pour boiling water over them and leave for about 2 minutes, then drain, peel and cut into small cubes. Put the crème fraîche into a saucepan and add the chopped rosemary and tomatoes, the sugar and a sprinkling of salt and black pepper. Put over a medium heat and stir, just under boiling point, for 4–5 minutes, to give the rosemary and tomato flavours time to develop. To serve, pour the sauce over the chicken marbles and garnish with the reserved parsley leaves.

Chickpeas with Chicken and Chorizo

SERVES 4 - 5

275g/10oz dried chickpeas

3 large cloves garlic

450g/1lb ripe tomatoes, the plum variety if available

4–5 skinless boneless chicken thighs

225–275g/8–10oz chorizo sausages

3 rounded teaspoons dried oregano

600ml/1 pint chicken stock

2–3 tablespoons extra virgin olive oil

salt

freshly ground black pepper

Unlike butterbeans, it is almost impossible to cook chickpeas to a stage where they break up. They are a particular favourite of mine for their lovely nutty flavour. This one-pot meal is ideal for a family supper as it is popular with children. Serve with a green salad and crusty bread.

Soak the chickpeas in water overnight. Drain and boil in plenty of water for 10 minutes. Now reduce the heat, cover the pan and simmer for about half an hour. Meanwhile, peel the garlic and chop finely. Put the tomatoes into a bowl, pour boiling water over them, leave for 2 minutes, then drain, peel and chop up fairly small. Cut the chicken into roughly 2.5cm/1in pieces and slice the chorizo sausages thinly. Preheat the oven to 170°C/325°F/gas mark 3.

Drain the parcooked chickpeas and put them into a heatproof casserole with all the prepared ingredients. Stir in the oregano and chicken stock and cover the casserole. Bring up to bubbling on top of the stove and then put on the centre shelf of the oven for 1½–2 hours, until the chickpeas are tender. Season to taste with salt and black pepper and, just before serving, trickle the olive oil over the top so that it mixes in roughly as you spoon the helpings out.

Pork and Chicken Meatballs with Pesto and Pine Kernels

SERVES 5 - 6

1 large red pepper

225g/8oz skinless chicken breast fillets

2–3 large cloves garlic

good handful fresh flat-leafed parsley

350g/12oz minced pork

50g/2oz pine kernels

2 rounded tablespoons pesto sauce

2 tablespoons groundnut oil

salt

black pepper

Jars of pesto sauce are now easily available and some supermarkets also sell tubs of fresh pesto; they are a boon for adding interest and flavour to quickly made dishes, as in these particularly good meatballs. They taste equally delicious cold, so are very practical to take on picnics.

Cut the pepper in half and remove the seeds and stem. Bring a pan of salted water to the boil, add the pepper halves, cover the pan and simmer for 6–8 minutes, until the pepper has softened. Drain and chop finely. Cut the chicken breast fillets into very small pieces. Peel the garlic and chop finely. Chop the parsley fairly small. Put the minced pork and the pine kernels (they are nicest if you toss them in a dry frying pan for a minute or two first just to brown) into a bowl and stir in the chopped pepper, chicken, garlic and parsley. Then add the pesto with a good seasoning of salt and black pepper and stir thoroughly.

Using wet hands, take up bits of the meat mixture and form into balls the size of large marbles. Heat the oil in a large, heavy frying pan over a medium heat. Add the meatballs and fry for 15–20 minutes, turning them around until browned all over. Transfer to a heated serving plate, pile up into a mound and serve.

Pesto Roast Chicken with Grilled Yellow Pepper Sauce

SERVES 7-8

1 large chicken, weighing
    2.5kg/5½lb

2–2½ tablespoons pesto sauce

knob of butter, at room temperature

1 medium yellow pepper

350ml/12fl oz chicken stock

1 dessertspoon sherry vinegar

6–8 fresh basil leaves

25g/1oz chilled butter

3–5 pinches cayenne pepper

salt

An ordinary chicken can be transformed really simply by putting pesto beneath the skin before roasting. With its smoky-sweet yellow pepper sauce, I find this an ever-popular dish for serving to family and friends at Sunday lunch. Accompany with new, sautéed or roast potatoes and a green vegetable.

Gently loosen the chicken skin by gradually easing your fingers between it and the flesh. If you are careful you can loosen the skin over the legs as well as the breast. Spoon the pesto sauce under the skin, then press the skin down on top to spread the sauce evenly over the flesh. Leave at cool room temperature for 1 hour before cooking.

To roast, preheat the oven to 190°C/375°F/gas mark 5. Smear the knob of butter all over the breast and legs. Put the chicken in a roasting pan with 4 tablespoons of water and cook for 2–2¼ hours, basting fairly often – the bird is cooked if the juices run clear when you insert a small knife close to the bone and the legs feel loosened from the body.

While the bird is cooking, cut the pepper in half, remove the seeds and stem and put the pepper halves under a hot grill, skin-side up, until blackened. Then wrap them in a plastic bag or tin foil and leave to cool. When cool, peel off the skin, put the pepper into a food processor with the stock and sherry vinegar and whizz until it is as smooth as possible.

Slice the basil leaves thinly across. Cut the chilled butter into small pieces and put it back in the fridge.

When the chicken is ready, turn off the heat, open the oven door a little and leave for 20 minutes to rest. Then remove the chicken from the roasting pan, emptying out any juices from inside the bird into the pan. Put the chicken on a carving board. Put the roasting pan on top of the stove over a high heat and bubble up the pan juices for 2–3 minutes to reduce them slightly. Then stir in the yellow pepper purée and bubble again for a minute or two. Finally, remove from the heat and whisk in the chilled butter, a few pieces at a time. Season to taste with the cayenne pepper and salt, stir in the sliced basil leaves and pour the sauce into a jug. Carve the chicken and serve with the sauce.

Pasta with Anchovy and Garlic Sauce and Toasted Breadcrumbs

SERVES 4

4 large cloves garlic

75ml/3fl oz water

3 tablespoons olive oil

150g/5oz fresh breadcrumbs

50g/2oz tin anchovies

350g/12oz pasta such as spaghetti or tagliatelle

large handful fresh flat-leafed parsley

sea salt

black pepper

In this pasta dish the anchovies add a wonderful flavour and the crunchy breadcrumbs a contrasting texture. This miraculous way of transforming anchovy fillets into a smooth cream can also be used as a base for many sauces and in dishes such as meat casseroles, or to transform the juices of chicken or meat.

Put 3 unpeeled garlic cloves into a small saucepan with the water, cover and simmer for about 10 minutes, until the garlic feels completely soft within its skin. Remove from the heat and leave on one side. Peel the remaining clove of garlic and chop very finely.

Heat 2 tablespoons of the olive oil in a large, heavy-based frying pan over a low heat. Add the chopped garlic and the breadcrumbs and stir until the breadcrumbs are a rich golden brown. Turn the mixture into a bowl and leave on one side.

Empty the anchovies and their oil into a bowl set over a pan of very hot water, but not over the heat. Add the remaining olive oil and stir the mixture constantly with a wooden spoon until the anchovies dissolve into a smooth, brown cream.

Pop the boiled cloves of garlic out of their skins (reserving the water in the pan) and into the anchovy mixture. Stir again thoroughly until the garlic breaks up and becomes amalgamated into the smooth anchovy cream. Then stir in the reserved garlic water a little at a time and season with salt if necessary and plenty of black pepper.

Leave the sauce on one side, still over the pan of hot water. Bring a large pan of salted water to the boil, add the pasta and cook until *al dente*. Meanwhile, chop the parsley fairly roughly. When the pasta is ready, drain it but leave it in the saucepan. Using a large wooden spoon, mix the anchovy sauce, parsley and toasted breadcrumbs into the pasta. Transfer to a warmed bowl and serve immediately.

My friend Franco lives in his old family house in Positano, southern Italy, now run as a comfortable hotel. Every year on his birthday Franco and his extensive family, plus a strong contingent of local Positanese and many friends from abroad, gather for a Sagra Della Pasta, literally a celebration of pasta.

This is a feast of pasta on an unbelievable scale. An infinitely long table holds 40 different pasta dishes. The guests walk up and down with a look of serious concentration, making sure they have taken all the varieties they want to try. Then, rather sheepishly, they return to their seats, holding a large plateful of what appears to be a Mount Vesuvius of pasta.

Pasta with Broccoli, Walnuts and Bacon

SERVES 4

675g/1½lb calabrese broccoli

2 large cloves garlic

225g/8oz rindless smoked streaky bacon

2 tablespoons extra virgin olive oil

350g/12oz pasta shapes

75g/3oz walnuts, roughly chopped

freshly grated Parmesan cheese, to serve

salt

black pepper

It is important to have a well-heated serving dish ready as pasta cools quickly.

Break the broccoli up into small florets. Discard any thick stalks likely to be tough and slice up the remaining stalks into small pieces. Steam or boil the broccoli for 3–6 minutes, until just tender and bright green. Rinse with cold water and leave on one side.

Peel the garlic and chop finely. Slice the bacon rashers crossways into small pieces. Bring a large pan of salted water to the boil. While the water is coming to the boil, put the olive oil into a largish, heavy-based saucepan over a fairly high heat, add the bacon pieces and stir around until crisp. Then add the chopped garlic and remove from the heat.

When the water is boiling, add the pasta and cook for 7–10 minutes, until *al dente*. When the pasta is nearly ready, put the saucepan containing the bacon back over a medium heat, add the broccoli and walnuts and stir for 2 or 3 minutes just to reheat the broccoli. Season with salt and plenty of black pepper. Drain the pasta well, turn it into a heated serving dish and stir in the broccoli and bacon mixture, with all of its flavourful fat. Serve with grated Parmesan.

Pasta with Parsnips and Kabanos Sausages

SERVES 4

2 large yellow peppers

225–275g/8–10oz pasta shapes, noodles or spaghetti

225g/8oz kabanos sausages

350g/12oz thin leeks

350g/12oz parsnips

4 tablespoons olive oil

freshly grated Parmesan cheese, to serve

salt

black pepper

Parsnips are far more versatile than you would imagine, as this easy recipe shows. With the smoky-sweet additions of grilled peppers and kabanos (thin Polish sausages with a spicy, smoked flavour), and the light, oniony taste of leeks, this is a wonderful combination.

Halve the peppers lengthways and discard the seeds and stem. Put the pepper halves under a hot grill, skin-side upwards, until blackened in patches all over. Wrap in a plastic bag or tin foil until cool enough to handle. Peel off the skin and cut the peppers lengthways into thin strips.

Cook the pasta in plenty of boiling salted water until *al dente*. Meanwhile, slice the kabanos sausages thinly. Cut the leeks into thin rings. Peel the parsnips and slice very finely across. Heat half the olive oil in a large, deep frying pan over a fairly high heat. Add the sausage and toss around for 1–2 minutes. Add the remaining oil and the leeks and stir for 1–2 minutes, until they begin to soften, then add the parsnips and stir for another minute. Lastly, stir in the peppers and season to taste.

Drain the pasta and place it in a warm serving bowl. Pour the sauce on top and serve with grated Parmesan cheese.

PASTA WITH BROCCOLI, WALNUTS AND BACON ▶

Lamb Paprika Pie with Potato Pastry

SERVES 4

675g/1½lb lamb fillets

1 large red pepper

175g/6oz chestnut mushrooms

2 large cloves garlic

15g/½oz butter

2 tablespoons olive oil

3 teaspoons paprika

2 rounded tablespoons plain flour

300ml/½ pint milk

300ml/½ pint soured cream

2 rounded teaspoons whole grain mustard

1 rounded teaspoon caster sugar

3–4 pinches cayenne pepper

salt

For the pastry:

100g/4oz plain flour

1 teaspoon baking powder

good pinch of salt

100g/4oz cold butter

175g/6oz cold mashed potato

a little milk for brushing

Pies always impress and excite. They offer an element of surprise, rather like opening a present. This potato pastry is a good way to use up leftover mashed potato, and it is also delicious.

Preheat the oven to 150°C/300°F/gas mark 2. Slice the lamb fillets across at 1.25cm/½in intervals. Halve the pepper, discard the seeds and stem and chop the flesh very small. Halve the mushrooms. Peel the garlic and chop finely.

Melt the butter and oil in a heatproof casserole over a medium heat. Add the paprika and stir for 1 minute, then add the chopped pepper, garlic, mushrooms and lamb. Using a wooden spoon, stir to coat them with oil, then remove from the heat and stir in the flour. Gradually add the milk and soured cream, then stir in the mustard and sugar. Add a sprinkling of salt and stir until smooth. Put the casserole back on top of the stove and bring to the boil, stirring all the time as the liquid thickens. When bubbling, cover and transfer to the centre of the oven. Cook for 1½ hours or until the lamb is tender, then add cayenne pepper to taste and more salt if necessary. Turn the mixture into a pie plate, deep flan dish or gratin dish, filling it almost to the top, and leave until cold.

Meanwhile, make the pastry. Sift the flour, baking powder and salt into a bowl. Cut the butter into small pieces and rub it into the flour until the mixture resembles breadcrumbs. Work in the mashed potato by hand and knead slightly until you have a smooth dough. Form it into a ball, wrap in cling film and leave in the fridge for 30 minutes.

Preheat the oven to 190°C/375°F/gas mark 5. Roll out the pastry on a floured board into a piece large enough to cover the dish of lamb. Moisten the edges of the dish. Roll the pastry back over the rolling pin and out again on to the dish. Trim the edges and make indentations round them with the back of the knife. Roll the trimmings out to make decorations for the top of the pie. Brush the pastry with milk and cook in the centre of the oven for 25–35 minutes, until golden brown.

Herb- and Spice-marinated Grilled Lamb Fillets

SERVES 6

3 tablespoons plain yoghurt

3 tablespoons sherry vinegar

2 tablespoons olive oil

1 heaped tablespoon tomato purée

3 teaspoons coriander seeds

1 teaspoon cumin seeds

4 bay leaves

2 large cloves garlic

good sprig fresh rosemary

675–800g/1½–1¾lb lamb fillets

salt

black pepper

Marinades can work wonders, enhancing flavours either subtly or dramatically depending on the ingredients. This marinade uses yoghurt as a base, which also tenderizes the meat.

Lamb neck fillets are a useful cut for all boneless lamb dishes, especially when grilled and eaten pink and juicy, as here. They are excellent for a barbecue.

Put the yoghurt, sherry vinegar, olive oil and tomato purée in a bowl and mix together. Put the coriander and cumin seeds and the bay leaves, roughly broken, into a coffee grinder and grind finely. Peel the garlic and pull the rosemary leaves from the stalk. Then chop the garlic and rosemary together finely. Stir the ground spices, garlic and rosemary into the yoghurt and vinegar mixture and season with salt and plenty of black pepper. Smear this mixture thoroughly over the lamb fillets, then leave them in a covered dish in a cool place for several hours.

Grill the lamb fillets over or under a very high heat for 8–12 minutes, turning them twice, until they are really dark brown on the outside. Then remove the fillets from the heat and leave to sit for a few minutes before cutting across in thin slices and arranging them on a warmed serving dish.

Kidneys with Apples, Sherry and Crème Fraîche

SERVES 4

8 lamb's kidneys

2 medium onions

3 dessert apples

juice of 1 lemon

bunch fresh flat-leafed parsley

25g/1oz butter

150ml/¼ pint sherry

3 teaspoons whole grain mustard

3 rounded tablespoons crème fraîche

salt

black pepper

The wonderful thing about kidneys is that they miraculously make their own sauce during the few minutes needed to cook them. With the addition of a little crème fraîche and sherry the sauce becomes even more luscious. Serve with mashed potatoes and a green vegetable. This is a perfect dish to make at the end of a busy day; quick but distinguished.

Remove the skin from the kidneys and slice them across fairly thinly. Peel the onions and slice thinly across. Peel and core the apples, halve them and then cut into thin half-moon slices, putting them straight into a bowl and sprinkling all over with the lemon juice. Chop the parsley – not too finely. Put a shallow serving dish in a very low oven to keep warm.

Melt the butter in a large, heavy-based frying pan over a medium heat, add the kidneys and sauté for only 2–4 minutes, until cooked on the outside but still pink in the centre. Using a slotted spatula, transfer them to the serving dish. Keep warm. Add the onions to the juices in the pan and cook gently until soft. Then add the sherry, mustard and apples and stir gently, at bubbling heat, for 2 minutes. Stir in the crème fraîche, bubble for another minute, then season with salt and black pepper. Stir in the chopped parsley and remove from the heat. Spoon the mixture over and amongst the kidneys in the dish. Serve at once.

Rabbit and Pumpkin with Mustard

SERVES 4

900g/2lb piece pumpkin

4 cloves garlic

2 level teaspoons dried or bottled green peppercorns

1 tablespoon olive oil

2 teaspoons caraway seeds

4 fresh rabbit joints

100g/4oz butter

3–4 teaspoons Dijon mustard

150ml/¼ pint white wine or cider

150ml/¼ pint soured cream

chopped fresh parsley, to garnish

salt

In this easy but popular autumnal recipe the pumpkin cooks down to form a lovely glowing sauce. As an alternative to parsley, small rocket leaves thrown in at the last moment are a nice touch.

Peel the pumpkin, scoop out and discard the seeds and chop up the flesh into small pieces. Peel the cloves of garlic and chop them up roughly. Lightly crush the green peppercorns with a pestle and mortar. Preheat the oven to 180°C/350°F/gas mark 4.

Heat the olive oil in a cast iron casserole over a medium heat, add the caraway seeds and stir for a moment. Then add the rabbit and brown on both sides. Add the garlic, stir for half a minute and then turn off the heat. Add the butter, cut into pieces. When the butter has melted in the hot casserole, add the pumpkin, green peppercorns, mustard, wine or cider and some salt and stir well. Cover with a tight-fitting lid and cook in the centre of the oven for 1¼ hours. Then stir to break up the pumpkin until it becomes a purée. Cover and continue cooking for 20 minutes.

Just before serving, pour the soured cream over the top and sprinkle with chopped parsley.

Pork and Apple Surprise

SERVES 6

450g/1lb Cox's apples

25g/1oz butter

1 teaspoon ground cinnamon

900g/2lb minced pork

1 large clove garlic

1 medium onion

about 1 dessertspoon chopped fresh rosemary

1 large egg, lightly whisked

75g/3oz goat's cheese

olive oil for brushing

4 tablespoons apple juice

150ml/¼ pint double cream

2 teaspoons lemon juice

salt

black pepper

This is like a particularly good and succulent meat loaf. It has the bonus of a moist surprise filling of apples and melted goat's cheese.

Preheat the oven to 180°C/350°F/gas mark 4. Peel and core the apples, then chop them into 1.25cm/½in pieces. Melt the butter in a large frying pan over a medium heat, add the apples and stir with a wooden spoon for 2–3 minutes. Stir in the cinnamon, remove from the heat and turn the mixture into a bowl. Put the minced pork into another bowl. Peel the garlic and onion, chop both finely and add to the pork, together with the rosemary. Season well, then add the egg and stir thoroughly.

Cut the goat's cheese into 1.25–2.5cm/½–1in pieces, mix it gently with the apples and season with a little salt and plenty of pepper. Using your hands, form the pork mixture into a large ball and put it in a lightly oiled roasting pan. Cut off the top of the ball and then, as if you were a potter, hollow out the meat with your hands and bring up the sides to form a bowl shape. Spoon the apple and cheese mixture into the cavity. Then replace the meat top and pat all over to give a roughly round shape. Brush with olive oil and cook in the centre of the oven for 1½ hours.

Remove the pork ball from the roasting pan and put it on a warmed serving plate. Add the apple juice to the juices in the roasting pan and bubble for a minute, then stir in the cream and bubble for another minute, until slightly thickened. Remove from the heat and stir in the lemon juice, then season to taste. Cut the loaf into thick slices from the centre like a cake and serve with the sauce.

RABBIT AND PUMPKIN
◀ WITH MUSTARD

Tossed Slices of Lamb Fillet and Kidneys with Mushrooms and Spring Onions

SERVES 4

450–550g/1–1¼lb trimmed lamb
neck fillets

8 lamb's kidneys

juice of 1 lemon

3 tablespoons soy sauce

1 rounded tablespoon tomato purée

225g/8oz brown-cap mushrooms

2 large cloves garlic

2.5cm/1in piece root ginger

1 bunch spring onions

25g/1oz butter

5 tablespoons olive oil

salt

black pepper

After marinating the meat, this is a quickly made supper or lunch dish. Lamb's kidneys become tough and rubbery if they are overcooked but sliced fairly thinly and tossed over the heat for only a minute or two they magically produce an instant, richly flavoured sauce around them. Here it combines wonderfully with the marinated lamb. Serve with rice or mashed potatoes to soak up the juices.

Slice the lamb fillets crossways in approximately 5mm/¼in strips. Skin the kidneys if necessary and then cut them across in thin slices like the lamb. Put the lemon juice and soy sauce into a bowl and stir in the tomato purée. Then add the lamb and kidneys and stir to coat with the marinade. Cover the bowl and leave in a cool place for several hours.

Shortly before you want to eat, slice the mushrooms across fairly thinly. Peel the garlic and ginger and chop finely. Slice the spring onions, using as much of the green part as possible. Heat the butter and 3 tablespoons of the oil in a large frying pan, add the mushrooms and stir until softened. Then add the garlic and ginger and stir for another 2–3 minutes. Remove from the heat, season with a little salt and pepper and spoon into a large serving dish. Cover with foil and keep warm in a very low oven.

Just before serving, put the remaining oil into the frying pan over a high heat. When the oil is smoking, add the lamb kidneys and marinade. Toss around for 2–4 minutes, really just to seal the meat – both lamb and kidneys should remain pink inside. Finally, stir in the spring onions and remove from the heat. Mix the lamb and kidneys with their sauce into the mushrooms. Taste, add salt and pepper only if necessary, and serve at once.

Chicken and Caper Quenelles

SERVES 4

350g/12oz skinless chicken breast
fillets

2–3 large cloves garlic

3 rounded teaspoons capers

75g/3oz fresh white breadcrumbs

finely grated rind of 1 lemon

2 small or medium eggs, separated

1 fresh red chilli

2–3 sprigs fresh flat-leafed parsley

200ml/7fl oz crème fraîche

sea salt

black pepper

Capers add their own unique flavour to food. I think of them as tasting a bit like seaweed but with a hint of earthiness. They have a sort of savoury piquancy that marries well with all sorts of other tastes.

These poached chicken quenelles are flavoured with capers, lemon rind and garlic, and enriched by a crème fraîche and egg yolk sauce with a slight bite of fresh chilli. They are irresistible. Serve with new potatoes and a green vegetable or salad.

Cut the chicken breast fillets into quarters and place in a food processor. Peel the garlic and press through a garlic crusher on to the chicken. Whizz until finely chopped. Roughly chop up the capers on a board. Turn the chicken into a bowl and, using a wooden spoon, stir in the chopped capers, breadcrumbs, lemon rind and egg whites. Stir thoroughly until well blended, then stir in some crushed sea salt and plenty of black pepper. Dampen your hands and form the chicken mixture into balls or small, fat sausage shapes. Bring a large pan of

FAMILY FAVOURITES

water to a vigorous boil, drop in the chicken quenelles and continue boiling hard for a few minutes, until they have all risen to the top. Lift them out with a slotted spoon and place closely together in an ovenproof dish. Cover with foil and keep warm in a low oven while making the sauce.

Cut the chilli open lengthways under running water, discard the seeds and stem and chop the flesh up finely. Chop the parsley leaves finely. Now put the crème fraîche into a saucepan with the egg yolks and heat very gently, stirring all the time, until the sauce thickens a little. Add the chopped chilli and stir for another minute or so. Finally, stir in the chopped parsley and season to taste with salt. Pour the sauce over the quenelles and serve at once.

Veal Cutlets Cooked with Chillies, Lemon Grass and Sweet Pepper

Small English veal cutlets are inexpensive but tend to be dry and bland when fried or grilled. Cooked like this, with a slightly piquant, creamy sauce, they are at their best. Serve with basmati rice or new potatoes and a green vegetable or salad.

Cut the chillies open lengthways under running water and discard the seeds and stems, then slice the flesh very thinly crossways. Top and tail the lemon grass stalk and remove any marked outer part, then slice very thinly across. Peel the garlic and chop finely. Cut the stalks off the peppers, remove the seeds from inside and slice the peppers thinly across in rings.

Melt the oil and 25g/1oz of the butter in a large casserole over a medium heat, then stir in the chillies, lemon grass, garlic and peppers. Stir around for 2 minutes, then stir in the flour, followed by the stock. Bring to the boil, stirring all the time until thickened. Add the veal cutlets and stir to mix in. Cover the casserole and leave on top of the stove over a low heat while you heat the oven to 140°C/275°F/gas mark 1. Put the gently bubbling casserole in the oven and cook for about 1½ hours or until the meat is very tender. Remove from the heat, taste the juices and add some salt if necessary. Then stir in the creamed smatana or soured cream. Melt the remaining butter in a small pan, add the paprika to it and stir around for a minute. Trickle this red liquid over the casserole just before serving.

SERVES 4

2 fresh red chillies

1 lemon grass stalk

3 large cloves garlic

2 medium to large yellow peppers

2 tablespoons sunflower oil

40g/1½oz butter

2 rounded tablespoons plain flour

300ml/½ pint chicken stock

900g/2lb small veal cutlets

150ml/¼ pint creamed smatana or soured cream

1 teaspoon paprika

salt

Pork and Tuna Rissoles with a Cream and Caper Sauce

SERVES 4

200g/7oz tin tuna in oil

350g/12oz minced pork

2 cloves garlic

7.5cm/3in sprig fresh rosemary

1 large egg, lightly whisked

plain flour for dusting

25g/1oz butter

2 rounded teaspoons capers

300ml/½ pint double cream

roughly chopped fresh parsley,
    to garnish

salt

black pepper

I don't like using the word 'tasty' but it is ideal for this dish. Serve with a bowl of tagliatelle or egg noodles and a green salad.

Put the tuna and its oil into a bowl with the pork and mix together thoroughly. Peel the garlic and take the rosemary spikes off the stem. Chop the garlic and rosemary together finely and add to the mixture, then stir in the egg, adding a sprinkling of salt and freshly ground black pepper. Using wet hands, form the mixture into small sausage shapes and roll lightly in a little plain flour.

Heat the butter in a large frying pan over a medium heat and add the rissoles. Fry for about 5 minutes on each side, turning carefully, until golden brown. Remove with a slotted spatula and put into a warmed serving dish. Roughly crush the capers. Add them to the frying pan with the cream, bring to the boil and bubble for about 2 minutes. Remove from the heat and season to taste. Pour the sauce over the rissoles, garnish with parsley and serve.

Veal and Tuna Sausages

SERVES 4

350g/12oz minced veal

200g/7oz tin light-meat tuna

1 large clove garlic

5–7.5cm/2–3in sprig fresh rosemary

1 rounded teaspoon bottled green
    peppercorns

1 egg

3 tablespoons olive oil

15g/½oz butter

chopped fresh parsley, to garnish
    (optional)

salt

Here I have taken the Italian idea of combining veal and tuna but using veal mince instead of expensive escalopes. The result is a simply made dish which children like as much as adults. Serve with new potatoes or egg tagliatelle and a green vegetable.

Put the veal and tuna into a mixing bowl. Peel the garlic and take the spiky leaves off the rosemary stalk. Chop both together as finely as possible and mix thoroughly into the veal and tuna. Roughly crush the green peppercorns and stir them into the mixture with a sprinkling of salt. Whisk the egg lightly and stir it in well. Using wet hands, form the mixture into short sausage shapes.

Put the olive oil and butter into a large, heavy-based frying pan over a medium heat. When the butter has melted, add the sausages and cook, turning carefully, for 10–12 minutes, until golden brown all over. Remove with a slotted spatula and put into a heated serving dish. Garnish with chopped parsley if you like.

**PORK AND TUNA
RISSOLES WITH A CREAM
AND CAPER SAUCE▶**

Double-Coriander Meatballs with Fresh Tomato Sauce

SERVES 4

675g/1½lb lean minced pork

2 teaspoons coriander seeds

2 large cloves garlic

stalks of 1 medium bunch fresh coriander

1 rounded tablespoon tomato purée

1 tablespoon sunflower oil

salt

black pepper

For the tomato sauce:

450g/1lb ripe tomatoes, the plum variety if available

25g/1oz butter

1 level dessertspoon caster sugar

3–4 pinches cayenne pepper

leaves from 1 medium bunch fresh coriander

This recipe should perhaps be called triple-coriander as the meatballs contain the seeds and stems and the tomato sauce the leaves. It is a very popular everyday dish for all the family and excellent with a bowl of tagliatelle or other pasta.

Put the minced pork into a bowl. Grind the coriander seeds as finely as you can with a pestle and mortar. Peel the garlic and chop finely. Slice the coriander stalks across finely. Add these ingredients to the pork with the tomato purée, a generous sprinkling of salt and plenty of black pepper. Using a wooden spoon, mix together very thoroughly. Then, with wet hands, form the mixture into small balls about the size of large marbles.

Heat the sunflower oil in a large frying pan and fry the meatballs over a low to medium heat for 15–20 minutes, turning them to brown all over. Using a slotted spoon, transfer the balls to a serving dish and keep warm in a low oven while you make the sauce. Pour excess fat from the pan but do not wash it.

To make the sauce, put the tomatoes into a bowl, pour boiling water over them and leave for about 2 minutes, then drain, peel and chop roughly. Melt the butter over a fairly low heat in the frying pan in which the meatballs were cooked. Add the chopped tomatoes and stir around for 8–10 minutes, until completely mushy. Then add the sugar, a good sprinkling of salt and the cayenne pepper. Stir around for another minute, then remove from the heat.

Roughly chop the coriander leaves and stir them into the sauce just before spooning it either directly on to the meatballs or into a separate bowl. Serve immediately.

Tagliatelle with Bacon and Quick Fried Spinach

SERVES 6

275–350g/10–12oz baby leaf spinach

225g/8oz lean rindless smoked bacon

2 large cloves garlic

350–400g/12–14oz tagliatelle

4 tablespoons olive oil

freshly grated Parmesan cheese, to serve

sea salt

black pepper

The quickness and popularity of most pasta dishes is a boon to any family. This recipe is so fast you should make sure everyone is ready to eat it before you start cooking.

First put a large serving bowl and a plate in a low oven to keep warm. Wash and drain the spinach and shake it in a cloth to dry it as much as possible. Cut the bacon into smallish pieces. Peel the garlic and slice it across as finely as possible.

Bring a large pan of salted water to the boil, drop in the tagliatelle and cook for 7–12 minutes, until just tender – it should still have a very slight bite to it.

As soon as you put the water on to boil, start cooking the other ingredients. Put half the olive oil in a large, deep frying pan over a fairly high heat. Add the bacon and stir around for 5–8 minutes, until crisp. Using a slotted spatula, transfer the bacon to the plate in the oven. Add the remaining olive oil to the frying pan and increase the heat to as high as possible. Then add the sliced garlic and stir for half a minute. Next add the spinach and stir around swiftly for barely a minute – just until the spinach has become limp. Season with black pepper and a little salt if needed.

When the tagliatelle is ready, drain it and put it into the warmed serving bowl. Pour the spinach, garlic and oil on top, add the fried bacon and mix everything in roughly with the tagliatelle. Serve with a bowl of grated Parmesan.

Pork Shoulder Steaks and Celeriac with Green Peppercorn Sauce

SERVES 6

6 large pork shoulder steaks

juice of 1 lemon, plus a little extra for the sauce

6–7 tablespoons white wine vinegar

2 large cloves garlic

about 450g/1lb celeriac

2 tablespoons olive oil

40g/1½oz butter

300ml/½ pint double cream

2 teaspoons bottled green peppercorns, roughly crushed

salt

black pepper

Pork can be dull and dry but marinating these steaks gives them a lovely sharpness and also adds tenderness. The sauce is luscious.

Put the shoulder steaks into a large, shallow, non-metallic dish. Put the lemon juice and 4 tablespoons of the vinegar into a bowl. Peel the garlic and crush it into the bowl, then add a generous sprinkling of black pepper. Stir the mixture and pour it over the shoulder steaks. Cover the dish and leave to marinate in the refrigerator for 8 hours or overnight, turning the meat over about half-way through.

Have a saucepan of water ready to which you have added 2–3 tablespoons of wine vinegar. Cut the knobbly peel off the celeriac, cut in half and then into thin slices, putting them straight into the saucepan. Bring to the boil and boil for 5 minutes, then drain and pat dry.

Drain the marinade from the meat and pat dry. Heat the olive oil and 15g/½oz of the butter in a large, heavy-based frying pan over a fairly low heat. Add the pork and fry gently for about 10 minutes on each side, until golden brown. Using a slotted spatula, transfer the pork to a shallow serving dish and keep warm, uncovered, in a low oven. Add the remaining butter to the frying pan and put back over a medium heat. When the butter has melted, add the celeriac slices and sauté for a few minutes, until browned on both sides. Arrange among the pork steaks and continue to keep warm. Don't wash out the frying pan; just before serving, empty the cream into the pan, add the crushed green peppercorns and season with salt. Bring to the boil and bubble for a minute, then stir in a small squeeze of lemon juice, pour the sauce over the pork and celeriac and serve at once.

SERVES 8

1.35–1.6kg/3–3½lb boneless pork joint

100g/4oz fresh spinach

5cm/2in piece fresh ginger

3 large cloves garlic

a little olive oil

225g/8oz gooseberries

1 heaped tablespoon caster sugar

juice of 1 lemon

300ml/½ pint lager

2–3 pinches cayenne pepper

1 bunch fresh chives, chopped

sea salt

black pepper

Roast Pork Spiked with Spinach and Ginger with Gooseberry Sauce

Pork can be a dry meat but spiking it with spinach and fresh ginger gives it both moisture and flavour. The gooseberry sauce, flavoured with lager and tasting both sharp and slightly sweet, complements the pork perfectly.

Preheat the oven to 230°C/450°F/gas mark 8. Using a sharp knife, make several deep incisions in the joint of pork. If the butcher has not already done it, score the thick skin thoroughly.

Wash the spinach and remove the stalks, then chop the leaves up finely. Peel the ginger and 2 cloves of the garlic and chop finely. Mix the chopped spinach, ginger and garlic together in a bowl and season with salt and black pepper. Press this mixture right down into the incisions in the meat with your fingers. Then smear olive oil all over the meat but not on the skin. Rub the skin with sea salt to give a good crackling and sprinkle with water.

Put the joint in a roasting pan with the skin upwards and cook on a high shelf of the oven for 20 minutes, then move it to the centre of the oven, turn the heat down to 170°C/325°F/gas mark 3 and cook for another 2 hours, basting occasionally and sprinkling the skin with a bit more water.

Meanwhile, top and tail the gooseberries and peel and chop the remaining clove of garlic. Put both into a saucepan with the caster sugar, lemon juice, lager, cayenne pepper and a little sprinkling of salt. Bring to bubbling over the heat, cover the pan and simmer very gently for 15–20 minutes or until the gooseberries have softened.

When the meat has been cooking for 2 hours, carefully pour just the fat out of the roasting pan and add the gooseberry mixture to the pan juices. Return to the oven for half an hour, then transfer the joint to a carving board. Stir the chopped chives into the gooseberry mixture and pour into a bowl to serve as a sauce with the carved pork.

Quick Indian Chicken and Courgettes in Coconut Milk

SERVES 6

300ml/½ pint full cream milk

75g/3oz coconut milk powder

450g/1lb smallish courgettes

6 medium-sized skinless chicken breast fillets

25g/1oz butter

1 tablespoon groundnut oil

3–5 teaspoons tikka paste or mild curry paste

handful fresh coriander or mint leaves

salt

One of the quickest curries you can make, and delicious. Serve with basmati rice.

Put the milk in a saucepan, bring just to the boil and remove from the heat. Stir in the coconut milk powder and whisk until smoothly dissolved. Then add a teaspoon of salt and leave on one side. Top and tail the courgettes, cut them in half and then into chip-shaped sticks. Slice the chicken breasts into strips 5mm/¼in wide.

Put the butter and oil in a large, deep frying pan over a medium to high heat. When the butter has melted, add the courgettes and chicken and stir around for a few minutes until the chicken is opaque and the courgettes have just softened – they should not have lost their bite. Now stir in the tikka or curry paste, adding more if you want a hotter curry. Lastly add the coconut milk, just to reheat it. Season with salt to taste and turn into a heated serving dish. Roughly chop the coriander or mint leaves and sprinkle them over the top before serving.

Saffron Lamb with Chicory

SERVES 6-8

about 900g/2lb lamb neck fillets

2–3 teaspoons caster sugar

2 tablespoons vegetable oil

4 plump chicory

3 large cloves garlic

1 medium red pepper

2 level tablespoons plain flour

600ml/1 pint milk

300ml/½ pint double cream

2 generous pinches saffron strands

4–5 pinches cayenne pepper

juice of ½ lemon

salt

This is a simple but deliciously creamy and interestingly flavoured casserole. Serve with new potatoes, egg noodles or basmati rice and a green salad or vegetable.

Slice the lamb fillets across at 2.5–4cm/1–1½in intervals. Sprinkle the sugar all over the pieces of lamb. Heat the oil in a large frying pan over a high heat. Add the lamb and stir around until well browned all over. Using a slotted spatula, transfer the lamb to a large casserole dish.

Cut the ends off the chicory and then slice in half lengthways. Peel the garlic and slice roughly. Cut the pepper in half, discard the seeds and stem and slice across as thinly as possible. Arrange the chicory, garlic and red pepper amongst the lamb in the casserole. Preheat the oven to 230°C/450°F/gas mark 8.

Put the flour into a saucepan, add a little of the milk and stir until smooth. Then gradually stir in the rest of the milk and the cream. Add the saffron and season with the cayenne pepper and salt. Bring to the boil, stirring all the time, and bubble, still stirring, for 2–3 minutes, until thickened. Then pour over the lamb and vegetables in the casserole dish. Cover and put in the centre of the oven. After 10–15 minutes, when the juices are simmering, turn the oven down to 150°C/300°F/gas mark 2. Cook for another 1¼–1½ hours, until the lamb is very tender. Before serving, stir the lemon juice into the casserole and check the seasoning.

QUICK INDIAN CHICKEN
AND COURGETTES IN
COCONUT MILK ▶

Pork, Pickle and Sweet Potato Shepherd's Pie

SERVES 6

675–800g/1½–1¾lb sweet
potatoes

50g/2oz butter, plus extra for
dotting over the pie

2 teaspoons caraway seeds

3 rounded tablespoons lime pickle

3 large cloves garlic

2 tablespoons groundnut oil

900g/2lb lean minced pork

1 bunch spring onions

1 large egg

salt

black pepper

A far cry from the grey mince and tasteless mash I had at school. I find that a thoughtfully made shepherd's pie is always popular, particularly this more exotic variation. The kind of sweet potatoes that have peach-coloured flesh are best (scratch the skin with your nails to check). Serve with a green salad.

Peel the sweet potatoes and cut them up roughly, then steam or boil until soft. Drain, turn into a bowl and mash, adding the butter, caraway seeds and a good seasoning of salt and black pepper. Leave on one side. Spoon the lime pickle out of the jar on to a board and slice any large pieces of lime fairly small. Peel the garlic and chop finely.

Preheat the oven to 180°C/350°F/gas mark 4. Put the groundnut oil into a large sauté pan over a fairly high heat, add the minced pork and dig around with a wooden spoon until the meat has separated and is browning slightly. Add the chopped garlic and stir for another minute, then stir in the lime pickle and remove from the heat. Taste the meat and add salt and black pepper as needed. Trim the spring onions and cut them across at 5mm/¼in intervals, using as much of the green part as possible. Stir them into the meat mixture and then turn it into a shallow ovenproof dish which it doesn't fill completely. Pat level.

Whisk the egg with a fork and stir thoroughly into the sweet potatoes. Then spoon the potatoes over the meat, flick the surface a bit and dot with a little extra butter. Cook on the centre shelf of the oven for 30–40 minutes, until well browned.

Slivers of Chicken Breast and Fennel with a Balsamic Vinegar Sauce

SERVES 4

4 fairly small cornfed chicken breast
fillets

2 medium to large bulbs fennel

2 cloves garlic

3 tablespoons olive oil

2 tablespoons sherry

2 tablespoons bottled green
peppercorns

300ml/½ pint double cream

1 tablespoon balsamic vinegar

salt

black pepper

This is a quickly made but excellent dish; it completely transforms chicken breasts which, although lean and tender, are often dull and dry. Not so here, combined with moist and mellow fennel in a cream sauce perfected by the unique sweet sharpness of balsamic vinegar. Serve with tagliatelle or waxy new potatoes and a green vegetable such as broccoli or petits pois.

Remove the skin from the chicken and slice the breasts fairly thinly cross-ways. Cut the base and top stalk off the fennel bulbs and remove any marked outer parts, then slice across thinly. Peel the garlic and chop finely. Heat the olive oil in a large, deep frying pan over a medium to low heat. Add the fennel and sherry and cook, stirring often, for 10–15 minutes, until the fennel has softened. Then add the chicken slices and chopped garlic and stir around with the fennel for about 8 minutes or until the chicken is opaque and cooked through. Season with salt and freshly ground black pepper and turn into a shallow serving dish, leaving the oil and juices in the pan. Keep warm in the lowest possible oven.

Roughly crush the green peppercorns. Put the frying pan back over a medium heat. Bubble up the oil and juices and then add the crushed peppercorns. After stirring around for 1–2 minutes, pour in the cream, increase the heat and bring to the boil. Bubble for another 2 minutes, stirring continuously. Then add the balsamic vinegar and bubble for a final minute. Season to taste with salt and black pepper, pour the sauce over the chicken and fennel and serve at once.

Potato, Cheese and Anchovy Dumplings with a Fresh Tomato Sauce

SERVES 4

675g/1½lb potatoes

50g/2oz butter

3 tablespoons milk

100g/4oz plain flour

2 cloves garlic

50g/2oz tin anchovies

175g/6oz strong Cheddar cheese, grated

2 medium eggs

freshly grated Parmesan cheese, to serve

salt

black pepper

For the sauce:

450g/1lb ripe tomatoes, the plum variety if available

75g/3oz butter

juice of 1 lemon

4–6 fresh basil leaves (optional)

A good supper dish, which I like to accompany with a green salad and hot crusty bread.

Peel the potatoes and cook them in boiling salted water until tender, then drain and mash smoothly, adding the butter and milk. Sift the flour on to the potatoes and stir in. Peel the garlic and press through a crusher on to the mixture.

Open the tin of anchovies, pouring the oil on to the potatoes. Cut the fillets up into small pieces. Add these pieces and the grated Cheddar to the potato mixture, then whisk the eggs lightly, season well with salt and black pepper and add to the potatoes. Stir all together thoroughly with a wooden spoon and leave to cool.

Meanwhile, make the sauce. Put the tomatoes in a bowl, pour boiling water over them and leave for about 2 minutes, then peel and chop them up roughly. Put the butter and lemon juice into a pan, add the tomatoes and cook in the open pan over a gentle heat, stirring now and then, until the tomatoes have turned into a mushy sauce. Season with salt and black pepper and keep the sauce warm over the lowest possible heat while you make the dumplings.

Warm a fairly large serving dish. Using well-floured hands, take up pieces of the potato mixture and form into pingpong-sized balls. Put a large saucepan of water over a high heat and bring to a fast boil, then drop in the potato balls. When they rise to the top (after about 5 minutes), take them out carefully with a slotted spoon and arrange in the warmed serving dish.

If you have any basil leaves, tear them into small pieces and stir them into the tomato sauce. Pour the sauce over the dumplings, sprinkle with grated Parmesan and serve.

vegetarian
inspirations

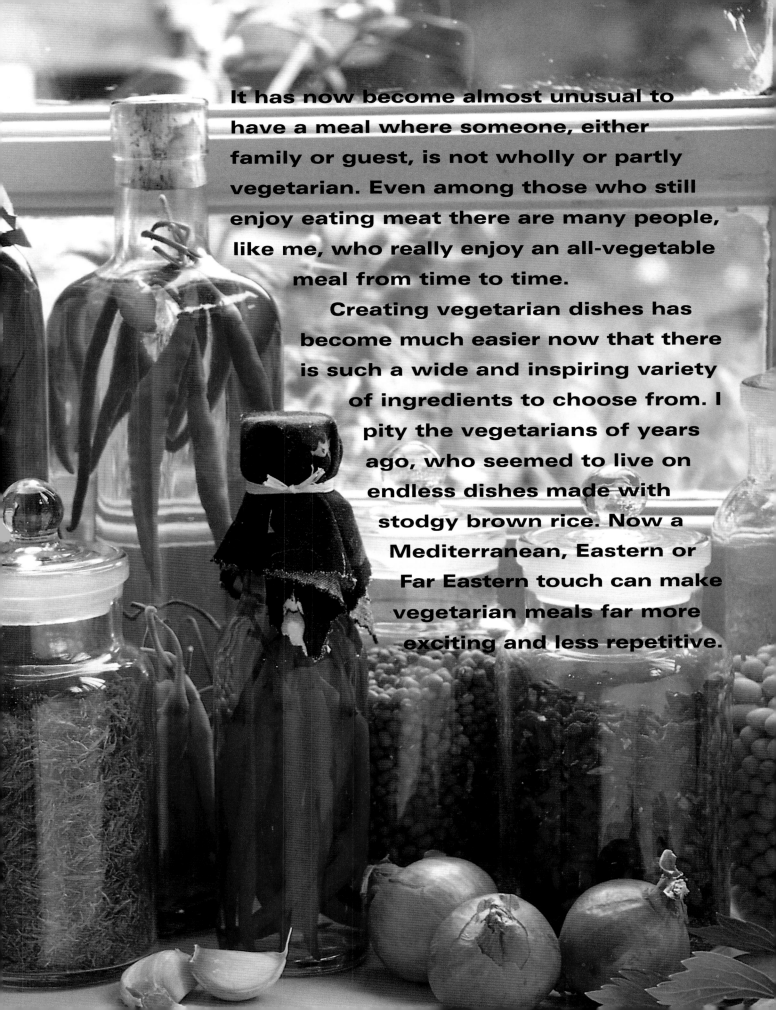

It has now become almost unusual to have a meal where someone, either family or guest, is not wholly or partly vegetarian. Even among those who still enjoy eating meat there are many people, like me, who really enjoy an all-vegetable meal from time to time.

Creating vegetarian dishes has become much easier now that there is such a wide and inspiring variety of ingredients to choose from. I pity the vegetarians of years ago, who seemed to live on endless dishes made with stodgy brown rice. Now a Mediterranean, Eastern or Far Eastern touch can make vegetarian meals far more exciting and less repetitive.

4 medium aubergines

675g/1½lb leeks

50g/2oz butter

2 teaspoons ground coriander

1 teaspoon cumin seeds

plain flour for coating

olive oil

100g/4oz mozzarella cheese

about 2 tablespoons freshly grated
    Parmesan cheese

salt

black pepper

Aubergine and Leek Pie

This is a good supper dish with Italian and Middle Eastern connotations, both areas where aubergines play a prominent part in the cuisine. Two layers of aubergine contain a filling of spiced leeks and cheese. The pie is excellent served with a tomato salad.

Top and tail the aubergines and slice them across thinly. Rub the slices on both sides with fine salt and leave in an unplugged sink for half an hour to drain. Meanwhile, wash the leeks thoroughly and slice across in 1.25cm/½in pieces, using as much of the green part as possible. Melt the butter in a large, heavy-based sauté pan, add the leeks, coriander and cumin seeds and cook over a low to medium heat, stirring often, until the leeks are really soft but not browned. Season with sea salt and plenty of black pepper and leave on one side.

Rinse the aubergine slices to get rid of all the salt and then pat them dry with absorbent paper. Put some plain flour into a mixing bowl and dip the slices into the flour to coat lightly. Heat a little olive oil in a large frying pan over a medium heat. Fry the aubergine slices for a few minutes on each side, until they feel soft when pierced with a knife. You will probably have to cook them in two or three relays, adding more oil as necessary and putting the cooked slices on absorbent paper on one side.

Preheat the oven to 190°C/375°F/gas mark 5. Put a thin layer of olive oil in a fairly shallow ovenproof dish and line it with about half the aubergine slices. Then slice the mozzarella cheese thinly and lay half the slices on top of the aubergines. Spoon in the leek mixture and top with the remaining slices of mozzarella. Cover with the remaining aubergine slices, sprinkle with the grated Parmesan and drizzle with olive oil. Bake near the top of the oven for about 20 minutes, until browned in patches.

New Potato and Spring Onion Pie

675g/1½lb new potatoes

1 bunch spring onions

generous bunch fresh dill

1 medium egg

4 rounded tablespoons crème fraîche

350g/12oz puff pastry

a little milk

salt

black pepper

This is suitable as a main dish for lunch or supper, simply accompanied by a salad. If you want to make it non-vegetarian, add thin slices of spicy kabanos or chorizo sausage among the potatoes.

Scrub the potatoes but do not peel them. Boil or steam until just tender right through, then drain, slice across thinly and put on one side in a bowl until cold. Trim the spring onions and slice across finely, using as much of the green part as possible. Roughly chop the dill. When the potatoes are cold, mix the spring onions and dill gently into them. In another bowl, whisk the egg lightly, then stir in the crème fraîche. Season well with salt and plenty of black pepper. Using a wooden spoon so as not to break up the potatoes, stir the cream and egg into the potato mixture.

Preheat the oven to 220°C/425°F/gas mark 7. Butter a 24–25cm/9½–10in loose-based flan tin, either fluted or plain. Cut the pastry in half and form each half into a ball. Roll out one half thinly and use to line the flan tin. Spoon in the potato mixture. Roll out the remaining pastry into a circle big enough to top the pie and lay it on the filling, trimming round the edge. Press the edges lightly together to seal them, then roll out any trimmings to cut out decorations. Moisten the decorations underneath and arrange on top of the pie. Cut 2 holes in the pastry to allow steam to escape. Brush the pie lightly with a little milk and cook in the centre of the oven for 30–35 minutes, until a rich, golden brown. Before serving, press the pie up out of the flan rim and, using a wide spatula, ease it carefully off the base on to a flat serving plate.

Shallot and Spring Onion Tart with Crunchy Hot Butter Pastry

SERVES 6

675g/1½lb shallots

2 tablespoons olive oil

1 bunch spring onions

1 large egg

2 egg yolks

150ml/¼ pint crème fraîche or double cream

2 teaspoons caster sugar

salt

black pepper

For the pastry:

100g/4oz plain flour

100g/4oz semolina

1 teaspoon salt

100g/4oz butter

1 tablespoon water

My family always teases me about my sensual descriptions of tarts but the very name makes it hard to avoid. I think onion is my favourite kind of savoury tart; they are sweet, soft and altogether irresistible – there I go again.

The pastry here is very easy. You do not have to roll it out and there is no advantage in baking it blind – it is naturally crisp.

To make the pastry, put the flour, semolina and salt into a bowl and stir to mix. Gently melt the butter with the water in a small saucepan, then pour the hot liquid on to the flour, stirring it with a wooden spoon until you have a warm dough. Take bits of the dough and press them evenly over the bottom and up the sides of a 24–25cm/9½–10in loose-based fluted flan tin, bringing the edge slightly up above the rim. Refrigerate while you prepare the filling.

Peel the shallots and slice them across in fairly thin rings. Put the olive oil into a large, heavy-based frying pan over a medium heat, add the shallots and cook, stirring often, for about 15 minutes or until really soft – if they begin to brown, reduce the heat. Leave on one side to cool a bit.

Preheat the oven to 220°C/425°F/gas mark 7. Trim the spring onions and slice across at 5mm/¼in intervals, using as much of the green part as possible. Whisk the egg and egg yolks together in a mixing bowl and then whisk in the cream. Season with salt and plenty of black pepper. Stir the cooled shallots and the spring onions into the egg and cream mixture and pour into the chilled pastry case. Level the surface and sprinkle with the caster sugar. Cook the tart towards the top of the oven for about 25 minutes, until it is just set in the middle and small specks of black have appeared on the surface.

Put the flan tin on top of a tin or jar, push the crumbly tart carefully up out of the rim of the tin and ease on to a serving plate with a spatula.

40g/1½oz butter

1 tablespoon clear honey

550g/1¼lb small turnips

salt

black pepper

For the pastry:

75g/3oz curd cheese

75g/3oz butter

2 teaspoons caraway seeds

175g/6oz plain flour

2 teaspoons baking powder

3 generous pinches cayenne pepper

Turnip Tart with Curd Cheese and Caraway Pastry

The peppery flavour of turnips is at its best in this glossy, caramelized upside-down tart. It can be served with a green salad or vegetable. The unusual pastry is very quick to make and full of taste.

To make the pastry, put the curd cheese and butter into a food processor and whizz together briefly. Then add the caraway seeds, flour, baking powder, cayenne pepper and a sprinkling of salt. Whizz again briefly until the mixture sticks together to form a dough. Press the dough into a ball, wrap in cling film and refrigerate while you prepare the filling.

Smear the butter thickly over the base and up the sides of a 23cm/9in round flan tin. Then drizzle the honey over the butter and sprinkle with salt and black pepper. Without topping and tailing or peeling them, slice the turnips very thinly lengthways and arrange a neat layer over the butter and honey. Continue layering with the remaining turnip slices, pressing them down evenly.

Preheat the oven to 200°C/400°F/gas mark 6. On a lightly floured surface, roll out the pastry to form a circle slightly bigger than the flan dish. Lay the pastry on top of the turnips and press the edges down inside the dish, making a thick rim. Pierce 2 small holes in the pastry to allow steam to escape.

Cook the tart on the centre shelf of the oven for 25–30 minutes, until the pastry has browned, then turn down the heat to 150°C/300°F/gas mark 2 and cook for another 30 minutes. Remove the tart from the oven and leave for about 5 minutes, then put a large, flat serving plate on top of the flan tin and turn them both upside down. Give a shake and turn the tart on to the serving plate, carefully lifting the tin off.

I frequently lament the advent of the English winter. Having acquired a taste for hot weather and brilliant light during my childhood, I find the long, damp, grey months of our northern winter hard to survive. On the other hand, if I lived in a hot country I'd miss the thrill of the changing seasons from winter to spring, and spring to summer. Another thing I'd miss would be our wonderful winter vegetables, with their rich sweetness, mellow flavours and enticing textures.

At a time when we need warmth and comfort as well as culinary pleasures, what could be better and more versatile than our own root vegetables? They can be boiled, stewed, fried, roasted, baked, mashed or finely puréed. In the past, many of them were used as animal feed – but today they are the object of many a gastronome's affections and favoured by some of the world's most sophisticated chefs.

about 10 large cloves garlic

450–550g/1–1¼lb onions, the
red-skinned kind if available

3 tablespoons olive oil

15g/½oz butter

225ml/8fl oz double cream

1 large egg

2 egg yolks

freshly grated Parmesan cheese

salt

black pepper

For the pastry:

175g/6oz plain flour

1 teaspoon salt

3 teaspoons dried oregano

100g/4oz butter

1 tablespoon water

Garlic and Onion Tart with Oregano Pastry

I adore onion tarts; a mixture of garlic and onion makes the flavour sweeter and even better. This has a foolproof crisp pastry which can be baked blind without shrinking. Serve with a salad for a light meal.

To make the pastry, sift the flour and salt into a bowl and stir in the oregano. Gently melt the butter with the water in a saucepan, then pour the hot liquid gradually on to the flour, stirring with a wooden spoon until the dough sticks together. Using your fingers, press pieces of the crumbly dough over the base and up the sides of a fluted, loose-based 24cm/9½in flan tin. Pat all over to make the pastry smooth and even, bringing the edges up just a little above the rim of the tin. Prick the base lightly all over with a fork, then refrigerate while you make the filling.

Preheat the oven to 220°C/425°F/gas mark 7. Put the cloves of garlic under the flat of a wide-bladed knife and press hard. The skins should now come off easily and the cloves will be slightly crushed. Peel the onions, cut them in half and slice across thinly. Heat the olive oil and butter gently in a large, deep frying pan. Add the whole cloves of garlic and the sliced onions and stir around almost constantly for 15–20 minutes, until soft. Keep the heat very low as you do not want them to burn. Remove from the heat and leave on one side.

Cook the chilled pastry case on the centre shelf of the oven for 10–12 minutes. Meanwhile, finish the filling: whisk the cream thoroughly in a large bowl with the egg and yolks and season with salt and plenty of black pepper. Then stir in the cooked garlic and onions.

Take the pastry case out of the oven and turn the heat down to 190°C/375°F/gas mark 5. Pour the filling into the pastry case and put back in the oven for 25–30 minutes, until the centre is only just set.

Spiced Spinach Pie with Coconut Milk Top

SERVES 4

1.1kg/2½lb fresh spinach

4–5cm/1½–2in piece fresh ginger

3 large cloves garlic

1 fresh red chilli

1 tablespoon groundnut oil

50g/2oz butter

2 teaspoons ground cinnamon

1 teaspoon ground cardamom

½ teaspoon ground cloves

juice of ½ lemon

cayenne pepper (optional)

sea salt

For the topping:

750ml/1¼ pints milk

75g/3oz coconut milk powder

40g/1½oz ground rice

2–3 pinches cayenne pepper

1 level teaspoon paprika

This vegetarian supper dish is one of my favourites. The spinach is topped with a delicious mixture made of ground rice and creamy coconut milk. If possible, use whole spices and grind them yourself in a coffee grinder – they will be far more aromatic.

To make the filling, remove any thick stalks from the spinach, then wash the leaves thoroughly. Put into a large saucepan, cover and put over a fairly low heat for a few minutes until the leaves are limp, stirring around once or twice. Drain the spinach well, pressing out excess water, and then chop up fairly small.

Peel the ginger and garlic. Cut the chilli open under running water, discard the seeds and stem, then put it on a board with the ginger and garlic and chop together finely. Heat the oil and butter in a large, deep frying pan over a medium heat. Add the chilli, ginger, garlic and ground spices and stir around for a minute or two. Then add the chopped spinach and lemon juice and stir over a gentle heat for about 5 minutes; any excess liquid should evaporate. Season to taste with crushed sea salt, adding a little cayenne pepper if wanted, and put into a wide, fairly shallow ovenproof dish.

Preheat the oven to 220°C/425°F/gas mark 7. To make the topping, pour the milk into a saucepan and bring to the boil. Remove from the heat and thoroughly stir in the coconut milk powder and a sprinkling of salt. Then stir in the ground rice. Put back over a medium heat until bubbling, stirring all the time, then simmer, still stirring, for 3–5 minutes until thickened – if it seems very thick, stir in a little extra milk. Remove from the heat, season with the cayenne pepper and more salt if needed and spoon over the spinach. Sprinkle the paprika over the centre of the topping. Put the dish just above the centre of the oven and cook for about 15 minutes, until the top begins to brown.

Sweet Pepper and Tomato Tart with Cheese Pastry

3 large red peppers

2 large cloves garlic

2 teaspoons coriander seeds

2 tablespoons olive oil

400g/14oz tin chopped tomatoes

1 tablespoon tomato purée

2 sprigs fresh rosemary

4–5 pinches cayenne pepper

2 teaspoons caster sugar

1 small yellow pepper

salt

For the pastry:

175g/6oz plain flour

1 teaspoon salt

75g/3oz butter

50g/2oz strong Cheddar cheese, grated

Rich in colour and flavour, this tart can be served with one or two accompanying vegetable dishes as the main course of a vegetarian meal or as a warm first course for eight people. For convenience, you can make it ahead and reheat it.

To make the pastry, sift the flour and salt into a bowl, cut the butter into small pieces and rub it into the flour with your fingers until the mixture is like breadcrumbs. Then stir in the grated cheese with a knife. Add a very little cold water, stirring until the dough just begins to stick together. Gather the dough into a ball, wrap in cling film and refrigerate for half an hour.

Meanwhile, make the filling. Cut the red peppers in half lengthways and discard the seeds and stems. Put the halves, skin-side upwards, under a hot grill until the skin is blackened. Then peel off the skin under cold running water and cut the peppers into 2.5cm/1in pieces. Peel the garlic and chop it finely. Crush the coriander seeds in a pestle and mortar.

Heat the olive oil in a large frying pan over a medium heat. Add the chopped garlic and crushed coriander seeds and stir for a minute or so. Then add the red peppers and tinned tomatoes. Stir in the tomato purée. Pull the rosemary leaves off their stalks, chop roughly and add to the tomato mixture. Cook gently for about 10 minutes, then increase the heat and let the mixture bubble strongly for a minute or two, until it is fairly thick. Remove from the heat and season to taste with salt, cayenne pepper and the caster sugar. Turn the mixture into a wide dish and leave until cold.

Butter a 25cm/10in loose-based fluted flan tin. Roll out the pastry on a floured surface and use to line the tin. Turn the overlapping edges over double but leave the top edge a little above the rim. Refrigerate until you are ready to cook the tart.

Preheat the oven to 200°C/400°F/gas mark 6. Spoon the filling into the pastry case and spread it level. Now cut the yellow pepper open lengthways, discard the seeds and stem and slice as thinly as possible lengthways. Fan the slices out in a starburst shape in the centre of the pie. Cook in the centre of the oven for 25–35 minutes, until richly browned in patches.

Beetroot and Swede Purée on Baby Spinach Leaves

SERVES 4-5

450–550g/1–1¼lb raw beetroot

350g/12oz swede

4–5 large cloves garlic

¼ whole nutmeg, grated

50g/2oz butter

juice of ½ lemon

225g/8oz baby spinach leaves, washed

dill or fennel leaves, to garnish

salt

black pepper

The sweetness of beetroot combines well with the slight pepperiness of swede, and if you are excited by colour as well as taste this is the dish for you. It is a symphony of scarlet and green and can be served for a light meal with bread and cheese – goat's cheese goes particularly well. If your beetroot still has fresh-looking stalks and leaves attached, they make a delicious vegetable on their own, cooked like spinach but with the scarlet stalks mixed with green leaves.

If necessary, cut any stalks and leaves off the beetroot. Wash the beetroot gently but thoroughly, without breaking the skin. Put the whole unpeeled beetroot into a large saucepan of unsalted water, bring to the boil, cover the pan and simmer for 1 hour. Meanwhile, peel the swede and cut into fairly large chunks. Peel the garlic.

After the beetroot has cooked for an hour, add the swede and garlic to the saucepan with a good sprinkling of salt. Continue simmering for another half an hour or until the swede is soft, then drain. Peel the beetroot and cut it into large chunks. Put the vegetables into a food processor – you may have to do this in two goes, depending on the size of your food processor. Add the nutmeg, butter, lemon juice, salt and plenty of black pepper and whizz to a smooth purée, checking for seasoning.

Arrange the baby spinach leaves in a shallow dish, overlapping the edges. Spoon the purée into the centre of the dish and garnish with dill or fennel leaves before serving.

Butterbean Purée with Onions and Garlic

SERVES 6

275g/10oz dried butterbeans

1 good sprig fresh bay leaves

1 medium onion

2 cloves garlic

75g/3oz butter, plus extra for dotting over the top

2 tablespoons olive oil

2 teaspoons caster sugar

2 rounded tablespoons fresh white breadcrumbs

1 tablespoon freshly grated Parmesan cheese

salt

black pepper

People are often rather scornful about butterbeans but their name is apt, as they do have a truly buttery flavour. Their only fault is that they break up easily, but this makes them particularly suitable for soups or purées. This is a good dish to serve with a salad or vegetables for a light meal.

Soak the butterbeans in cold water for 8 hours or overnight, then drain. Put them in a saucepan with the bay leaves and cover with plenty of water. Bring to the boil and boil briskly for 10 minutes, then reduce the heat, cover and simmer gently for 1–1½ hours, until very soft.

Meanwhile, peel and thinly slice the onion. Peel and finely chop the garlic. Melt 25g/1oz of the butter with the olive oil in a frying pan over a medium heat. Add the onion and cook, stirring, until soft and golden brown. Then stir in the caster sugar, remove from the heat and put on one side.

Preheat the oven to 200°C/400°F/gas mark 6. Drain the cooked butterbeans and put them into a food processor with the garlic and the remaining butter. Whizz thoroughly to a smooth purée and then season to taste with salt and black pepper. Stir in the fried onion with its butter and oil, then spoon the mixture into a shallow earthenware dish. Mix the breadcrumbs with the grated Parmesan cheese and spoon all over the top of the purée, dotting with small knobs of butter. Cook towards the top of the oven for 20–30 minutes, until the top is speckled with brown.

Carrot and Parsnip Crumble

SERVES 4

100g/4oz brown bread

675g/1½lb carrots

450g/1lb parsnips

100g/4oz butter or 4 rounded tablespoons fromage frais

¼–½ nutmeg

75g/3oz Cheddar cheese, grated

25g/1oz Parmesan cheese, freshly grated

2 rounded teaspoons dried oregano

3 tablespoons olive oil

sea salt

black pepper

The first time I made this, people licked their plates clean. It really is an excellent lunch or supper dish, served with a simple green salad or vegetable.

Whizz the bread to crumbs in a food processor – don't bother to cut off the crusts – then put them in a bowl and set aside. Scrape the carrots and chop them roughly. Peel and chop the parsnips. Either steam or boil them together until very soft, then drain and put them in the food processor (you may have to do this in 2 lots if your processor is small) with the butter or fromage frais. Whizz to a smooth purée, grate in the nutmeg and add salt and black pepper to taste – a generous amount of freshly ground black pepper is best. Now turn the mixture into a shallow ovenproof dish and spread level.

Preheat the oven to 230°C/450°F/gas mark 8. Stir the grated cheeses, dried oregano and olive oil into the breadcrumbs. Spread this mixture evenly all over the top of the puréed vegetables. Put the dish near the top of the oven and cook for 15–25 minutes, until the topping is golden brown and crisp.

225g/8oz dried chickpeas

1 teaspoon cumin seeds

2 teaspoons coriander seeds

3 large cloves garlic

450g/1lb tomatoes

2 rounded teaspoons tamarind paste

150ml/¼ pint hot water

2 tablespoons groundnut oil

50g/2oz butter

1 teaspoon ground turmeric

2 teaspoons mustard seeds

¼ teaspoon cayenne pepper

450g/1lb fresh spinach

4 medium or large eggs

handful fresh coriander leaves,
    roughly chopped

salt

Chickpea and Spinach Curry with Soft Eggs

This dish combines two of my favourite ingredients – chickpeas and spinach. You can buy tamarind paste (which adds a lovely sharp taste), mustard seeds and the herbs and spices at Indian or oriental grocer's shops or in large supermarkets. The curry is a meal in itself and needs only some Indian bread such as nan or chapatis to go with it.

Soak the chickpeas in water overnight. Drain and boil in plenty of water until really soft. This can take anything from 45 minutes to over 2 hours, depending on the age of the chickpeas. Drain well.

Grind the cumin and coriander seeds finely. Peel the garlic and chop roughly. Put the tomatoes in a bowl, cover with boiling water and leave for 2 minutes, then peel and chop roughly. Put the tamarind paste into a measuring jug, add the hot water and stir to mix.

Put the oil and butter in a wide, heavy, heatproof casserole over a medium heat. Then stir in the turmeric and the ground cumin and coriander. Next add the garlic and chopped tomatoes, the tamarind water, mustard seeds, cayenne pepper and a sprinkling of salt. Add the cooked chickpeas, cover the dish and cook gently on top of the stove, stirring once or twice, for about 15 minutes.

Meanwhile, wash the spinach and add the whole leaves to the casserole. Cover again and continue cooking for about 5 minutes, until the spinach is soft. Remove the lid and, if the mixture is slightly liquid, bubble it for a few minutes, stirring in the open dish until it is fairly thick and mushy.

Lower the heat and make 4 depressions in the chickpea and spinach mixture. Break the eggs carefully into these depressions. Cover again and cook for 6–8 minutes, until the eggs are just set – they should still be runny in the centre. Sprinkle with roughly chopped coriander leaves and serve immediately.

When my parents became the first foreigners on the volcanic island of Lanzarote, then completely undeveloped, about 39 years ago, they employed a cook called Maria – a tiny woman as wide as she was tall. Her husband had fallen to his death from a roof while drunk and she lived in one room with her seven children, but she seemed to laugh all the time. She also turned out to be a wonderfully natural cook and is still remembered for her chickpea dishes.

In the centre of the island, planted in black volcanic ash, were fields of chickpeas. Their grey-green foliage looked so striking that my mother, an artist, did several paintings of them. I, meanwhile, wandered among the plants and opened their short, hairy pods to eat the fresh seeds which would become the dried, nutty chickpeas that we know. They were delicious.

Eggs in Spiced Coconut Milk Sauce

SERVES 4

8 large eggs

1 medium onion

1 large clove garlic

2 ripe tomatoes, the plum variety if available

1 fresh red chilli

1 small bunch spring onions

4 rounded tablespoons coconut milk powder

600ml/1 pint milk

25g/1oz butter

1 teaspoon ground turmeric

salt

This simple lunch or supper dish has a sauce which is an irresistible fusion of flavours. It is best served with basmati rice or oriental noodles and a green salad. If you like, you can use fresh coriander leaves instead of the spring onions.

Put the eggs into a saucepan of cold water, bring to the boil and simmer for 4 minutes. Drain and immerse in cold water. When cool, peel the eggs and cut them in half lengthways.

Peel and finely chop the onion and garlic. Put the tomatoes into a bowl, pour boiling water over them and leave for about 2 minutes, then drain, peel and chop up fairly small. Cut the chilli open lengthways under running water and discard the seeds and stem. Chop the flesh up finely. Trim the spring onions and slice across finely, using as much of the green part as possible. Put the coconut milk powder and 2 teaspoons of salt into a bowl. Heat the milk until just below simmering point and then pour it on to the coconut milk powder, stirring until smooth.

Melt the butter in a large frying pan over a low heat, add the onion and garlic and cook gently, stirring all the time, until soft and golden. Then add the tomatoes and turmeric and cook until the tomatoes are soft and mushy. Stir in the coconut milk and boil for half a minute. Pour the mixture into a food processor and whizz until smooth. Return the smooth sauce to the frying pan and add the chopped chilli and the halved, cooked eggs. Bubble gently for 2–3 minutes and then turn into a warmed serving dish. If necessary, you can cover it with foil and keep warm in a low oven for up to 1 hour. Just before serving, sprinkle with the chopped spring onions.

Dandelion Bud Omelette

SERVES 2

handful dandelion buds

15–20 very young dandelion leaves

4 large eggs

25g/1oz unsalted butter

sea salt

black pepper

There is something very satisfying about using edible flowers to cook with; it makes one feel both resourceful and inspired. You should pick dandelion buds which are showing yellow about half way down the bud.

Remove any stems from the dandelion buds, wash and drain. Rinse the leaves, drain and chop roughly. Break the eggs into a bowl and whisk lightly, then stir in the chopped leaves and season with crushed sea salt and black pepper.

Melt the butter in a fairly large omelette pan over a moderate to high heat. Add the dandelion buds and sauté until they start to burst open. Pour in the egg mixture and, as the eggs begin to cook around the edges of the pan, pull them back with a wooden spoon, letting the liquid egg run to the sides. Remove from the heat when the sides of the omelette are set but the centre is still soft. Using a spatula, fold the omelette over in thirds, cut in half across and turn quickly out on to warmed plates.

Fried Eggs on Spiced Sprouting Broccoli

SERVES 4

675g/1½lb sprouting broccoli or spring greens

2.5–4cm/1–1½in piece fresh ginger

3 large cloves garlic

1–2 fresh red chillies

3 tablespoons groundnut oil

50g/2oz butter

2 heaped teaspoons ground coriander

1 teaspoon cumin seeds

3 tablespoons lemon juice

4 large eggs

1 teaspoon paprika

salt

This is wonderful if you can use young purple sprouting broccoli but, unless you grow it yourself, this lovely vegetable is sometimes hard to find these days. Otherwise use spring greens. Quickly made, this dish is lovely for supper or lunch, accompanied by good crusty bread.

Wash the broccoli or greens and cut off the lower stalks of the broccoli or the base of the greens. If using greens, slice them across thinly. Peel the ginger and garlic and chop them together finely. Cut open the chillies lengthways under running water, discard the seeds and stems and then slice the halves finely across.

Bring a saucepan of salted water to the boil, add the broccoli or greens and boil for 5–7 minutes, until soft but still bright green. Drain well and leave on one side. Put 1 tablespoon of the oil and half the butter in a large frying pan over a medium heat. When the butter has melted, stir in the ginger, garlic, chillies, coriander and cumin seeds. Stir around for a minute or two, then add the cooked broccoli or greens and the lemon juice. Stir over a gentle heat for about 5 minutes, then season to taste with salt if necessary and spread out in a warmed shallow serving dish. Keep warm in a low oven while you cook the eggs.

Put the remaining oil in a frying pan over a medium heat. Fry the eggs 2 at a time, basting them with the oil until the white is only just set. Remove the eggs with a slotted spatula and put them on top of the spiced broccoli or greens. Finally, melt the remaining butter in a small saucepan and stir in the paprika. Just before serving, trickle this red butter over the eggs.

SERVES 6

225g/8oz lasagne sheets

450g/1lb fresh spinach

6 medium bulbs fennel

2 large cloves garlic

2 teaspoons green peppercorns in brine

2 tablespoons olive oil

3 teaspoons fennel seeds

225g/8oz small, round white goat's cheese with rind

1 rounded tablespoon cornflour

2 tablespoons milk

150ml/¼ pint Greek-style yoghurt

2 tablespoons freshly grated Parmesan cheese

salt

black pepper

The sauce for this lasagne is made from yoghurt, giving the dish a lighter texture. It has a wonderful combination of flavours. Use either fresh lasagne sheets or the type that needs no pre-cooking.

Put the lasagne sheets (unless you are using the fresh kind) into a sink of hot water into which you have sprinkled a little cooking oil and leave them to soak – they should not be left for longer than 20 minutes or they will become too soft.

Wash the spinach, then boil it in salted water until limp. Drain thoroughly, pressing out excess liquid, and chop up small.

Cut the tough stalks and base off the fennel, and any marked outer parts, reserving the green leaves. Chop the fennel up into fairly small pieces and boil in salted water for a few minutes until softened. Drain well. Peel and finely chop the garlic and roughly crush the green peppercorns in a pestle and mortar.

Heat the olive oil over a medium heat in a large, deep frying pan or a wide, heatproof casserole dish, add the garlic and fennel seeds and stir around for a minute. Add the fennel, stir around for another 3–4 minutes and then remove from the heat. Stir in the crushed peppercorns and drained chopped spinach and season with salt and a little black pepper.

Drain the soaked lasagne sheets, placing them in a single layer on absorbent kitchen paper. Butter a rectangular ovenproof dish measuring roughly 27.5 x 20cm/11 x 8in. Slice the goat's cheese across thinly without cutting off the rind.

Arrange a layer of lasagne sheets in the dish, then spoon one third of the fennel and spinach mixture over the lasagne. Arrange one third of the goat's cheese slices on top. Lay on more lasagne and continue as before, ending with a layer of lasagne sheets.

Preheat the oven to 200°C/400°F/gas mark 6. Put the cornflour into a saucepan, add the milk and stir until smooth. Then stir in the yoghurt. Put on to the heat and bring to the boil, stirring constantly in one direction only. Allow to bubble, still stirring, for 2–3 minutes. Season with salt and black pepper. Then spoon the stabilized yoghurt evenly over the lasagne and sprinkle with the grated Parmesan.

Cook the dish in the centre of the oven for about 35 minutes, until speckled brown on top. Garnish the edges with chopped fennel leaves before serving.

Semolina Gnocchi Roll with Broccoli and Mozzarella

SERVES 4

600ml/1 pint milk

100g/4oz fine semolina

25g/1oz butter

75g/3oz mature Cheddar cheese, grated

¼ nutmeg, grated

2 egg yolks

1 large clove garlic

450g/1lb broccoli, with plenty of head

2 tablespoons olive oil

150–175g/5–6oz mozzarella cheese

freshly grated Parmesan cheese

salt

black pepper

The first time I tasted semolina gnocchi I was amazed that something as ordinary as semolina could be turned into such an irresistible dish. I find it perfect to serve if I have vegetarian friends to supper. A tomato salad or just a bowl of small cherry tomatoes goes well.

Put the milk and semolina in a heavy saucepan and bring to the boil, stirring constantly. Simmer, still stirring, for 3–4 minutes, until the mixture is very thick. Remove the pan from the heat and stir in the butter, grated cheese, nutmeg and egg yolks. Season with salt and plenty of black pepper. Smear a Swiss roll tin or baking sheet (about 23 x 33cm/9 x 13in) lightly with oil and spread the gnocchi mixture evenly all over. Leave to cool, then chill in the fridge for half an hour or more.

Meanwhile, peel the garlic and chop finely. Trim just the base of the stalk off the broccoli. Cut off the thick part of the stalk, peel it and then chop into very small pieces, with the head of the broccoli. Heat the olive oil in a large frying pan over a medium heat. Add the broccoli and cook, stirring frequently, for 7–8 minutes. Then add the garlic and continue to stir over the heat for another 2 minutes or until the broccoli is just cooked but still crunchy. Season with a little salt and black pepper and leave on one side.

Slice the mozzarella thinly. Spread the broccoli all over the chilled gnocchi mixture and arrange three-quarters of the mozzarella on top. Then, using your fingers, carefully and loosely roll up the gnocchi mixture like a Swiss roll, enclosing the broccoli. Using a wide spatula and the palms of your hands, transfer the roll to an oiled shallow ovenproof dish – don't worry if it cracks a bit, you can just press it together again. Put the remaining slices of mozzarella on top and then sprinkle grated Parmesan cheese generously over the whole roll. Keep in the fridge until ready to cook.

Preheat the oven to 240°C/475°F/gas mark 9. Cook the roll at the top of the oven for 15–20 minutes, until a rich golden brown.

Basmati Rice with Aubergines and Currants

SERVES 4-5

225g/8oz basmati rice

50g/2oz currants

1 tablespoon white wine vinegar

2 small to medium aubergines

50g/2oz butter

1 tablespoon olive oil

4–5 cardamom pods, roughly crushed

1 teaspoon salt

just over 300ml/½ pint water

black pepper

In the Himalayas, fields of basmati rice are said to perfume the air with their fragrance. It is wonderful that this king of rice is so widely available now, because its flavour and texture are hard to match. This recipe makes a delicious accompaniment to stews, casseroles or curries, or even a roast chicken for Sunday lunch.

Put the rice into a sieve and wash through well with running water. Then put it into a bowl with the currants and 600ml/1 pint of salted water and leave to soak for 30 minutes–1 hour. Meanwhile, put the vinegar into a medium saucepan of salted water and bring to the boil. Top and tail the aubergines and cut them into 1.25cm/½in cubes. Add the aubergines to the boiling water and boil for 5–8 minutes, until soft. Drain, pat dry with absorbent paper and leave on one side.

Heat the butter and olive oil in a saucepan over a medium heat, add the aubergines and cardamom pods and stir for 4–5 minutes. Drain the rice and currants, add to the aubergine mixture and stir for another minute. Add the salt and a good sprinkling of black pepper to the water, pour it into the saucepan and stir around. Bring to bubbling, then reduce the heat, cover the pan and cook over the lowest possible heat for 10–12 minutes, until the rice is soft but still has a bite to it. Using a fork, turn out onto a warm serving plate.

Tagliolini with Lemon Cream Sauce

SERVES 4

150ml/¼ pint double cream

finely grated rind and juice of 1 small lemon

225g/8oz tagliolini or tagliatelle

1 tablespoon olive oil

freshly grated Parmesan cheese

salt

black pepper

This simple and easy-to-prepare dish was the best I had on a gastronomic trip to Perugia in Italy. Use a high-quality Italian pasta.

Before you start to cook the pasta, put the cream and grated lemon rind in a saucepan on one side. Then plunge the pasta into a saucepan of boiling salted water and boil, uncovered, for a few minutes, testing until it is just cooked *al dente* – still with a slight bite to it. Drain the pasta and put it back in the warm saucepan with the olive oil while you make the sauce.

Bring the cream and lemon rind to the boil and bubble for a minute or two. Remove from the heat and gradually stir in the lemon juice. Season with a little salt and plenty of pepper. Pour the sauce on to the pasta in the saucepan, toss around to coat it, then turn out into a heated serving dish and serve immediately, accompanied by a bowl of freshly grated Parmesan cheese or just a hunk of Parmesan with a grater.

Chicory and Sun-dried Tomato Risotto

SERVES 4

2 plump chicory

1 small onion

10–12 sun-dried tomatoes

about 1.5 litres/2½ pints good vegetable stock

75g/3oz butter

3 tablespoons olive oil

1 level tablespoon golden caster sugar

350g/12oz risotto rice, such as arborio or carnaroli

25g (1oz) Parmesan cheese, freshly grated

A creamy risotto, made with proper risotto rice such as the arborio or carnaroli varieties, is always a treat. Risottos do need stirring almost constantly while you cook but they are ideal for an informal kitchen meal and need no other accompaniment, except perhaps a leaf or two of green salad. If possible, use home-made stock – if it is good it makes a great difference.

Cut the base off the chicory and slice across fairly thinly. Peel the onion and chop small. Slice the sun-dried tomatoes in half lengthways. Heat the stock to simmering point and keep on a burner at a low simmer while you make the risotto.

Melt 50g/2oz of the butter with the olive oil in a large, heavy-based pan over a medium heat. Add the prepared chicory and onion and fry gently until soft and golden. Then stir in the sun-dried tomatoes and caster sugar, add the rice and stir around for 1–2 minutes, until the rice is opaque. Now add a ladleful of the simmering stock and stir until it has been absorbed by the rice. Continue adding stock, a ladleful at a time, waiting for it to be absorbed before adding more. Keep stirring all the time for 20–25 minutes, until the rice is soft but still has a central bite to it. You should add enough stock for the rice to be slightly loose, not solid.

Finally, stir in the grated Parmesan and the remaining butter, with salt and black pepper to taste. Serve immediately.

Crusted Baked Fennel

SERVES 4

4 large firm bulbs fennel

butter for the dish

2 large cloves garlic

75g/3oz fresh white breadcrumbs

4 tablespoons extra virgin olive oil

2 rounded tablespoons freshly grated Parmesan cheese

sea salt

black pepper

This is similar to the wonderful Italian way of baking fennel with Parmesan cheese. I find the smell of fennel, garlic, olive oil, Parmesan and toasting breadcrumbs emerging from the oven almost unbearably mouthwatering. Serve with a tomato salad.

Preheat the oven to 200°C/400°F/gas mark 6. Cut the top, stalks and base off the fennel bulbs and remove any marked outer leaves. Cut the bulbs into quarters, or sixths if they are very large, then boil in salted water until just soft all the way through. Drain and lay the pieces of fennel in one layer in a generously buttered shallow ovenproof dish.

Peel the garlic and chop as finely as possible. Put the breadcrumbs into a bowl and then stir in the olive oil, grated Parmesan, garlic, a sprinkling of crushed sea salt and plenty of coarsely ground black pepper. Scatter this mixture evenly over the fennel pieces and cook at the top of the oven for 20–30 minutes, until golden.

CHICORY AND SUN-DRIED TOMATO RISOTTO ▶

Cauliflower Cheese Flan

SERVES 6

450g/1lb cauliflower florets

225g/8oz curd cheese

2 medium or large eggs

2 egg yolks

2 tablespoons whole seed mustard

25g/1oz mature Cheddar cheese, grated

salt

black pepper

An alternative and more interesting way of serving cauliflower cheese; it may even convert those who have bad memories of the sometimes infamous nursery dish. Serve with a green salad.

Preheat the oven to 180°C/350°F/gas mark 4. Reserve one floret of cauliflower and steam or boil the rest until soft. Chop up the cooked cauliflower as finely as possible and put it into a bowl with the curd cheese. Add the eggs and egg yolks and whisk together thoroughly. Then stir in the mustard and season with salt and black pepper. Pour the mixture into a buttered 23cm/9in round ovenproof dish and cook in the centre of the oven for 20–25 minutes, just until set.

When the flan is ready, remove from the oven and turn the heat up to 240°C/475°F/gas mark 9. Slice the reserved cauliflower floret lengthways as thinly as possible and arrange the slices in a circle on top of the flan. Sprinkle with the grated cheese. Put the flan back on the top shelf of the oven for 8–10 minutes, until the cheese is speckled brown.

Jerusalem Artichoke Stir-fry

SERVES 4

2 large cloves garlic

4–5cm/1½–2in piece fresh ginger

generous bunch fresh parsley

675g/1½lb large, fresh-looking Jerusalem artichokes

3–4 tablespoons olive oil

salt

black pepper

Unfortunately the wondrous Jerusalem artichoke induces flatulence in most stomachs – sometimes quite severe and even painful. But if you are lucky enough not to be affected or if, like me, the delicious taste of the artichoke makes it worth the discomfort now and then, do try this way of cooking them. Despite any amount of inner turbulence it is my favourite.
If you have a wok, use it, otherwise a large, heavy frying pan will do. Ginger is said to reduce wind – I'm not sure about this but it tastes very good anyway.

Peel the garlic and ginger, chop very finely and put to one side. Chop the parsley fairly finely. Wash the artichokes, cut off any shrivelled-looking bits and then scrub, but don't bother to peel. Using a sharp knife, slice the artichokes across as thinly as you can.

Heat the olive oil in a frying pan over a fairly high heat, add the artichokes and stir constantly for 2–5 minutes (depending on the thickness of the slices), until just beginning to soften at the edges – the slices should still be crunchy in the centre. Now add the chopped garlic and ginger and stir for another minute. Add the chopped parsley, stir to mix and then remove immediately from the heat. Add salt and pepper to taste, turn into a heated serving dish and serve at once.

Sautéed Cauliflower with Chilli, Ginger and Pine Kernels

SERVES 4

450g/1lb cauliflower florets

1 fresh red chilli

2.5cm/1in piece fresh ginger

2 cloves garlic

25g/1oz pine kernels

2 tablespoons olive oil

40g/1½oz butter

roughly chopped fresh coriander leaves, to garnish

salt

Cauliflower is often thought of as a dull vegetable; this recipe proves that it need not be. For a vegetarian meal, serve with one or two other vegetable dishes. Alternatively, serve as an accompaniment to roast chicken or game birds.

Slice the cauliflower florets downwards fairly thinly. Plunge into boiling salted water and cook for 2–3 minutes only, until slightly softened. Drain and dry thoroughly. Cut the chilli open lengthways under running water, discard the seeds and stem and slice the flesh across as thinly as possible. Peel the ginger and garlic and chop together finely. Put a large sauté pan over a high heat, add the pine kernels to the dry pan and toss briefly until browned. Turn on to a plate and leave on one side.

Now put the olive oil and butter into the sauté pan over a medium to high heat, add the cauliflower and stir around for 3–4 minutes. Then lower the heat a bit, add the chilli, ginger and garlic and stir around for another 2 minutes. Finally, stir in the pine kernels and a sprinkling of salt and remove from the heat. Turn into a heated serving dish and scatter the roughly chopped coriander on top.

Sautéed Potatoes with Fresh Ginger and Spices

SERVES 6

900g/2lb new potatoes

3 cloves garlic

5cm/2in piece fresh ginger

3 tablespoons groundnut oil

25g/1oz butter

2 teaspoons paprika

2 teaspoons ground cinnamon

3 teaspoons cumin seeds

1 level teaspoon cayenne pepper

good handful chopped fresh coriander leaves or parsley

sea salt

I really think potatoes are my favourite vegetable. I wouldn't mind a meal entirely made up of them, and indeed Antoine Augustin Parmentier, who converted the French to potatoes in the late 18th century, once presented distinguished guests with a meal consisting only of potatoes, cooked in 20 different ways.

These spicy potatoes are especially good. You can serve them with other vegetable dishes or as an accompaniment to a non-vegetarian meal.

Scrub the potatoes but don't peel them. Steam or boil until they are just cooked, then drain and cut them in half, or into quarters if they are fairly large.

Peel the garlic and ginger and chop together finely. Heat the oil and butter in a large, deep frying pan or a wok over a medium heat. Add the garlic, ginger and spices and stir around for a minute. Then add the potatoes and sauté over a medium heat for about 8 minutes. Finally, stir in a sprinkling of sea salt and the chopped coriander or parsley, remove from the heat and turn into a heated serving dish.

Sweet Potato and Leek Cakes

SERVES 6

900g/2lb sweet potatoes

100g/4oz butter

1 rounded tablespoon thick plain yoghurt

2 tablespoons whole seed mustard

2 level teaspoons caraway seeds

6 small to medium leeks

100g/4oz fresh breadcrumbs

groundnut oil for frying

sea salt

black pepper

There are several types of sweet potato but the ones I like best are those with a thin reddish/orange skin and clear, pale-orange flesh, which becomes richer and deeper when cooked. Before buying, scrape a little skin off with your nail to make sure they are not the white-fleshed kind. Serve these cakes for lunch or supper, with a mixed leaf salad.

Peel the sweet potatoes, cut them up roughly and steam or boil until very soft. Then drain and mash thoroughly with 50g/2oz of the butter. Mix in the yoghurt, mustard and caraway seeds and season to taste.

Trim the leeks and chop up fairly small, using as much of the green part as possible. Wash the chopped leeks and drain thoroughly. Melt the remaining butter in a deep frying pan over a gentle heat, add the leeks and cook in the open pan until just soft, stirring often. Now mix the leeks and their butter into the mashed sweet potatoes and leave until cold.

Using wet hands, mould the mixture into fish cake shapes. Have the breadcrumbs in a bowl on one side and as you form the cakes dip each one in the breadcrumbs to cover it.

To cook, pour 1.25cm/½in groundnut oil over the base of a large frying pan and put over a medium heat. Fry the cakes until rich golden brown on both sides and remove to a warmed serving dish with a slotted spatula.

Chickpea Purée with Red Onion and a Parmesan and Garlic Crust

SERVES 4

275g/10oz dried chickpeas

1 medium red onion

75g/3oz butter

4 tablespoons olive oil

2 teaspoons caster sugar

½ nutmeg, grated

2 cloves garlic

2 rounded tablespoons fresh white breadcrumbs

1 rounded tablespoon freshly grated Parmesan cheese

salt

black pepper

Soak the chickpeas in plenty of cold water overnight. Drain, put in a saucepan and cover generously with water. Boil until completely soft.

Meanwhile, peel the onion, cut in half and slice finely. Melt a third of the butter with half the olive oil in a frying pan over a medium heat. Add the sliced onion and cook, stirring, until soft but not browned. Stir in the caster sugar, remove from the heat and leave on one side.

Drain the cooked chickpeas and put them into a food processor with the remaining butter and the nutmeg. Whizz thoroughly until smooth. Season to taste with salt and black pepper, then stir in the fried onion with its butter and oil and spoon into a small earthenware dish.

Preheat the oven to 200°C/400°F/gas mark 6. Peel the garlic and chop finely. Put the breadcrumbs into a bowl and stir in the grated Parmesan and garlic. Then thoroughly stir in the remaining olive oil. Spoon this mixture evenly over the top of the chickpea purée. Cook near the top of the oven for about 20 minutes, until speckled brown on top.

The salad can be
anything from a light
accompaniment or first course to
a whole meal. Gone are the days when it meant
limp lettuce and woolly tomatoes. Nowadays even
fussy children are tempted by salads. They can be
made from raw, cooked or partly cooked ingredients,
and can be cold, warm or fashionably *tiède*. The choice
is wide. I particularly like chilled salads that have some
sizzling ingredient added to them at the last moment.

Picnics, at least the informal ones I am used to,
demand not salads but food that can be eaten in the
hand and emphatic flavours that satisfy a keen
outdoor appetite.

salad days and perfect picnics

Asparagus and Grilled Red Pepper Salad with Pine Kernels

2 medium red peppers

450g/1lb thin green asparagus

25g/1oz pine kernels

For the vinaigrette:

2 tablespoons white wine vinegar

1 tablespoon strained lemon juice

finely grated rind of 1 lemon

2 teaspoons clear honey

6 tablespoons extra virgin olive oil

sea salt

black pepper

This salad makes a perfect first course, arranged on individual plates. If you like, you can grill the asparagus instead of steaming it.

Cut the peppers in half and remove the seeds and stems. Put them, skin-sides up, under a hot grill until the skin has blackened. Then wrap in a plastic bag or tin foil and leave on one side – this will make them easy to peel.

Unless they look coarse, cut only about 1.25cm/½in off the asparagus stalks. Steam or boil them until just tender, then rinse immediately with cold water to cool and stop the cooking.

Put a dry frying pan over a high heat, add the pine kernels and stir for about a minute until toasted brown. Turn out of the pan and leave to cool. Peel the skin off the red peppers and, using a sharp knife, cut them lengthways into thin strips.

When ready to assemble the salad, arrange the asparagus on 4 serving plates, crossed with strips of pepper and sprinkled with toasted pine kernels. Put all the vinaigrette ingredients except the salt and pepper into a jam jar. Seal with a lid and shake vigorously to mix, then add salt and pepper to taste. Just before serving, shake the jar again and spoon the dressing evenly over the salad.

Broad Bean Kernel, Avocado and Bacon Salad

800g/1¾lb fresh broad beans or 350g/12oz frozen broad beans

1½ tablespoons white wine vinegar

2 teaspoons French mustard

4 tablespoons extra virgin olive oil

3–4 pinches cayenne pepper

2 avocados (ripe but not too soft)

175g/6oz thin rashers rindless smoked bacon

bunch fresh dill, chopped

salt

If you use fresh broad beans for this delicious salad, make sure they are small and only recently picked. If you decide to use frozen, there is no need to boil them; simply put them in a bowl, pour boiling water over and leave for a minute or two, then drain and press them out of their skins as for the fresh beans.

Pod the fresh broad beans. Bring a saucepan of water to the boil, put in the beans and cook for only 3–4 minutes, then drain. Pop the green insides out of their skins into a salad bowl. Put the vinegar, mustard and olive oil into a jam jar with the cayenne pepper and some salt.

Shortly before you eat, cut the avocados in half, remove the stones and carefully peel off the skin. Then cut them thinly across in half-moon slices and put into the salad bowl with the broad beans. Shake the dressing in the jar and mix it into the broad beans and avocado. Slice the bacon up fairly small. Put a dry frying pan over a fairly high heat and toss the bacon pieces around until crisp. Add to the salad together with the chopped dill and serve immediately.

Creamy Monkfish, Bacon and Two-Cress Salad

SERVES 4

1 bunch watercress

1 carton cress

approximately 550g/1¼lb monkfish

1 bunch spring onions

175g/6oz rindless smoked streaky bacon

1 tablespoon olive oil

150ml/¼ pint double cream

2 teaspoons bottled green peppercorns, roughly crushed

2 teaspoons chopped fresh tarragon

salt

Hot salads are best for informal lunches and suppers, since they need last-minute attention but can be made quickly. For a big meal you can serve them as a first course but many are substantial enough to be the main course of a light meal, accompanied by hot, crusty bread. This is a luscious combination of hot ingredients set on a bed of chilled cresses.

Take the thick stalks off the watercress and put the leafy sprigs into a large, fairly shallow serving bowl. Mix in the cress and then refrigerate. Cut away any central bone from the monkfish, then slice the flesh into 2.5cm/1in chunks. Trim the spring onions and slice them into 1.25cm/½in pieces, using as much of the green part as possible. Slice the bacon up into fairly small pieces.

Heat the olive oil in a large frying pan and fry the bacon over a fairly high heat until crisp. Remove with a slotted spatula and leave on a plate in a warm oven to keep hot. Turn the heat down to medium and add the monkfish and spring onion to the bacon fat. Toss around gently for 4–6 minutes, until the monkfish is just cooked. Pour the cream into the pan, adding the green peppercorns and tarragon. Season with salt. Allow the cream just to bubble, then add the fried bacon, turn the mixture out on to the bed of cresses and serve at once.

Dandelion and Bacon Salad

SERVES 4

large handful unopened dandelion flower buds

1 bunch (about 2 large handfuls) young dandelion leaves

4 rashers rindless smoked streaky bacon

3–4 tablespoons extra virgin olive oil

1 tablespoon wine vinegar

1 teaspoon caster sugar (optional)

salt

black pepper

I have never grown out of my student thrill at finding free food. This salad is for early summer, when the dandelions are fresh and young.

Wash the dandelion flowers and leaves and pat them dry between paper towels. Cut the bacon into small pieces, fry in a dry pan over a fairly high heat until crisp and then drain on paper towels. Toss the dandelion flowers in the bacon fat over a medium heat until the buds are just open, then drain on paper towels. Put the dandelion leaves in a salad bowl and mix in the fried bacon and flowers.

Put the oil, vinegar and sugar, if using, in a small screw-top jar and season with salt and pepper. Seal the jar and shake well, then add to the salad and toss lightly.

Nasturtium and Lettuce Salad with a Raspberry and Hazelnut Dressing

SERVES 4

2–3 Little Gem lettuces

good handful of small nasturtium leaves

8–10 nasturtium flowers

1 good tablespoon chopped fresh dill (optional)

50g/2oz raspberries

1 tablespoon raspberry vinegar

4 tablespoons hazelnut oil

salt

black pepper

The peppery leaves and brilliant flowers of the nasturtium can either be thrown whole into salads or chopped and folded into mayonnaise. They can be bought in supermarkets but are the easiest thing to grow from seed, even if you only have a flowerpot on your windowsill. This simple summer-to-early-autumn salad combines them with raspberries, raspberry vinegar and hazelnut oil. Remember that all nut oils become stale quickly, so buy the smallest possible bottles and store in the fridge. If you are making the salad at a time when the first cob nuts have appeared in the shops, roughly chop a few and add them to the mixture.

Pull the leaves of the lettuces apart, wash and dry them and put into a salad bowl. Lightly mix in the nasturtium leaves and flowers and the chopped dill, if using.

To make the dressing, press the raspberries through a sieve into a small bowl. Add the raspberry vinegar and hazelnut oil and mix together thoroughly with a fork. Season to taste with salt and black pepper and dress the salad with the mixture just before serving, making sure that plenty of the nasturtium flowers are visible on top.

Hot Potato, Cool Cucumber

SERVES 4

450g/1lb new potatoes

1 small cucumber

4 tablespoons plain yoghurt

2–3 pinches cayenne pepper

2 tablespoons white wine vinegar

6 tablespoons extra virgin olive oil

1–2 tablespoons whole seed mustard

large handful fresh parsley, finely chopped

salt

black pepper

The best potatoes you can get for this during the winter are the Italian new potatoes, which have a good waxy texture and slightly yellow colour. Otherwise, use other salad-type potatoes, and Jersey potatoes during the summer.

Scrub the potatoes but don't peel them. Cut them in half, or in quarters if they are large, and steam or boil until tender. Meanwhile, peel the cucumber, cut it into cubes and mix in a bowl with the yoghurt, cayenne pepper and some salt. Make a vinaigrette dressing by putting the wine vinegar, olive oil and mustard into a jam jar and seasoning with salt and black pepper. Close the jar and shake to mix well.

When the potatoes are cooked, put them in a mixing bowl and add the vinaigrette dressing. Turn gently with a wooden spoon so that the dressing is absorbed into the hot potatoes. Then add the cucumber and yoghurt mixture and the chopped parsley, mix roughly together, turn into a serving bowl and serve at once.

NASTURTIUM AND
LETTUCE SALAD WITH
A RASPBERRY AND
HAZELNUT DRESSING ▶

Exotic Egg and Cucumber Salad

SERVES 4

2.5cm/1in piece fresh ginger

2 cloves garlic

5 cardamom pods

300ml/½ pint milk

2 rounded tablespoons coconut milk powder

6 large eggs

100g/4oz whole-milk yoghurt

2 fresh red chillies

good handful fresh coriander

½ cucumber

salt

With its spice-scented sauce of yoghurt and coconut milk, this is an especially good way of serving cold eggs. Accompanied by fresh bread and new potatoes it makes a delicious light lunch.

Peel the ginger and garlic and chop finely. Crush the cardamom pods and put them into a saucepan with the ginger, garlic and milk. Sprinkle with salt. Bring to the boil, bubble gently for 2 minutes, then remove from the heat, stir in the coconut milk powder until dissolved and leave to cool.

Meanwhile, put the eggs in a saucepan of water, bring to the boil, then bubble for 1 minute. Remove from the heat and leave to cool in the water. When the coconut milk mixture is cold, strain it through a sieve into a mixing bowl and stir in the yoghurt. Cut the chillies open lengthways under running water, discard the seeds and stem and chop the flesh across in very thin strips. Roughly chop the coriander leaves, reserving a sprig or two for garnish. Then stir the chopped coriander leaves and chillies into the sauce. Peel the eggs and slice across in rounds. Peel the cucumber and cut into smallish cubes.

Arrange the egg slices and cucumber in a fairly shallow serving dish. Spoon the coconut and yoghurt mixture over the top, put a whole leaf or two of coriander in the centre and refrigerate until ready to serve.

Potato Salad with Red Pesto and Fresh Basil Leaves

SERVES 4

450g/1lb waxy potatoes

6 rounded teaspoons red pesto

1 small clove garlic, crushed

3 tablespoons extra virgin olive oil

10–12 fresh basil leaves or handful fresh dill

Red pesto is a fairly new invention. It has the same delicious mixture of basil, olive oil, garlic, pine kernels and Parmesan cheese as traditional pesto but it also includes sun-dried tomatoes. It has a slightly sweeter taste which I have found to be the perfect answer for an easy dressing for potato or other salads.

Wash the potatoes well but do not peel them. Cut in half or in very thick slices, according to size, then steam or boil until tender. Meanwhile, spoon the pesto into a bowl, add the crushed garlic and olive oil and stir together.

When the potatoes are ready, drain them, put them into a large bowl and pour over the pesto dressing. Turn around gently with a wooden spoon to coat the potatoes thoroughly. Leave until cold. Then slice the basil leaves across in thin strips (or chop the dill, if using), mix roughly in with the potatoes and transfer to a serving bowl.

Pea Salad with Ginger, Olives and Sweet Pepper

SERVES 8

100g/4oz pitted black olives

1 large red pepper

generous 5cm/2in piece fresh ginger

3 large cloves garlic

675g/1½lb frozen peas

100g/4oz chopped candied peel

4 tablespoons lemon juice

175ml/6fl oz extra virgin olive oil

2 heaped teaspoons paprika

good bunch fresh mint

good bunch fresh flat-leafed parsley

salt

black pepper

I've never known anyone, very young or old, who didn't like this rather unlikely sounding combination of ingredients. Apart from its taste, the great advantage of this cooked salad is that it can be made well in advance, so it is practical for larger gatherings. You can serve it with cold chicken or meat or, for a light meal, simply on its own, accompanied by good crusty bread.

Slice the olives roughly. Cut the pepper in half lengthways, discard the seeds and stem, then slice across very thinly, using a food processor. Peel the ginger and garlic and chop finely. Now put these prepared ingredients into a saucepan with all the remaining ingredients except the mint, parsley and seasoning. Cover the pan and cook gently, stirring around once or twice, for 15 minutes. Then remove from the heat, season to taste with salt and black pepper and leave to cool.

Chop the mint finely and the parsley rather less so. Stir the herbs into the cooled pea mixture and spoon into a serving bowl. If the salad has been sitting in the bowl for some time before you eat, stir it again to coat it with the juices at the last moment. Eat at room temperature, not chilled.

Potato Salad with Rocket, Shallots and an Anchovy Cream Dressing

SERVES 4

50g/2oz tin anchovy fillets

2 teaspoons plus 4 tablespoons extra virgin olive oil

1 small clove garlic, crushed

4–6 shallots (depending on size)

2 good handfuls rocket leaves

450g/1lb Pink Fir apple potatoes or other small waxy potatoes

1½ tablespoons sherry vinegar

black pepper

During my childhood the idea of a potato salad used to make my heart sink. Now it makes it leap. The first potato salads I had were at school: small white cubes of wet potato coated in sour-tasting salad cream. It was not until years later that I realized a good potato salad can be an infinitely variable gastronomic thrill. Here is an example that is also practical and portable for taking on picnics.

Empty the anchovies and their oil into a bowl set over a pan of water that has just boiled and been taken off the heat. Add the 2 teaspoons of olive oil and the crushed garlic and stir for a few minutes until the anchovies turn into a smooth cream. Leave on one side.

Peel the shallots and slice across as thinly as possible in rounds. Chop the rocket leaves roughly, or leave whole if small. Wash the potatoes but do not peel. Cut into slices 5mm/¼in thick and steam or boil until tender. Drain and turn into a bowl with the shallots and rocket – the rocket should wilt on contact with the hot potatoes. Stir the remaining 4 tablespoons oil and the vinegar into the anchovy cream and season with coarsely ground black pepper – no salt should be needed because of the anchovies. Pour this dressing over the potatoes and turn all the ingredients around gently with a large wooden spoon to coat them. Then leave until cold and transfer to another serving dish if you like.

Salmon, Blood Orange and Chicory Salad

SERVES 4

550g/1¼lb salmon fillet, skinned

3 blood oranges

3–4 chicory

juice of 1 small lemon, strained

handful fresh dill or flat-leafed parsley

at least 6 tablespoons extra virgin olive oil

sea salt

black pepper

Beautiful blood oranges are worth making the most of whenever they are in season. They are wonderful in salads, and orange has an affinity with fish. If you can't get blood oranges, use small normal ones. This salad makes a complete light meal served with crusty white bread to mop up the delicious juices. Ask the fishmonger to fillet and skin a tail piece of salmon for you.

Put the salmon into a fairly shallow heatproof dish, such as a cast iron gratin dish, and cover completely with salted water. Bring gradually to the boil, bubble for only a minute, then remove from the heat and leave the fish to cool in the water at room temperature. When the fish is cold, drain well, break into fairly large flakes and put on one side.

Cut the skin off the blood oranges with a small, sharp knife so that you remove all the white pith. Then slice across in very thin circles, removing any pips. Cut the base off the chicory and then slice across at 1.25cm/½ in intervals. Arrange the pieces of salmon, circles of orange and chicory prettily in a wide, shallow dish. Just before serving, pour the lemon juice over the salad and season with crushed sea salt and freshly ground black pepper. Chop up the dill or parsley fairly small and scatter over liberally. Finally, gradually spoon plenty of extra virgin olive oil over the salad.

Fennel and Greengage Salad with Smoked Oysters

SERVES 4

2 large bulbs fennel

3–4 tablespoons extra virgin olive oil

1 tablespoon wine vinegar

1 teaspoon caster sugar (optional)

225g/8oz greengages

50–75g/2–3oz pitted black olives

1 tin smoked oysters

pretty salad leaves, to serve

salt

black pepper

During the late summer I sometimes feel I've eaten rather too many raw salads. If you add cooked vegetables or even fruit to salads there is a much wider range of appetizing possibilities. This is one of them. It can be served as a first course or as part of a cold lunch.

Trim the base off the fennel bulbs and remove any marked outer parts. Cut the fennel lengthways into fairly thin slices and steam for 8–10 minutes, until just soft. Meanwhile, put the oil, vinegar and sugar, if using, in a small screw-top jar and season well with salt and pepper. Seal the jar and shake well to make a dressing. Put the fennel into a bowl and pour some of the dressing over it while hot. Leave until cold.

Cut the greengages into quarters, removing the stones. Chop the olives roughly. Mix the greengages and olives with the fennel and stir in the smoked oysters and their oil. Turn into a serving dish or on to individual plates and garnish with a few pretty salad leaves. Spoon some more dressing over the salad just before serving.

SALMON, BLOOD ORANGE AND CHICORY SALAD ▶

Two-Tomato and Spiced Aubergine Salad with Toasted Pine Kernels

SERVES 4

approximately 550g/1¼lb aubergines

2 tablespoons white wine vinegar

4–5 sun-dried tomatoes

1 small clove garlic, crushed

1 tablespoon sherry vinegar

1 teaspoon paprika

1 teaspoon ground cumin

1½ teaspoons tomato purée

1 tablespoon sunflower oil

2–4 pinches cayenne pepper

450–550g/1–1¼lb well-flavoured tomatoes

8–10 fresh basil leaves

1 tablespoon pine kernels

extra virgin olive oil for drizzling

sea salt

black pepper

This is a part-cooked salad that can be prepared well in advance. Serve for a light lunch accompanied by good bread, and a green salad as well if you like.

Cut the unpeeled aubergines lengthways into quarters and then into 2.5–5cm/1–2in chunks. Put the aubergine pieces into a saucepan with the white wine vinegar, a good sprinkling of salt, and water to cover. Cover the pan, bring to the boil and simmer for only 4–5 minutes, until soft, then drain well. Slice the sun-dried tomatoes across in thin strips.

Now put the crushed garlic, sherry vinegar, paprika, cumin, tomato purée and sunflower oil into a bowl, adding cayenne pepper and salt to taste. Stir to mix and then add the hot aubergine and the strips of sun-dried tomato and toss gently to coat in the dressing. Leave to become cold.

Meanwhile, slice the tomatoes thinly and arrange on a large flat serving dish, leaving a space in the centre. When the aubergine mixture is cold, spoon it into the empty space, ensuring the mixture comes right up to the edge of the tomatoes. Slice the basil leaves across in thin strips and scatter them over the tomatoes.

Put the pine kernels in a dry frying pan over a high heat and toss around for a moment or two, just to brown. Then sprinkle them over the aubergines. Sprinkle the tomatoes with sea salt and coarsely ground black pepper. Do not refrigerate. Just before serving, drizzle olive oil all over the tomatoes and a little over the aubergines.

Warm Cinnamon Chicken and Curly Endive Salad

SERVES 4-5

1 curly endive (frisée)

medium bunch fresh coriander or mint

4 skinless chicken breast fillets

1 lemon

1 large clove garlic

5 tablespoons extra virgin olive oil

2 rounded teaspoons ground cinnamon

3–4 pinches cayenne pepper

salt

I love the mixture of warm cooked ingredients with fresh leaves. Served with good crusty bread, this salad is ideal for a light lunch or supper.

Discard the outer dark green leaves of the curly endive. Separate the pale and mid-green leaves, wash and dry them and put into a large salad bowl. Pull the leaves from the coriander or mint and chop only a little before mixing in with the endive. Using a sharp knife, slice the chicken breasts across as thinly as you can. Finely grate the rind of the lemon and squeeze the juice into a cup. Peel and finely chop the garlic.

Shortly before eating, put the olive oil into a frying pan over a medium heat, add the chopped garlic and stir around, then add the slices of chicken and toss for 2–3 minutes until the chicken is opaque all over. Now add the grated lemon rind and the ground cinnamon and stir about for another minute. Finally stir in the lemon juice with cayenne pepper and salt to taste and leave, covered, for a short time only, as it mustn't get cold. Just before you eat, empty the chicken mixture with the oil and juices on to the bowl of endive and toss around lightly.

Spicy Chicken Strip Salad

SERVES 4

1 large crisp Cos or Webbs lettuce

4 medium skinless chicken breast fillets

juice of 1 lemon

4 tablespoons groundnut oil

1 teaspoon ground cinnamon

1 teaspoon ground coriander

1 rounded teaspoon paprika

4 pinches cayenne pepper

50g/2oz crystallized ginger

2 large cloves garlic

1 tablespoon red wine vinegar

handful fresh coriander leaves

salt

This hot and cold salad is a light meal in itself, served with new potatoes or just good bread. It is best prepared in advance so the spices have time to penetrate the chicken. But it then needs only 5 minutes cooking before you eat.

Pull apart the lettuce, put it into a large serving bowl and refrigerate. Slice the chicken breast fillets into thin strips. Put the lemon juice and 2 tablespoons of the groundnut oil in a mixing bowl. Stir in the cinnamon, coriander, paprika and cayenne pepper, then season with salt. Add the strips of chicken, turning them to coat with the mixture, then cover the bowl and leave at cool room temperature for at least an hour.

Meanwhile, slice the crystallized ginger across thinly and keep on one side. Peel the garlic, cut into thin slices and keep separately from the ginger.

Just before you eat, heat the remaining groundnut oil in a large frying pan over a medium heat. Add the chicken strips with their juices and the sliced garlic. Toss around in the pan for about 5 minutes, until the chicken is just cooked. Then stir in the crystallized ginger and the wine vinegar, toss around for another minute and remove from the heat. Stir in the coriander leaves, spoon the mixture into the bowl of chilled lettuce leaves, toss briefly to mix and serve at once.

WARM CINNAMON CHICKEN AND CURLY ENDIVE SALAD ▶

Spiced Carrot Salad with Red Pepper, Mint and Lovage

SERVES 4

350g/12oz young carrots

1 medium red pepper

3 large cloves garlic

2.5cm/1in piece fresh ginger

juice of 1 lemon and 1 small orange

2 teaspoons raspberry or cider vinegar

1 teaspoon paprika

1 teaspoon ground coriander

3–5 pinches cayenne pepper

1 teaspoon cumin seeds

generous handful fresh mint leaves

about 10 fresh lovage leaves

6 tablespoons extra virgin olive oil

salt

black pepper

Every year I wait for the lovage to spring up in my garden and I use as much of it as possible before it gets rather old in mid to late summer. It is strongly flavoured and goes especially well with spices, as do the sweet, cooked carrots in this recipe. This is a good salad to serve with other vegetables or with fish.

Top and tail the carrots and slice them thinly. Cut the pepper in half, discard the seeds and stem and chop the flesh up into the smallest possible pieces. Peel the garlic and ginger and chop together finely. Put all these ingredients into a saucepan and strain in the lemon and orange juice. Then stir in the vinegar and spices and cover the pan. Put over a fairly low heat and let the liquid barely simmer for 8–10 minutes, until the carrots are just soft but still have a slight resistance. Then remove from the heat, cover the pan and leave until cold.

Meanwhile, chop the mint leaves finely. Slice the lovage leaves across in thin strips, reserving 2 or 3 whole ones for garnish. When the carrots are cold, stir in the chopped mint and strips of lovage, followed by the olive oil. Season to taste with salt and black pepper and turn into a serving dish shortly before you eat. Garnish with the reserved lovage leaves.

Onion and Potato Omelette with Dill and Parmesan

SERVES 6-8

350g/12oz salad-type potatoes

550g/1¼lb onions

2 cloves garlic

2 tablespoons olive oil

25g/1oz butter

10 large eggs

50g/2oz Parmesan cheese, grated

generous bunch fresh dill, chopped

salt

black pepper

SPICED CARROT SALAD WITH RED PEPPER, MINT AND LOVAGE

To me, this is perfect picnic food. The omelette is thick in the Spanish style, so you can cut it in slices like a cake and eat it with your fingers. Wrapped in greaseproof paper and lots of newspaper it will keep warm – or you can take the whole pan on your picnic, also well wrapped in newspaper.

Scrub the potatoes but don't bother to peel them. Then steam or boil until tender, drain and cut into small pieces. Peel the onions, cut them in half and slice finely. Peel and finely chop the garlic. Put the olive oil and butter into a large, deep, heavy-based frying pan about 25cm/10in in diameter. Add the onions and garlic and cook over a fairly low heat, stirring around occasionally, until the onions are very soft and golden. Then add the potatoes, stir to mix and remove from the heat.

Break the eggs into a bowl and whisk lightly. Stir in the Parmesan and dill, then season generously with salt and black pepper. Pour this mixture over the onions and potatoes in the frying pan, stir once and return to a low heat. Cook for about 15 minutes, until all but the central part has set, then cover the pan with foil or a lid and continue cooking for a few more minutes, until the centre feels set to a light touch. If you want, you can sprinkle a little more grated Parmesan cheese on top of the omelette and put it under a hot grill to brown.

SERVES 4-5

Turkish Pasties with Yoghurt Pastry

275g/10oz leeks

100g/4oz new potatoes

1 large clove garlic

1 tablespoon olive oil

15g/½oz butter

2 teaspoons ground coriander

2 pinches cayenne pepper

salt

For the pastry:

100g/4oz butter

1 tablespoon olive oil

1 small egg

150g/5oz carton plain yoghurt

275g/10oz plain flour

¼ teaspoon bicarbonate of soda

1 teaspoon salt

1 egg yolk, beaten

These are not in fact a traditional dish, though Turkey has many good little pies to offer. The delicious yoghurt pastry came from some Turkish friends of mine in Istanbul and the filling, which is full of flavour, contains two of my favourite vegetables – potato and leek. Being small, the pies are ideal to take on picnics, still warm if possible. They can be made ahead and reheated.

Make the filling first. Wash the leeks and slice across in thin rounds as far up the stalk as possible. Chop the slices in half. Scrub the potatoes and cut into small cubes. Peel the garlic and chop finely. Heat the oil and butter in a large frying pan over a medium heat. Add the potatoes and cook, stirring often, for 5–7 minutes, until just tender. Stir in the coriander, garlic and leeks. Stir for 2–3 minutes, until the leeks are softened. Season well with cayenne pepper and salt and remove from the heat.

To make the pastry, melt the butter in a saucepan over a gentle heat and leave on one side. Put the olive oil and egg into a mixing bowl and whisk lightly. Stir in the yoghurt. Using a wooden spoon, slowly stir the melted butter into the yoghurt and egg mixture.

Sift the flour with the bicarbonate of soda and salt and gradually stir it into the yoghurt and butter mixture. Lightly knead the rather soft dough for a few minutes and then roll it out to 5mm/¼in thick. Cut out circles of pastry with a 7.5cm/3in plain pastry cutter or the rim of a wide glass. Spoon about 2 teaspoons of the filling on to one side of each circle, then fold to form semi-circles and press the edges to seal. Re-roll the pastry as necessary.

Preheat the oven to 200°C/400°F/gas mark 6. Lightly grease a large baking sheet, lay the pasties on it and brush with the beaten egg yolk. Cook just above the centre of the oven for about 20 minutes, until golden brown.

TOP: FETA CHEESE, SUN-DRIED TOMATO AND OREGANO PIES (PAGE 142)

BELOW: TURKISH PASTIES WITH YOGHURT PASTRY ▶

Beef, Horseradish and Anchovy Tart with Potato and Oregano Pastry

SERVES 6

450g/1lb potatoes

75g/3oz butter

175g/6oz plain flour

2 teaspoons dried oregano

1 medium onion

675g/1½lb lean minced beef

1 rounded tablespoon horseradish
  sauce

2 tablespoons tomato purée

¼ nutmeg, grated

50g/2oz tin anchovy fillets

salt

black pepper

I devised this recipe years ago and often take it on picnics, as both children and adults enjoy it enormously and it is just as good cold or hot. I usually wrap it in several layers of newspaper so it is still just warm when we reach our picnic spot. It is also ideal for a simple supper, accompanied by a salad.

Peel the potatoes and boil them in salted water until soft, then drain well and mash smoothly, adding the butter. Sift in the flour and sprinkle in the oregano. Stir thoroughly with a wooden spoon to form a dough. Butter a 23cm/9in earthenware flan dish. Gather the potato dough up in a lump and press it evenly over the base and up the sides of the dish. Preheat the oven to 200°C/400°F/gas mark 6.

Peel the onion and chop finely. Then put the minced beef in a bowl and add the chopped onion, horseradish sauce, tomato purée and grated nutmeg. Season with salt and black pepper and mix everything together with a wooden spoon. Spoon the mixture into the flan dish and arrange the anchovy fillets in a criss-cross pattern on top, pressing them down lightly. Pour the oil from the tin all over the meat. Cook the tart on the centre shelf of the oven for 25–30 minutes.

Feta Cheese, Sun-dried Tomato and Oregano Pies

MAKES 12

75ml/3fl oz double cream

3 egg yolks

3–4 pinches cayenne pepper

100g/4oz feta cheese

2 teaspoons dried oregano

6–8 sun-dried tomatoes

salt

For the pastry:

175g/6oz plain flour

¼ teaspoon salt

100g/4oz butter

1 egg white

These light little pies are a treat for a picnic and can be eaten without plate or fork. With their crisp pastry they are nicest eaten warm; you can reheat them and take them to your picnic well wrapped in newspaper.

Make the pastry first. Sift the flour and salt into a bowl. Gently melt the butter and pour it into the flour, stirring with a wooden spoon to mix evenly. Add the egg white and continue to stir until you have a smooth, soft dough. Leave the dough in the bowl for about 5 minutes, until it has cooled slightly. Then divide the still-warm dough into 12 pieces and roll into balls. Put one in each patty tin and press it to line the tin so that it comes a little over the edge. Refrigerate for half an hour or more.

Meanwhile, prepare the filling. In a mixing bowl, whisk the cream and egg yolks together until slightly thickened. Whisk in the cayenne pepper and a very little salt. Crumble in the feta cheese, add the oregano and stir to mix. Slice the sun-dried tomatoes into small pieces and stir into the mixture.

When the pastry is chilled, preheat the oven to 190°C/375°F/gas mark 5. Spoon the filling into the pastry-lined tins and cook in the centre of the oven for about 20 minutes, until the pastry and filling are a rich brown. Then remove the pies from the oven and leave in the tins for a few minutes before edging them out on to a plate.

Tender Slices of Marinated Lamb Fillet with Fresh Mint

SERVES 6

handful fresh mint leaves

2 large cloves garlic

2 tablespoons olive oil

juice of 1 lemon

2 tablespoons tomato purée

2 teaspoons ground cinnamon

2 teaspoons ground coriander

3–4 pinches cayenne pepper

4–5 well-trimmed lamb neck fillets, weighing about 675–800g/ 1½–1¾lb

For the dressing:

3 tablespoons extra virgin olive oil

1 tablespoon sherry vinegar

cayenne pepper

sea salt

This is a much more interesting way of serving cold meat, and ideal for picnics. As long as you don't overcook them, lamb fillets are an excellent way of serving cold boneless lamb. They are cooked whole at the highest heat so that their centre remains pink and juicy.

Chop the mint leaves finely and put them into a bowl. Peel and crush the garlic. Add the garlic, olive oil, lemon juice, tomato purée and spices to the mint and mix very thoroughly together. Put the lamb fillets into a roasting pan and rub all over with the mixture. Cover the pan with foil and leave in the fridge for at least 6 hours or overnight. Remove the lamb fillets from the fridge to bring them to room temperature about an hour before you cook them.

Preheat the oven to 240°C/475°F/gas mark 9. Remove the foil from the roasting pan and turn the lamb to make sure it is still evenly covered with the marinade. Cook at the very top of the oven for 15 minutes, turning the fillets once half way through. Immediately after cooking, remove the fillets from the pan and leave on a plate in a cool place until cold.

Before taking on your picnic, cut the fillets crossways into very thin slices, using your sharpest knife. Put them into a bowl or a container that you can take with you. Mix the dressing ingredients together in a cup with a fork, adding cayenne pepper and salt to taste. Then mix into the cold meat.

Spicy Chicken and Pork Sausages

SERVES 6

450g/1lb skinless chicken breast fillets

3 cloves garlic

2.5cm/1in piece fresh ginger

1 rounded tablespoon curry powder

2 rounded tablespoons tomato purée

50g/2oz fresh breadcrumbs

225g/8oz minced pork

1 small onion, roughly chopped

small handful fresh coriander or mint leaves

groundnut or sunflower oil for grilling

salt

These sausages are really practical and versatile for a picnic. You can cook them beforehand and wrap them well to keep warm, although they are also good cold. Alternatively, you can grill them at the picnic site if you have a portable barbecue or if you make a fire. The sausages can be eaten with your fingers and are good dipped into a bowl of seasoned yoghurt.

Cut the chicken breasts up roughly and put them in a food processor. Peel and chop the garlic and ginger and add to the chicken. Whizz until the chicken is well chopped, then add the curry powder, tomato purée, breadcrumbs, minced pork, onion and coriander or mint leaves. Season with salt and whizz again until it forms a pasty mixture.

Using wet hands, form the mixture into smallish sausage shapes. Smear them all over with oil and grill, turning often, until richly brown all over.

Sun-dried Tomato and Mozzarella Bread with Olive Oil and Sage

SERVES 4—6

about 12 sun-dried
tomatoes

1 Italian mozzarella cheese

10–12 fresh sage leaves

350g/12oz strong unbleached
white flour

1 sachet Easyblend dried yeast

4 teaspoons crushed sea salt, plus
extra for sprinkling

4 tablespoons extra virgin olive oil,
plus extra for drizzling

175–225ml/6–8fl oz warm water

One of the best uses for sun-dried tomatoes is to add flavour. This easily made bread is excellent on a picnic to go with salami or Parma ham and quarters of Little Gem lettuce. It is nicest of all eaten warm, so keep it in the oven until you leave and then wrap in several layers of newspaper. The bread is also good made with feta or goat's cheese instead of mozzarella.

Smear a deep 20cm/8in round cake tin with olive oil. Slice the sun-dried tomatoes across fairly thinly. Cut the mozzarella cheese into small pieces. Chop the sage leaves finely.

Sift the flour into a mixing bowl and stir in the yeast and salt. Then, using a wooden spoon, stir in the sun-dried tomatoes, mozzarella and sage, followed gradually by the olive oil and warm water, adding enough water to form a soft, slightly sticky dough. Using floured hands, gather up the dough and knead lightly on a floured surface for 5–8 minutes, until smooth and elastic. Form the dough into a ball, put it into the cake tin and flatten slightly – it doesn't matter if the surface is uneven. Using a sharp knife, make a few deep criss-cross lines in the dough. Trickle a little olive oil all over and sprinkle with a little salt. Put the tin into a large plastic bag and fold the bag in under the tin, trapping plenty of air so that the bag is puffed up well above the bread. Leave at room temperature for 1–2 hours, until the dough has risen well.

Preheat the oven to 220°C/425°F/gas mark 7. Bake the bread for 25–30 minutes, until a rich brown. Turn it out of the tin on to a rack and cool a little. If you have made the bread earlier, reheat it before your picnic.

Venison Burgers

SERVES 4

550–675g/1¼–1½lb minced
venison

1 tablespoon horseradish sauce

2 rounded teaspoons capers,
chopped

2–4 pinches chilli powder

groundnut or sunflower oil for
grilling

salt

Supermarkets sometimes sell minced venison. Alternatively you can ask your butcher to mince it for you, or do it yourself in a food processor. I think it is better than beef for making hamburgers. As it is so lacking in fat, it is best for quickly fried, well-seasoned or spiced hamburgers or meatballs, which should still be pink and juicy in the middle. These burgers are ideal for a picnic where you can make a fire or have a portable barbecue. You won't need plates because you can put the burgers between buns and just serve them with a bowl of cherry tomatoes and maybe a salad leaf or two.

Put the venison, horseradish sauce, capers and chilli powder into a bowl and season with salt. Mix well with a wooden spoon. Using wet hands, divide the mixture into 4 and pat into burgers about 1.25cm/½in thick. Smear all over with oil, then grill over a very hot fire for not more than 2 minutes on each side – they should be pink to red inside.

SUN-DRIED TOMATO AND
MOZZARELLA BREAD WITH
OLIVE OIL AND SAGE ▶

traveller's tastes

I have been a traveller since the age of four. At seven years old I began to realize that food was one of the excitements of life. By the time I had my first cooking

lesson at an English boarding school I realized that, as a result of living in different countries, I would never be satisfied with just learning how to make rock buns. As soon as I was able to I experimented on my own, adding to simple dishes the spices and flavours I had come to love.

Still today, whenever I return from abroad I try to recreate tastes I have enjoyed in a way that is suitable for the home cook. Travelling has always been my main source of culinary inspiration and will, I'm sure, remain so.

Burmese Chicken Noodles with Cashew Nuts

SERVES 4

2 large skinless chicken breast fillets or 4–6 boneless skinless chicken thighs

1–2 fresh red chillies

2 tablespoons oyster sauce

1 level tablespoon dark muscovado sugar

225g/8oz Chinese egg noodles

350g/12oz carrots

5cm/2in piece fresh ginger

2 large cloves garlic

2 tablespoons groundnut oil

1 teaspoon ground turmeric

75g/3oz unsalted cashew nuts

leaves from 1 small bunch fresh coriander

This is a recipe that I put together from memory after a wonderful trip to Burma. It came with a specially good bowl of noodles from a little noodle shop near the market in Rangoon. It makes a light meal in itself but you could serve a green salad on the side. Oyster sauce is available in supermarkets or from oriental grocers.

Cut the chicken breasts or thighs across in thin slices. Cut the chillies open lengthways under running water and discard the seeds and stem. Cut each piece of chilli again in half lengthways and then slice across as thinly as possible. Put the pieces of chicken in a bowl with the chillies and stir in 1 tablespoon of the oyster sauce and all the brown sugar until the chicken is evenly coated. Cover the bowl and leave on one side.

Cook the noodles according to the directions on the packet, then drain and leave on one side. Peel the carrots and slice across very finely, using a food processor if possible. Peel the ginger and garlic and chop together finely.

Put the oil into a wok or large flameproof casserole over a medium heat. Add the ginger, garlic, turmeric and cashew nuts and stir around for a minute. Then add the chicken mixture and stir for 3–4 minutes until the chicken is just about cooked through. Add the sliced carrots, stir for another minute and then add the noodles and the remaining oyster sauce. Stir for another minute or so until the noodles are warmed through. Lastly, roughly mix in the coriander leaves and serve immediately.

Chicken with an Anchovy and Garlic Cream Sauce

SERVES 6

6 medium skinless chicken breast fillets

5 large cloves garlic, unpeeled

5–6 fresh bay leaves

300ml/½ pint white wine

strained juice of 1 lemon

50g/2oz tin anchovy fillets

300ml/½ pint double cream

handful fresh parsley

salt

black pepper

The Italians seem to recognize the true worth of anchovies. This recipe relies on their wonderful ability to turn to a cream over the heat. The garlic, cooked whole, adds a mild sweetness. The dish is delicious served with a bowl of tagliatelle or new potatoes and a crisp green vegetable.

Preheat the oven to 170°C/325°F/gas mark 3. Slice each chicken breast lengthways into 3. Arrange the slices in a single layer in a gratin dish or a shallow roasting pan. Put the garlic cloves among them and also the bay leaves, some under the chicken and some on top. Heat the wine and lemon juice in a saucepan until bubbling, then pour it over the chicken breasts, cover the dish or pan tightly with foil and cook on the centre shelf of the oven for 35–45 minutes, until the chicken is cooked and the garlic feels soft when you stick a small knife into a clove. Then, using a slotted spatula, take out the chicken pieces and arrange them in a large, fairly shallow serving dish. Cover loosely with foil and leave in a very low oven to keep warm while you make the sauce.

Empty the anchovies and their oil into the top of a double boiler or a bowl set over a saucepan of hot water. Stir over simmering water until the anchovies seem to melt into a brown cream.

Take the bay leaves from the cooking liquid and discard. Pop the cloves of garlic out of their skins into a sieve, then rub them through the sieve into the anchovy mixture. Next, pour the chicken poaching liquid into a saucepan and bubble fiercely over a high heat until well reduced and almost syrupy. Stir in the anchovy and garlic mixture and the double cream and bring to the boil again for 2–3 minutes. Remove from the heat and season to taste with black pepper and some salt if necessary. Finely chop the parsley, stir it into the sauce and pour the sauce over the chicken – if the chicken has been in the oven for some time and created more liquid, add this to the sauce first.

Persian Chicken with Apricots, Almonds and Saffron

SERVES 4

600ml/1 pint chicken stock

10–12 strands saffron

1 very large onion

25g/1oz butter

1 tablespoon olive oil

1 teaspoon ground cinnamon

4 chicken breast joints on the bone

100g/4oz dried apricots, halved

25g/1oz sultanas

50g/2oz whole almonds, unskinned

salt

black pepper

As you grow older, more and more of your life becomes history. When I first visited Iran it was still known as Persia and, apart from an incredible feast of large, pale-grey, glistening caviar to which we were treated one evening, my most vivid memories of the food are the combination of chicken or meat with fruit and the ethereal quality of the rice. I still try to recapture those tastes, as in this recipe, which goes perfectly with basmati rice.

Bring the stock to the boil in a pan, stir in the saffron and leave on one side. Peel the onion and chop into small pieces. Melt the butter and olive oil in a large, heavy, flameproof casserole over a medium heat. Add the onion and cook for a few minutes until soft, stirring now and then. Stir in the cinnamon and then, using a slotted spoon, transfer the onion to a plate and leave on one side. Increase the heat under the casserole slightly and add the chicken joints. Fry on each side just to brown. Return the onion to the casserole dish together with the apricots, sultanas and almonds. Sprinkle with black pepper. Give the stock and saffron a good stir and pour into the casserole. Bring to the boil, then cover and simmer very gently for 40–50 minutes, until the chicken is really tender. Before serving, season to taste with salt and black pepper.

Chicken, Prawn and Noodle Hotpot

SERVES 4

100g/4oz thin Thai or Chinese wheat noodles

5cm/2in piece fresh ginger

3 large cloves garlic

4–5 kaffir lime leaves (optional)

2 fresh red chillies

2 skinless chicken breast fillets

1.2 litres/2 pints chicken stock

50g/2oz coconut milk powder

juice of 1 lemon

mixture of salad leaves and plenty of fresh mint, to serve

2 tablespoons groundnut oil

225g/8oz beansprouts

225g/8oz large cooked peeled prawns

good handful fresh coriander leaves

salt

Almost every meal I had when I was travelling in Vietnam included a delicious soup, or hotpot as they often call them there. I created this recipe as a memory of those soups.

At a Vietnamese meal all the dishes are put on the table at once, rather than one following the other as in a Chinese meal. However, this kind of hotpot is perfect as a light meal in itself. If you can get all the ingredients prepared in advance it only needs a little last-minute cooking.

Boil the noodles in salted water until just soft, then drain in a sieve, run through with cold water and leave on one side. Peel the ginger and garlic and chop finely. Chop the lime leaves finely, if using. Cut the chillies in half under running water, discard the seeds and stem, and cut into very thin strips. Slice the chicken breasts across fairly thinly. Bring the chicken stock to boiling point, add the coconut milk powder and stir to dissolve. Add the lemon juice.

Before cooking, mix up the salad leaves and mint and put them into a serving bowl. Put them on the table where you will eat.

Heat the groundnut oil in a wok or large saucepan over a medium heat, add the ginger, garlic and chicken, and stir around for about 2 minutes. Then add the lime leaves, if using, the chillies and beansprouts and stir around for another minute or two, until the beansprouts are limp. Now pour in the chicken stock mixture and stir in the cooked noodles. Bring up to bubbling, remove from the heat and add the prawns. Taste and add salt if necessary. Chop the coriander leaves roughly, add to the soup and pour into a heated tureen or large bowl. Serve at once and tell people to throw a good handful of the salad leaves and mint into their bowls.

Every morning all over Vietnam, even in remote villages, you see freshly baked French baguettes for sale. If you are travelling early (life in Vietnam is bustling at 5am), you will see sandwich stalls by the roadside where you can stop for breakfast. Your sandwich will be a perfect example of how the French of the old Indo-China have left their mark on Vietnam: a small baguette is split lengthways and spread with coarse liver pâté, which has a typically French country flavour – but then the Far East creeps in with a sprinkling of nuac nam (a sauce made from fermented anchovies, the most characteristic seasoner of Vietnamese food), slivers of red chilli, pieces of spicy fish cake and coriander leaves. Surprisingly, the combination is excellent.

The French culinary legacy also includes all kind of charcuterie, many of them wrapped and cooked in banana leaves, as well as daubes, civets, ragouts, and soupes to which chilli, nuac nam and other flavourings give a Vietnamese touch.

Spiced Chicken with Chickpeas and Lemon Peel

SERVES 6

225g/8oz dried chickpeas

2 medium onions

3 large cloves garlic

100g/4oz mushrooms

675–900g/1½–2lb boneless skinless chicken thighs

75g/3oz butter

2 teaspoons ground cinnamon

2 teaspoons paprika

2 teaspoons ground turmeric

1 lemon

5cm/2in piece fresh ginger

600ml/1 pint chicken stock

cayenne pepper

generous handful fresh coriander or parsley leaves

salt

This chicken casserole is aromatic with spices evocative of both India and North Africa, two of my favourite places and cuisines. Serve with a crisp green vegetable or a salad. If you cook this for part of the time early in the day and then complete the cooking later on it seems to taste even better.

Soak the chickpeas in water overnight. Drain and boil in plenty of water until soft. This can take anything from 45 minutes to 1½ hours, depending on the age of the chickpeas. Drain well. Meanwhile, peel the onions and garlic, put them into a food processor with the mushrooms and whizz until chopped as finely as possible.

Preheat the oven to 140°C/275°F/gas mark 1. Cut the chicken thighs in half. Melt the butter in a large, flameproof casserole dish over a fairly high heat. Add the cinnamon, paprika and turmeric and stir around once or twice before adding the onion mixture from the food processor. Stir around for a minute or two, then add the chicken thighs and the drained chickpeas and remove from the heat. Cut the lemon in half and squeeze out the juice into the casserole. Then scrape as much pith as possible from the lemon peel and cut the peel into small pieces. Peel the ginger and slice finely. Mix the lemon peel and ginger slices into the casserole. Lastly, pour over the chicken stock.

Cover the casserole dish, put it back on the stove over a high heat and bring up to simmering point. Then transfer to the oven and cook for 2½ hours, until all the ingredients are meltingly tender. Season to taste with cayenne pepper and salt. Just before serving, slice the coriander or parsley leaves roughly and scatter into the casserole.

If you are a worldwide traveller, you may have realized that fresh coriander is the most commonly used herb. In the markets of southern Europe, North Africa, the Middle East, India, South-east Asia, China, Japan, Mexico and South America, little bundles of broad- or feathery-leafed coriander are an inevitable sight.
Once you taste these fragrant green leaves you can become almost addicted – which should not matter as coriander is reputedly highly nutritious. When you buy a bunch don't throw away the stalks as they can be chopped and added to stews, soups, stir-fries and fresh chutneys.
Dried coriander seeds are described in the Bible as 'like manna'. They have a completely different taste from the fresh herb – mild, warm and slightly orangey. If you grow your own coriander during the summer you will benefit from being able to catch the seeds when they have just formed and are still green. This is the brief moment when their taste is an exquisite combination of the flavours of both leaf and seed.

Chicken Slowly Poached in Tea and Aromatics

SERVES 6

1 x 900g–1kg/2–2¼lb free range or cornfed chicken

4 large cloves garlic

5cm/2in piece fresh ginger

7.5cm/3in piece cinnamon stick

1 rounded teaspoon cayenne pepper

3–4 whole star anise

1 tablespoon sesame oil

6 Earl Grey or Lapsang Souchong teabags

1 bunch spring onions

dark soy sauce

The nearest I have been to China is Hong Kong, where you can feast on every variety of regional Chinese food. My many visits to restaurant kitchens there made me appreciate their ingenious ways of cooking. This method of cooking chicken to eat cold produces a more succulent result than any other, as it must be the gentlest way there is (you may have done much the same thing with a whole salmon in a fish kettle).

You will need four metal skewers for this recipe. The chicken is cooked slowly by the heat from the skewers and the cooling hot water. Only use small chickens so that the skewers generate the heat right through the flesh, and never use frozen birds. If you are cooking for a crowd, use two or three chickens and cook them in a large preserving pan.

Insert the metal skewers crossways right through the body and legs of the chicken and put it into a large saucepan. Add enough cold water to cover the chicken. Peel the garlic and chop roughly. Cut the unpeeled piece of ginger across fairly thinly. Break up the cinnamon stick roughly. Put the garlic, ginger and cinnamon into the saucepan and add the cayenne pepper, star anise, sesame oil and teabags. Bring to the boil and boil fiercely for 3 minutes. Then cover the pan, turn off the heat and leave the chicken in the covered pan until the water is cold. Remove the chicken and chill thoroughly in the fridge.

To serve, remove the skewers, carve the chicken in very thin slices and arrange on a flat serving dish. Chop the spring onions and scatter them all over the chicken. Just before serving, trickle a few lines of soy sauce across the slices of chicken.

'Ncapriata (Dried Broad Bean Purée with Green Vegetables)

SERVES 4

225g/8oz skinless dried broad beans

2 medium potatoes

about 3–5 tablespoons extra virgin olive oil

350g/12oz spring greens

2 small to medium chicory

sea salt

black pepper

This is a well-known peasant dish from Puglia, in the heel of Italy. In spite of its simplicity we voted it a star turn during a gastronomic trip to the region. Dried broad beans are not as easy to find in Britain as they are in Puglia but Cypriot and Greek grocers often have them. You can use butterbeans instead but will then have to sieve the purée to remove the skins. Since it is difficult to get the long stems of dark leaf chicory with which the purée is usually served in Italy, I used spring greens mixed with our usual chicory.

In Puglia this dish is served as one of several, but I found it was perfect on its own as a light meal, accompanied by a tomato salad, cheese and bread.

Soak the broad beans in cold water for an hour or more, then drain and put into a flameproof casserole or heavy saucepan. Peel the potatoes, cut them into fairly thick slices and lay evenly on top of the beans. Add cold water to come about 5cm/2in above the level of the potatoes, but no salt. Bring the water to the boil, skim off any scum, then cover and simmer gently for 2 hours. Check once or twice and add a little more boiling water if necessary. By the end, a lot of the water should have been absorbed but not all of it.

When the beans are ready, beat the mixture vigorously with a fork to turn it into a purée, beating in the olive oil to taste. Season with salt and coarsely ground black pepper. Turn the mixture into a wide heated serving dish, cover loosely with foil and leave in a very low oven to keep warm.

To prepare the vegetables, wash the spring greens and slice just the leaves across fairly thinly. Cut the base off the chicory and then slice lengthways in quarters or thirds. Bring a large pan of salted water to the boil, add the spring greens and chicory and boil for 10–15 minutes, until both greens and chicory are soft. Drain and put them on top of the bean purée towards the middle, so that you can see the purée round them. Then sprinkle the vegetables with salt and pepper and drizzle some more extra virgin olive oil all over.

'Le Sirenuse' Meatballs with Pine Kernels and Raisins in Fresh Tomato Sauce

SERVES 4

2 medium-thick slices white bread

1 large clove garlic

50g/2oz pine kernels

handful fresh flat-leaf parsley

500g/1lb 2oz lean minced beef

150g/5oz Parmesan cheese, freshly grated

2 medium eggs

50g/2oz small seedless raisins

plain flour for sprinkling

sunflower oil for frying

salt

black pepper

For the sauce:

500g/1lb 2oz ripe tomatoes, the plum variety if available

1 medium onion

4 tablespoons olive oil

2 level tablespoons Italian tomato purée

2 teaspoons caster sugar

My friend Franco still lives in his family house overlooking the sea at Positano in Southern Italy – though it is now a luxurious hotel, Le Sirenuse. It was on a visit to see Franco that I had these Neapolitan meatballs. The addition of soaked bread gives them a lovely soft consistency and the pine kernels and raisins are included in many local dishes.

Unfortunately, the tomatoes available in Britain are unlikely ever to rival the wondrously intense flavour of the small plum tomatoes I had on the Amalfi Coast, so a little tomato purée is needed to add strength to the sauce.

Cut the crusts off the bread, put the slices in a dish, cover with water and leave to soak for 3–5 minutes. Then squeeze the bread in your hands to drain it. Peel the garlic and chop finely.

Heat a dry frying pan, add the pine kernels and toss about briskly over a high heat until slightly browned. Turn out on to a work surface to cool. Chop the parsley finely.

Put the minced beef into a large bowl and add the squeezed-out bread, garlic, parsley and Parmesan cheese. Whisk the eggs and add to the mixture with some salt and black pepper. Using your hands, blend the mixture thoroughly for several minutes, adding the pine kernels and raisins halfway through. Form the mixture into balls a little smaller than pingpong size and sprinkle lightly all over with flour. Pour a generous amount of sunflower oil into a large frying pan and put over a medium heat. Add the meatballs and fry until golden brown on all sides. Remove from the heat while you make the sauce.

Put the tomatoes into a bowl, pour boiling water over them and leave for about 2 minutes, then drain, peel and chop up fairly small. Peel the onion and chop finely. Put the olive oil into a deep-sided frying pan over a medium heat. Add the onion and fry, stirring often, until fairly soft and golden. Then add the chopped tomatoes and any juice and stir in the tomato purée and caster sugar. Cook gently for 15–20 minutes, stirring until mushy, then add the meatballs and cook them in the sauce without stirring for another 10 minutes. Turn into a heated serving dish and serve.

Glossy Lamb Tagine with Okra and Almonds

SERVES 6

1 kg/2¼lb lamb neck fillet

1 large red pepper

2 large cloves garlic

5cm/2in piece fresh ginger

2 teaspoons ground cinnamon

2 teaspoons paprika

50g/2oz butter

approximately 900ml/1½ pints water

350g/12oz fresh okra

75–100g/3–4oz whole almonds, unskinned

juice of 1 lemon

1 rounded tablespoon honey

salt

black pepper

The Moroccans have an enticing way of combining ingredients with aromatic spices, and sweetness is often mixed with savoury to great effect. Their cooking is a combination of simplicity and sophistication. Their tagines (simply a stew cooked in an earthenware dish with a pointed lid which collects and adds moisture) can be as easy to make as an Irish stew but are much more exciting to look at, and wonderful to eat. Serve this tagine with a bowl of couscous or chickpeas and a simple salad. If you like, sprinkle it with a few whole coriander leaves before serving. This recipe is adapted for a kitchen that does not have a traditional Moroccan tagine – if you do have one, you can use it as the serving dish.

Cut the lamb into 5cm/2in pieces and put them into a large, heavy-based saucepan. Cut the pepper in half, remove the seeds and stem and then cut the flesh in strips lengthways. Peel and roughly chop the garlic. Peel the ginger and slice it thinly.

Add the red pepper, garlic and ginger to the meat, together with the spices and the butter. Season with salt and black pepper and add the water, which should just cover the meat. Cover the pan and bring to the boil, then lower the heat and simmer gently for about 1½ hours or until the meat is meltingly tender.

Using a slotted spoon, transfer the meat, red pepper, slices of ginger etc. to a heated, rounded serving dish, leaving the liquid in the saucepan. Cover the meat mixture loosely with foil and keep warm in a very low oven.

Cut the tops off the okra and put them in a saucepan of boiling salted water for about 3 minutes, until just tender and bright green. Drain and keep on one side.

Add the almonds, lemon juice and honey to the juices in the saucepan. Bring to the boil, stirring to dissolve the honey, then boil fiercely without stirring, for 10–20 minutes, until the sauce is reduced and syrupy. Pour off any fat from the top. Now mix the cooked okra with the meat, spoon the sauce and almonds all over the tagine and serve immediately.

The Maharani Mohini Kumari's Lamb Pie

SERVES 4-5

2 cloves garlic

2.5cm/1in piece fresh ginger

4 medium onions

675g/1½lb lamb fillets

40g/1½oz butter

3 teaspoons ground coriander

2 teaspoons ground cumin

½ level teaspoon chilli powder

1 rounded tablespoon plain flour

300ml/½ pint milk

2 teaspoons tamarind paste
(available from Indian and
oriental grocers)

1 tablespoon sugar

1 rounded tablespoon unsweetened
desiccated coconut

4 tablespoons Greek-style yoghurt

225–350g/8–12oz puff pastry

egg yolk or milk, to glaze

salt

Ten tigers watched over me as I ate dinner in the cathedral-like dining room of the Wankaner Palace. Everything else in this vast and elaborate Edwardian edifice, standing on its hill above the town of Wankaner in Gujarat, India, is slightly dusty but the 95 beasts' heads high up on every wall still look glossy and almost alive.

A member of the Wankaner royal family gave me this recipe, which is typical of the many Anglo-Indian-style dishes that the family have eaten since the days of the British Raj. I like the pie best with just a green vegetable or a salad.

Peel the garlic and ginger and chop finely. Peel the onions, cut them in half and slice fairly thinly in half rings. Cut the lamb fillets into roughly 5cm/2in pieces. Preheat the oven to 180°C/350°F/gas mark 4. Melt the butter in a flameproof casserole over a medium heat. Add the onions and cook, stirring quite often, until softened and well browned. Then stir in the ground spices and chopped garlic and ginger and continue stirring for a minute or so. Next, add the lamb pieces, stir them around to coat in the butter and remove from the heat. Stir in the flour and then gradually add the milk, followed by the tamarind paste, sugar and desiccated coconut. Put back over the heat and stir until the juices bubble and thicken.

Cover the casserole and cook in the centre of the oven for 1½ hours or until the lamb feels very tender when you test it with a knife. Then remove from the oven, stir in the yoghurt, add salt to taste and spoon into a pie dish or deep earthenware flan dish which the mixture fills to the top. Leave until cold.

Preheat the oven to 220°C/425°F/gas mark 7. Roll out the pastry into a piece big enough to cover the pie dish. Moisten the edges of the pie dish and lay the pastry on top. Trim the edges neatly and press round them with your fingers. Use the pastry trimmings to make decorations. Cut 2 holes in the pastry to let the steam escape, then brush with egg yolk or milk to glaze and cook in the centre of the oven for 25–30 minutes, until the pastry is a rich brown.

Venison Curry with Lamb's Kidneys

SERVES 6-8

900g/2lb boneless venison from shoulder or neck

2 medium red peppers

2 medium onions

6 cloves garlic

5cm/2in piece fresh ginger

2 fresh red chillies

3 tablespoons groundnut oil

1 teaspoon ground cardamom

2 teaspoons ground cumin

3 teaspoons ground coriander

50g/2oz butter

400g/14oz tin chopped tomatoes

600ml/1 pint beef stock

6 lamb's kidneys

handful fresh coriander leaves

salt

All game takes well to Indian-style dishes. In this luscious curry the venison is cooked gently in an aromatic sauce that is thickened and enriched by the addition of juicy kidneys at the last moment. If possible, spices should always be bought whole and then ground freshly, either in a coffee grinder or a pestle and mortar. Serve the curry with basmati rice and a green vegetable or salad.

Cut the venison into 4–5cm/1½–2in cubes. Cut the red peppers in half lengthways, discard the seeds and stems and then slice across very thinly. Peel the onions, garlic and ginger and chop finely. Cut the chillies in half under running water, remove the seeds and stems and then chop finely.

Preheat the oven to 150°C/300°F/gas mark 2. Put the oil into a large, heavy-based frying pan over a high heat, then add the venison and cook, turning, until browned all over. Using a slotted spatula, transfer the meat to a large flameproof casserole dish. Add the ground spices to the oil in the frying pan and stir around for half a minute, then add the butter and lower the heat to medium. When the butter has melted, add the red peppers, onions, garlic, ginger and chillies and fry, stirring, until the peppers and onions have just begun to soften. Then add this mixture, including the spices and fat, to the venison in the casserole. Empty in the tinned tomatoes and the beef stock, season with salt and stir. Put the casserole on top of the stove and bring to the boil, then cover and cook just below the centre of the oven for about 2 hours or until the venison is very tender.

Meanwhile, cut the kidneys in half and roughly chop the coriander leaves. When the venison is tender, put the casserole on top of the stove again. With the juices bubbling very gently, add the kidneys and stir for 2–3 minutes – they must remain pink and juicy in the centre. Remove from the heat, sprinkle in the chopped coriander leaves and serve immediately.

The hunting scene is a common subject in the Mogul miniatures of India. Skittish deer prance about on brown hills, a domed palace is seen in the distance and a group of turbaned huntsmen point their rifles at the next feast.

Centuries later game shooting continues in India. I was once given a lift by a group of huntsmen, travelling through the night from Lucknow to Agra, where I was to have my first sight of the Taj Mahal. By incredible luck our arrival coincided with a full moon, still high in the sky; the perfect moment to view this white marble wonder of the world. It looked almost luminous as we walked up the long avenue and entered the echoing central chamber. I had thought the huntsmen in their shooting kit looked incongruous in this magical setting, but even more bizarre was a motor cyclist in a huge helmet, the stamp of whose boots made a thunder of echoes all around us.

Indian Quails with Eggs and Spinach

SERVES 6

2 medium to large onions

4 large cloves garlic

1 fresh green chilli

3 teaspoons coriander seeds

2 teaspoons cumin seeds

2 blades mace

5–6 whole cloves

1 teaspoon fennel seeds

piece cinnamon stick, approximately 2.5cm/1in long

2 bay leaves

1 teaspoon ground turmeric

2 medium to large red peppers

2 tablespoons groundnut oil, plus extra for brushing

75g/3oz butter

400g/14oz tin chopped tomatoes

1 level tablespoon tamarind paste

2 teaspoons caster sugar

6 quails

chilli powder

6 large eggs

450g/1lb fresh spinach

fresh coriander leaves, to garnish

salt

This was inspired by my many trips to India, where quails are often cooked with spices and aromatic sauces. The dish should be accompanied by basmati rice and a bowl of yoghurt. If you don't have all the spices, simply add a little more of the ones you do have. The spices and tamarind paste should be available from oriental grocer's, good delicatessens and some large supermarkets. Buying whole spices and grinding them freshly makes all the difference as they will be far more aromatic.

Peel the onions and garlic, cut them up roughly and put into a food processor. Cut open the green chilli under cold running water, discard the seeds and stem and put the chilli halves in the food processor with the onions and garlic. Whizz very thoroughly until the mixture has become as smooth a mush as possible.

Put the whole spices and the bay leaves into a coffee grinder and whizz until finely ground. Mix these spices with the ground turmeric. Cut the peppers in half lengthways, discard the seeds and stem and slice thinly. Preheat the oven to 180°C/350°F/gas mark 4.

Put the oil and butter into a large cast iron casserole over a high heat. When melted, add the ground spices and then the onion mixture. Allow to bubble in the open casserole, stirring on and off, for about 5 minutes. Then add the chopped tomatoes, sliced peppers and tamarind paste and season with the sugar and some salt. Cover the casserole and cook in the centre of the oven for half an hour. Then brush the quails with a little oil and dust with salt and a very little chilli powder. Remove the casserole from the oven, place the quails on top of the sauce, cover and return to the oven for another hour. Uncover for the last 20 minutes or so to allow the quails to brown a little.

Meanwhile, semi-hardboil the eggs, then plunge them into cold water, peel and cut in half lengthways. Wash the spinach, remove any thick stalks and chop up only roughly. After the quails have cooked for an hour, take them out of the casserole and set aside on a plate. Stir the spinach into the hot sauce just until limp. Check the seasoning and add salt and a little chilli powder if needed. Then replace the quails on top of the sauce, interspersed by the halved eggs yolk-side upwards. Cover the casserole again and cook for 8–10 minutes, until the spinach is quite soft. Just before serving, roughly chop some coriander leaves and sprinkle them over the top.

SERVES 4

1–2 fresh red chillies

generous handful fresh coriander leaves

handful fresh mint leaves

225g/8oz peeled prawns

2 heaped teaspoons Thai shrimp paste without chilli (available from oriental grocers) or anchovy essence

100g/4oz beansprouts

6 large eggs

6 tablespoons cold water

groundnut oil for frying

salt

Hue Omelettes

Even though it was one of the main areas of combat during the Vietnam war, Hue, the old imperial city, is still a magically beautiful place. When I watched these omelettes being made, the whole of Hue had a power cut and as the tiny restaurant serving this speciality possessed just two oil lamps it was quite hard to work out the exact method and ingredients. Also, since the charming family who ran the restaurant were all deaf and dumb, explanations were limited. However, my memory served me quite well and these light and crispy omelettes, stuffed with prawns, beansprouts and other Vietnamese flavours, make a delicious light supper or snack. Incidentally, they also taste good cold so would be excellent for a picnic.

Prepare the filling first. Cut open the chillies under running water and discard the seeds and stems. Slice the chillies across as finely as possible. Roughly chop the coriander and mint leaves. Put the prawns into a bowl and mix in the shrimp paste or anchovy essence. Have the beansprouts ready. Put 4 serving plates into a very low oven to warm, putting a piece of absorbent paper on each one.

To make the omelettes, break the eggs into a bowl and whisk lightly with a fork. Then whisk in the water, season with salt and stir in the sliced chillies and 2 teaspoons of the chopped coriander. Pour a layer of groundnut oil at least 1.25cm/½in deep into a small frying pan and put over a high heat until smoking. Then pour in about a quarter of the egg mixture and swirl around to form a circle. When the omelette has bubbled up right through to the centre and is very brown and crispy underneath, quickly pile a quarter of the prawns, beansprouts, coriander and mint leaves on one side of the omelette, then fold over to enclose the filling. Using a wide spatula, transfer carefully to one of the warmed serving plates.

The first person to be served should really start eating at once, or you can keep the omelettes warm in a low oven until you have cooked all of them. Before serving, gently lift the omelettes with a spatula and ease the absorbent paper from underneath.

SERVES 2

1–2 fresh red chillies

2–3 good sprigs fresh coriander

2 small shallots

2–3 firm tomatoes, the plum variety if available

4 large eggs

25g/1oz butter

salt

Masala Omelette

When travelling in India it is quite usual to find only rather unprepossessing places to stop and eat at along the road. In these cases the one dish that never fails is masala omelette – a simple omelette with a dash of chilli, fresh coriander leaves, little onions and tomatoes. Eggs in India are good and the omelette is made freshly in front of you.

Back at home, this is an ideal dish to remember if you want to make yourself a quick snack.

Cut open the chillies under running water, discard the seeds and stems and slice the halves finely across. Remove any large stalks from the coriander sprigs and chop the leaves only very roughly. Peel the shallots and slice across as finely as possible. Put the tomatoes in a bowl, pour boiling water over them and leave for about 2 minutes, then drain, peel and cut into small cubes. Mix all these ingredients together.

Have 2 warmed serving plates ready. Break 2 eggs into each of 2 bowls and whisk together with a fork. Divide the chopped ingredients in two and stir into each bowl of eggs. Season each with salt.

Put half the butter into an omelette pan over a fairly high heat until foaming. Then add the contents of one bowl and stir with a fork for a few seconds until it starts to thicken. Working quickly, move the egg that has set at the side of the pan so that the uncooked egg pours into the space made and sets too. Cook for a minute or two, until the top is about to set but still slightly runny. Then tilt the pan to one side and, using a spatula, fold over the omelette and slide it carefully out of the pan on to one of the warmed serving plates. Add the remaining butter to the pan and repeat the procedure with the second bowl of eggs.

Bhikoo's Poached Eggs

SERVES 4

2.5cm/1in piece fresh ginger

3 cloves garlic

1 fresh green chilli

1 large onion

1 tomato, the plum variety if available

3 tablespoons groundnut oil

4 medium-sized firm bananas

½ teaspoon ground turmeric

4 large eggs

salt

Bhikoo lives in Delhi and shares the deep interest most Indians have in food and cooking. One day she made me this unusual variation on poached eggs. They are cooked in a delicious spiced banana mixture and the result is a quick and excellent supper dish.

Peel the ginger and garlic. Cut the chilli open under running water and remove the seeds and stem. Finely chop the ginger, garlic and chilli together. Peel the onion and slice thinly in rings. Cut up the tomato into small cubes.

Heat 2 tablespoons of the oil in a large frying pan over a low heat and fry the onion gently until soft. Then add the ginger, garlic, chilli and tomato and sauté over a medium heat for 2–3 minutes. Remove from the heat.

Peel the bananas and slice thinly. Add the remaining oil to the frying pan, put back over a medium heat, add the sliced bananas and the turmeric and sauté for 1 minute. Then make 4 hollows in the mixture and break an egg into each. Sprinkle all over with salt, cover the pan with a lid or foil and cook over a low heat for 3–5 minutes, until the whites of the eggs have just set – it is important that the yolks are still runny. Serve straight from the pan, accompanied by a green salad and warmed nan bread.

Stuffed Meatballs with Indian Spices

SERVES 4-5

450g/1lb lean minced beef or lamb

8 cardamom pods

2 teaspoons coriander seeds

6–8 cloves

1 level teaspoon ground turmeric

3–4 pinches chilli powder

3 large cloves garlic

1 small to medium egg

100g/4oz curd cheese or fromage frais

1 tablespoon vegetable oil

small handful fresh coriander leaves

salt

As in the Middle East, you find all kinds of meatballs in India, perhaps because whole pieces of meat can be tough. But since minced meat cries out for this kind of aromatic spicing, their meatballs are among the best you could have. This variation offers an exciting surprise, as when you bite into the meatballs a centre of melted white cheese oozes out. Serve them on a bed of leaves accompanied by buttered basmati rice and a tomato salad.

Put the minced meat into a bowl and mash with a large wooden spoon until slightly softened. Extract the seeds from the cardamom pods and put them into a coffee grinder with the coriander seeds and cloves. Grind finely and stir into the beef with the turmeric and chilli powder. Peel the garlic and chop finely. Whisk the egg lightly. Stir the garlic and egg into the mixture and season with salt.

Using dampened hands, form the mixture into pingpong-sized balls. Then flatten them into circles on an oiled surface. Put a level teaspoon of curd cheese or fromage frais on each circle and carefully bring the meat up around it to encase the cheese, thus making the balls larger than before. Heat the vegetable oil in a frying pan over a medium heat. Fry the meatballs for about 5–7 minutes on each side, turning carefully, until browned all over. Transfer the balls to a serving dish and, if necessary, keep them warm in a low oven until ready to eat. Before serving, sprinkle with roughly chopped coriander leaves.

Far Eastern Turkey Pie

about 1.35kg/3lb cooked boneless turkey meat

5–7.5cm/2–3in piece cinnamon stick

4–5 cardamom pods

2 star anise

1–2 fresh red chillies

5cm/2in piece fresh ginger

3 large cloves garlic

2 thin lemon grass stalks

3–4 kaffir lime leaves

3 rounded tablespoons coconut milk powder

225ml/8fl oz warm water

100g/4oz butter

1 bunch spring onions

generous handful fresh coriander leaves

350g/12oz filo pastry

salt

I concocted this as a vehicle for leftover turkey but you can use cooked chicken if you have enough; in fact the pie is so good that it would be worth cooking some turkey or chicken meat from scratch. I first started using these flavourings after enjoying the delicate cuisine of Vietnam. Putting them in a filo pastry pie is very cross-cultural, of course, but it works well.

Remove any skin from the turkey meat, chop the flesh roughly and put it into a large mixing bowl. Break up the cinnamon stick and put it into an electric coffee grinder with the cardamom seeds extracted from their pods and the star anise. Grind finely. Cut open the chillies lengthways under running water and discard the seeds and stems. Peel the ginger and garlic. Chop the chillies, ginger and garlic together finely. Cut the base and top and any marked outer part off the lemon grass and then slice across very finely. Chop the lime leaves very finely. Put the coconut milk powder into a measuring jug with a teaspoon of salt. Add the warm water and stir to mix smoothly.

Put a dry frying pan over a medium heat, add the ground spices and stir for half a minute. Add 15g/½oz of the butter and, when it melts, add the chillies, ginger, garlic and lemon grass. Stir over the heat for a minute, then stir in the coconut milk and the chopped lime leaves. Stir thoroughly and remove from the heat before it boils. Pour over the turkey meat and mix together.

Slice the spring onions at 5mm/¼in intervals, using as much of the green part as possible. Roughly chop the coriander leaves. Stir the spring onions and coriander leaves into the turkey mixture and season with salt.

Gently melt the remaining butter in a saucepan and then remove from the heat. Brush a large round or rectangular ovenproof dish with some of the butter and lay a sheet of filo pastry in the dish, leaving the edges hanging over the sides. Brush the filo pastry thinly with butter. Then lay on a second sheet, spoon in the turkey mixture and spread level. Fold the sides of the pastry in over the turkey filling. Lay another sheet of pastry on top and fold in. Brush with butter and continue with layers of pastry and butter until you have only one sheet of pastry left. Put this on top but crumple roughly instead of folding in the edges. Brush lightly with butter.

Preheat the oven to 170°C/325°F/gas mark 3 and cook the pie for 30–40 minutes, then increase the heat to 230°C/450°F/gas mark 8 and cook for a further 5–10 minutes, until the pastry is a rich golden brown.

Hot and Sour Pork and Chicken Meatballs

SERVES 15-20

AS CANAPÉS OR 4-6 AS A MAIN COURSE

675g/1½lb minced pork

225g/8oz boneless skinless chicken breasts or thighs

5 large cloves garlic

5–6cm/2–2½in piece fresh ginger

4–6 fresh kaffir lime leaves (optional)

juice of 1 lemon

6 teaspoons *tom yum* sour shrimp paste (available from oriental grocers)

6 rounded tablespoons coconut milk powder

handful fresh coriander leaves

salt

I devised these meatballs to be eaten as canapés at the launch party for a friend's book about Indo-China; they were to bring back memories for all the old Indo-China hands. As it was a large gathering, I made 550 little meatballs and they disappeared astonishingly fast.

If you serve the meatballs as a main course, accompany them with Chinese noodles and steamed, sliced spring greens with soy sauce.

Put the pork into a mixing bowl. Chop the chicken very finely either by hand or in a food processor and then mix it thoroughly into the pork with a wooden spoon. Peel the garlic and ginger and chop together finely. If using kaffir lime leaves, chop them as finely as possible with a very sharp knife. Strain the lemon juice into a small saucepan and heat slightly. Stir in the sour shrimp paste until smooth, then remove from the heat and stir into the meat mixture together with the garlic, ginger and kaffir lime leaves. Add a small sprinkling of salt. Lastly, vigorously work in the coconut milk powder so that it mixes evenly.

Preheat the oven to 180°C/350°F/gas mark 4. Using dampened hands, take small bits of the mixture and roll into balls about the size of large marbles. Arrange the balls, close together but not touching, in a large, lightly oiled roasting pan and cook just above the centre of the oven for 20–25 minutes. Using a slotted spatula, transfer the meatballs to an ovenproof serving dish and spoon the pan juices over them. If not serving immediately, you can reheat the balls in a low oven later. Just before serving, chop the coriander leaves and sprinkle over the meatballs.

Sweetbread Curry

SERVES 4

450–550g/1–1¼lb sweetbreads

1 tablespoon vinegar

2 large onions

2.5cm/1in piece fresh ginger

2 small fresh red chillies

2 teaspoons ground coriander

½ teaspoon ground cardamom

75g/3oz butter

juice of ½ lemon

handful fresh coriander leaves

salt

In India, one of my favourite dishes is brain curry but in Britain it is easier to buy sweetbreads, unless you live near a Halal butcher. However, sweetbreads also work very well made into a mildly spiced dish which has the same soft creaminess as brains. Serve with basmati rice and a green vegetable – petits pois are nice. If possible, use whole spices which you grind yourself.

Soak the sweetbreads in water for an hour or two, changing the water once or twice to get rid of all traces of blood. Then pull off as much of the thin, membrane-like skin as you can – but don't bother to take too much trouble over this. Finally soak the sweetbreads again for about 30 minutes in cold water with the vinegar added to it.

Meanwhile, peel the onions and slice in rings. Peel the ginger and chop finely. Cut the chillies open under running water, discard the seeds and stem and slice into very thin strips.

When the sweetbreads have soaked, drain them and leave on one side.

Put a large, heavy frying pan over a medium heat, add the ground spices and then add 50g/2oz of the butter. When the butter has melted, add the onions and cook, stirring, until soft and golden, then add the ginger and chillies and continue stirring for another minute or two. Add the remaining butter and turn the heat down as low as possible. Add the drained sweetbreads, put a lid or a piece of foil over the pan and cook gently, stirring occasionally, for 10–15 minutes.

Then uncover, stir in the lemon juice, remove from the heat and season with salt. Transfer to a warmed serving dish. If necessary, cover and keep warm in a very low oven while you cook the rice and vegetables. Just before serving, roughly chop the coriander leaves and stir them lightly into the sweetbreads.

Pork and Veal Meatballs with a Light Cream and Balsamic Vinegar Sauce

SERVES 4

225g/8oz minced pork

225g/8oz minced veal

100g/4oz rindless smoked bacon

6–8 fresh sage leaves

50g/2oz Parmesan cheese, freshly grated

¼–½ nutmeg, grated

1 tablespoon olive oil

25g/1oz butter

300ml/½ pint double cream

1 tablespoon balsamic vinegar

a little chopped fresh parsley

salt

black pepper

I worked out the recipe for this delicately flavoured dish from the memory of an exceptionally good meal I ate with an Italian family at their farmhouse between Modena and Parma – the homes of balsamic vinegar and Parmesan cheese respectively. For the sauce, this family used their own, well-aged balsamic vinegar made with grapes from their vineyard. The many-coursed meal lasted happily for four hours.

Put the minced pork and veal into a bowl. Chop the bacon and sage leaves up finely and add them to the minced meat, together with the grated Parmesan. Grate in the nutmeg, season with salt and plenty of black pepper and mix thoroughly with a wooden spoon. Using wet hands, form the mixture into little meatballs, about the size of a marble.

Put the olive oil and butter into a large, heavy-based frying pan and melt over a fairly high heat. Then add the meatballs and fry, stirring gently, for 8–10 minutes, until they are cooked through and well browned all over. Using a slotted spatula, transfer the meatballs to a plate and put in a warm place on one side.

Add the cream to the pan juices, bring to the boil and bubble for about 2 minutes, stirring around. Then stir in the balsamic vinegar and bubble for another minute. Remove from the heat and season to taste with salt and black pepper, adding a little more balsamic vinegar if you like. Just before serving, put the meatballs back in the pan and bring the sauce to bubbling point again, then stir in a little chopped parsley and turn into a heated serving dish.

Vietnamese Steamed Squid with a Ginger and Chilli Dipping Sauce

SERVES 4

900g/2lb ready-prepared small squid

2 rounded teaspoons black peppercorns

1 fresh red chilli

1.25cm/½in piece fresh ginger

3 tablespoons Chinese rice vinegar (available from oriental stores and major supermarkets)

good handful fresh mint leaves

2 level teaspoons caster sugar

coarsely ground sea salt, crushed

The seafood in Vietnam is sweeter and more succulent than anywhere I can remember. I ate this simple but lovely dish in a café overlooking the endless white sands of China Beach, made famous by American soldiers during the war, who took time off here while the Vietcong kept watch on them from their cave hideouts in the Marble Mountains nearby.

As long as you cook the squid very briefly and add a hint of sugar you can make this one of the most pleasurable quick summer meals. The best type of steamer to use is the wide stainless steel two-tiered kind or the Chinese basket kind which stacks on top of a saucepan. Ready-prepared small squid are now sold in major supermarkets and by some fishmongers.

Slice the squid thinly across in rings, leaving the tentacles whole. Crush the peppercorns coarsely in a pestle and mortar. Cut the chilli open lengthways under running water and discard the seeds and stem. Peel the ginger, then chop both chilli and ginger together very finely. Mix them with the rice vinegar and transfer to a very small, shallow serving bowl to put on the table. Chop the mint leaves up roughly.

To cook the squid, put it in the top of a wide steamer, or 2 smaller ones – the steamer should not be over the water at this stage. Bring the water to a fierce boil, then put the steamer basket over the water and cover. Steam for literally just a minute or two, until the squid has turned opaque. Then turn the squid into a mixing bowl, add the caster sugar, coarse black pepper, a sprinkling of crushed sea salt and the chopped mint. Pile into a heated serving dish and serve immediately, with the dipping sauce.

My favourite guide during my journey in Vietnam was Tue from Hue. He was 22, and spoke charmingly idiomatic English picked up entirely from the BBC World Service.

In Hue market we bought a picnic for our sampan journey down the Perfumed River to see the old emperor's tombs. The market is on the river bank and seems to continue on to the sampans themselves, where many families live. Amidst the sea of Vietnamese conical hats there is an unbelievable wealth of produce: at least 10 different types of rice, countless varieties of salad leaves, all manner of crisp-looking vegetables and exotic fruits, and an abundance of fresh fish and shellfish.

Apart from Vietnam-style baguette sandwiches and that particularly delicious tropical fruit, the mangosteen, we found the prettiest picnic ingredient I have ever seen – intricately folded little boxes made of banana leaves, containing glutinous rice stuffed with fruit and coconut.

Eastern Fish Terrine

**AS A LIGHT MEAL,
8 AS A STARTER**

225g/8oz kipper fillets

10 cardamom pods

5 cloves

1 teaspoon ground turmeric

½ teaspoon cayenne pepper

1–2 fresh green chillies

2 cloves garlic

50g/2oz butter

juice of 1 lemon

1 tablespoon tomato purée

2 rounded teaspoons gelatine

4 large eggs

425g/15oz plain yoghurt

fresh coriander leaves, to garnish

salt

This fluffy and exotically flavoured terrine was inspired by the taste of some fish which was caught and cooked on a boat I was on in the Bay of Bengal, while visiting the remote Andaman Islands. No one would guess that it is based on that most English of fish, the kipper. Neither does it taste too assertive in any way; delicate and sophisticated is a better description. If you wish to do so, the terrine can be made at least a day in advance.

Remove the skin from the kipper and chop the flesh finely. Put the whole cardamom pods and the cloves in a coffee grinder and grind finely. Sieve and then mix with the turmeric and cayenne.

Cut the chillies open lengthways under running water and discard the seeds and stems. Peel the garlic and chop finely with the chillies. Melt the butter gently in a pan, add the mixed spices and stir briefly. Add the chillies and garlic and stir for half a minute, then add the kipper, lemon juice and tomato purée. Cover the pan and cook over a very gentle heat for 10 minutes.

Sprinkle the gelatine into 4 tablespoons of barely simmering water and stir until dissolved. Add this liquid to the fish mixture and remove the pan from the heat. Separate the eggs, stirring the yolks into the fish mixture. Return the pan to a very low heat and stir constantly for 3 minutes, without allowing it to bubble. Remove from the heat. Taste now, taking into account that it will be slightly diluted by the egg whites, and add salt only if necessary. Turn the mixture into a large bowl and leave to cool.

When the mixture is just cool and not yet setting, whisk the egg whites until they stand in soft peaks and, using a large metal spoon, fold them gently into the fish mixture a third at a time. Oil a loaf tin or a rectangular dish of about 600ml/1 pint capacity, turn the fish mixture into it and spread level. Chill thoroughly until set.

Shortly before serving, dip the tin in hot water and, giving it a good shake, turn the terrine out on to a board. Spread a thin layer of the yoghurt on to each serving plate, cut the terrine into thickish slices and lay them in the centre of the yoghurt. Arrange the coriander leaves around the edge of the terrine slices.

Anthony's Fish Moilee

SERVES 4

4 rounded tablespoons coconut milk powder

600ml/1 pint hot water

1 medium onion

4 large cloves garlic

2–3 small fresh green chillies

generous 5cm/2in piece fresh ginger

3 tablespoons sunflower oil

½ teaspoon ground turmeric

1 rounded teaspoon plain flour

juice of 3 limes

675–800g/1½–1¾lb thick swordfish or monkfish steaks

10–12 curry leaves

generous handful fresh coriander leaves

salt

Anthony is tall and lean; he has dark-rimmed spectacles which almost hide his warm, twinkling eyes, and a neat, greying moustache. He looks like a professor out of a children's story book. But Anthony is a cook. He comes from Kerala, the lush, tropical and predominantly Christian state in the southwest of India, where he cooks for English friends of mine in the old coastal city of Cochin.

Fish is plentiful and varied in Kerala. Anthony used seer fish for this recipe, an excellent meaty fish with fine, pure white flesh. Swordfish or monkfish make good alternatives. This lovely, creamy dish is popular all over Kerala; tomatoes are often added, but not in Anthony's version. His sauce is also slightly thickened, which I like very much. Serve with basmati rice and a green vegetable or salad. Curry leaves are always used in Kerala but are not essential. However, they are available in Britain in Asian grocery shops and some supermarkets, fresh or dried.

Put the coconut milk powder into a bowl, add the hot water and 2 teaspoons of salt, stir until smooth and leave on one side. Peel the onion, cut it in half and then crossways into thin slices. Peel the garlic and chop finely. Under running water, cut a slit down the length of the chillies with a small sharp knife and extract all the seeds with your fingers. Drain the chillies but leave them whole. Peel the ginger, cut it in quarters lengthways and then slice into very thin strips.

Put the oil into a fairly large casserole over a medium heat, add the onion, the whole chillies and the ginger and stir around until the onion has just softened. Then add the turmeric and garlic and stir around for another 2–3 minutes. Remove from the heat and stir in the flour, followed by the lime juice. Then gradually stir in the reserved coconut milk. Return to the heat and bring to the boil, stirring all the time. Bubble, still stirring, for 2–3 minutes as the sauce thickens. Then add the fish steaks and curry leaves, cover the casserole and simmer very gently for about 15 minutes, until the fish has lightly cooked through. Meanwhile, roughly chop the coriander leaves. Stir them into the casserole just before serving.

In the face of ever-changing and, in my opinion, neurosis-causing theories put forward about which foods are good for you and which are bad, the beneficial effects of garlic remain uncontested. From ancient times to the present day it has been alleged to cure all manner of ills and to keep people healthy.

But it is because of what it does to my food rather than to my body that I feel I could not live, or cook, without it. It has a highly complex flavour, enhancing beyond measure so many other tastes. When cooked to a mellow sweetness it has a very different character from the assertive strength of the raw bulb. A mixture of garlic cooked for a long time and a little raw garlic added at the end can be wonderful, while to me the smell of garlic cooking is one of the best kitchen aromas in the world.

Salmon Steaks in Coconut Milk with Star Anise, Fresh Chilli and Ginger

SERVES 4

4 thick salmon steaks

1 medium-sized yellow pepper

1 fresh red chilli

2.5cm/1in piece fresh ginger

2 large cloves garlic

4 whole and 1 broken-up star anise

400ml/14fl oz tin coconut milk

juice of 2 limes

handful fresh coriander leaves

sea salt

This luscious, aromatic dish is extremely simple to prepare. Salmon, normally associated with the Northern cuisines of its habitat, nevertheless goes well with more exotic flavours from the Far East. If you prefer, you can use any other fish steaks. Serve with basmati rice and a green vegetable.

Place the fish steaks in a fairly shallow ovenproof dish with a lid, into which they fit quite closely. Cut the pepper in half lengthways, discard the seeds and stem and slice across as thinly as you can – use a food processor for extra thinness. Cut the chilli in half lengthways under running water, discard the seeds and stem, and slice as finely as possible across the flesh. Peel the ginger and garlic and cut into small, very thin slices. Scatter the chilli, ginger and garlic all over and around the fish and then place the sliced pepper evenly over the top. Put a whole star anise on each steak and the broken pieces in between. Empty the coconut milk into a bowl, add a good sprinkling of sea salt and gradually stir in the lime juice. Pour gently over and around the fish.

Preheat the oven to 150°C/300°F/gas mark 2. Cover the dish and place in the oven for about 50 minutes, until the fish is just cooked. If you are using salmon, insert a small, sharp knife into the centre of one of the steaks to test it – if the flesh is a slightly darker pink in the centre, it is perfectly cooked. Remove from the oven. Chop the coriander leaves roughly and scatter them on top of the fish.

Within a few hours of my arrival in Trinidad I realized that I was surrounded by many of my favourite things: the aromatic spices that I use in so much of my cooking; chocolate, a lifetime passion; tropical sun and warmth; exotic vegetation with its colours and smells; music; and an ethnic mix of people with the cross-cultural food that it creates.

During a late-night drive through the streets of Port of Spain, Western gastronomic influences on Trinidad became apparent. Neon lights spelled out names such as 'Pizza Boys', 'Burger Boys', 'Wok Roll', 'Meaty Needs', 'St James Meat Cottage', 'Chunkey's Nite-Bite', and even 'Munch King's Ice Cream Parlour', where a favourite flavour, apparently, is Guinness. But a touch of spice crept into almost everything, and I learned that Angostura bitters, the secret herb and spice mixture invented by a German doctor in the Venezuelan jungle and brought to Trinidad 140 years ago, not only creates pink gin but enhances soups, stews, salad dressings, sauces for both fish and meat as well as creamy puddings, ice creams, and fruit compotes.

winter
warmers

A real winter of storms, cold and general gloom can bring its own rewards by making your house seem a warm haven, and home food a true comfort. Chill winds make your appetite keener and the pleasure of working in the kitchen is increased as eating becomes more than ever one of the best things in life.

Parsnip-topped Italian Villa Pie

SERVES 6

550g/1¼lb parsnips

225g/8oz potatoes

2 teaspoons ground cumin

6 tablespoons olive oil

900g/2lb minced pork

6 rounded teaspoons tomato pesto

2 rounded tablespoons tomato purée

7.5cm/3in sprig fresh rosemary

225g/8oz fresh spinach

1 large egg

freshly grated Parmesan cheese, for
     sprinkling

salt

black pepper

So called because it is a far-flung variation of a cottage pie with Italian influences. It tastes so good that it can be served either for a family lunch or at an informal dinner party, and needs only a green salad as an accompaniment. The pie has a moistening layer of spinach between the topping and the minced pork.

Peel the parsnips if necessary. Peel the potatoes. Chop both up roughly, cutting the potatoes quite a lot smaller than the parsnips. Boil in salted water until they are both soft. Drain and mash thoroughly in a bowl, adding the ground cumin and 4 tablespoons of the olive oil, plus salt and black pepper to taste. Leave on one side.

Preheat the oven to 180°C/350°F/gas mark 4. Put the minced pork into another mixing bowl and add the pesto and tomato purée. Pull the spikes off the rosemary, chop finely and add to the pork mixture. Season with salt and plenty of black pepper. Put another tablespoon of the olive oil in a large, heavy frying pan over a high heat. Add the pork mixture and fry for 8–10 minutes, digging at the meat all the time with a wooden spoon until it has separated. If there are still juices in the pan, bubble fiercely until evaporated. Remove from the heat, taste and add more salt and pepper if needed.

Spoon the mixture into a large, rather shallow ovenproof dish and pat level. Chop the spinach leaves very finely and spread them on top of the meat. Whisk the egg thoroughly with a fork and mix it into the mashed parsnip mixture with a wooden spoon. Spread this mixture on top of the spinach layer and make flicks or patterns with a fork. Trickle the remaining tablespoon of olive oil over the top and sprinkle with grated Parmesan. Cook the pie on the centre shelf of the oven for 40–50 minutes, until a deep golden brown.

Creamy Chicken and Apple Pie with Cardamom

550–675g/1¼–1½lb boneless skinless chicken thighs

4–5 cardamom pods

25g/1oz butter

3–4 pinches cayenne pepper

1 rounded tablespoon plain flour

300ml/½ pint cider

finely grated rind and juice of 1 small lemon

150ml/¼ pint double cream

2 dessert apples

salt

For the pastry:

225g/8oz strong plain flour

½ teaspoon salt

100g/4oz butter

50g/2oz vegetable fat

2 tablespoons very cold water

milk, to glaze

Chicken pies are an old-fashioned favourite. This one, with its luxuriously creamy sauce, crumbly pastry and aroma of cardamom, is a great favourite. Serve with broccoli, if possible, which goes well with the sauce.

Make the pastry first. Sift the flour and salt into a bowl. Cut the butter and fat into small pieces, add them to the flour and crumble with your fingertips until the mixture looks like rough breadcrumbs. Add the water and stir with a knife until the dough begins to stick together. Shape into a ball, wrap in cling film and refrigerate.

Preheat the oven to 180°C/350°F/gas mark 4. To make the filling, cut each chicken thigh into 3 pieces. Remove the seeds from the cardamom pods and grind with a pestle and mortar. Melt the butter in a flameproof casserole over a medium heat. Remove from the heat and stir in the chicken pieces and ground cardamom until the chicken is coated with butter. Sprinkle with the cayenne pepper and some salt, then stir in the flour. Gradually stir in the cider with the lemon rind and juice. Put the casserole back over a higher heat until the juices bubble and thicken, stirring all the time, then cover, place in the centre of the oven and cook for 1 hour. Remove from the oven and stir in the cream. Check the seasoning.

Peel and core the apples, slice thinly in semi-circles and add to the casserole. Transfer the mixture to a pie dish or earthenware flan dish and leave to cool.

Preheat the oven to 200°C/400°F/gas mark 6. Knead the pastry lightly, then roll it out thickly on a lightly floured surface into a piece big enough to cover the top of the pie dish. Moisten the edges of the dish and lay the pastry on top. Press the edges down lightly and trim neatly. Reroll the trimmings and use to make decorations. Cut 2 holes in the pastry to allow steam to escape, brush all over with milk and cook in the centre of the oven for 25–35 minutes, until well browned.

Pork with Prunes, Juniper Berries and Pernod

SERVES 4-5

675–900g/1½–2lb boneless pork

100g/4oz pitted prunes

25g/1oz butter

3 tablespoons extra virgin olive oil

2 teaspoons ground mace

2 teaspoons juniper berries, roughly crushed

400g/14oz tin chopped tomatoes

150ml/¼ pint Pernod

juice of 1 orange

3–4 bay leaves

1 bunch spring onions

salt

black pepper

Pork can be a dull and dry meat, but not so in this simply made casserole, which has a lovely fusion of flavours. Serve with potatoes or egg tagliatelle and a green vegetable, such as spring greens. Pernod, with its taste of aniseed, makes this much more than an ordinary casserole.

Preheat the oven to 170°C/325°F/gas mark 3. Slice the pork into largish pieces. Chop the prunes up fairly small. Melt the butter and olive oil in a flameproof casserole over a medium heat, then add the ground mace and stir for a minute. Next, stir in the pork, juniper berries and prunes. Add the chopped tomatoes, Pernod, orange juice and bay leaves. Season with salt and plenty of black pepper, bring to bubbling, then cover the casserole, put it in the oven and cook for 1¾–2 hours, until the meat is very tender.

Trim the spring onions and cut across at 5mm/¼in intervals, using as much of the green part as possible. Before serving, check the casserole juices for seasoning, then stir in the chopped spring onions.

Steamed Venison Pudding

SERVES 6

675g/1½lb boneless venison from shoulder or neck

25g/1oz plain flour

2 onions

175g/6oz chestnut mushrooms

50g/2oz butter

1½ teaspoons ground cinnamon

½ teaspoon ground cloves

1½ teaspoons roughly crushed juniper berries

1 level tablespoon coarse-cut marmalade

225ml/8fl oz Guinness

2 teaspoons soy sauce

250g/9oz belly of pork

salt

black pepper

For the pudding crust:

175g/6oz self-raising flour

100g/4oz fresh white breadcrumbs

2 heaped teaspoons mustard seeds (optional)

175g/6oz vegetable or beef suet

1 egg

It is often forgotten what a pleasure steamed savoury puddings can be. I think the combination of this light crust (the secret is in the addition of breadcrumbs) and richly flavoured venison filling makes a wonderful winter dish, well worth preparing for a weekend meal when you have time to cook.

Slice the venison into roughly 2.5cm/1in pieces. Put the flour into a large bowl, add the sliced venison and stir around to coat all over with flour. Peel and slice the onions and cut the mushrooms in half. Melt 40g/1½oz of the butter over a medium heat in a large casserole. Add the sliced onions and fry until dark brown, then add the mushrooms and continue frying for a few minutes until browned. Using a slotted spoon, remove the onions and mushrooms from the pan and keep on a plate on one side.

Preheat the oven to 240°C/475°F/gas mark 9. Add the remaining butter to the casserole, then add the floured venison and turn around to brown the meat all over. Stir in the ground spices, followed by the juniper berries, the onions and mushrooms and any leftover flour from the bowl. Finally stir in the marmalade, Guinness and soy sauce and season with a little salt and plenty of black pepper. Increase the heat and bring the juices up to boiling point, stirring around several times as you do so. Allow to bubble for 2–3 minutes while stirring, then cover the dish and put into the oven. After about 10 minutes, turn down the heat to 150°C/300°F/gas mark 2. Cook for 1 hour.

Meanwhile, cut the skin from the belly of pork and slice the flesh into small pieces. When the venison has been cooking for 1 hour, add the pork and cook for another 30 minutes. Check for seasoning, then leave until cold.

To make the crust, mix together the flour, breadcrumbs, mustard seeds, if using, and suet. Season with salt and black pepper. Beat the egg with a fork in a measuring jug and make it up to 175ml/6fl oz with water. Gradually stir the liquid into the flour and breadcrumb mixture to form a soft, elastic dough. Gather up the dough and cut off a quarter of it to use for a lid.

Generously butter a 1.2 litre/2 pint pudding basin. Form the larger piece of dough into a ball and roll it out fairly thinly on a floured surface into a large circle. Fold the circle in half and then in half again. Lift into the prepared basin with the pointed end of the pastry downwards. Unfold in the basin, gently pressing it against the sides and leaving it hanging over the edge.

Spoon in the cooled venison filling and fold the overlapping edges of pastry back over the filling. Then roll out the remaining pastry into a circle big enough to form a lid. Moisten the pastry edges and place the lid on top, pressing the edges together to seal.

Cover the basin with a piece of buttered greaseproof paper, then a piece of foil. Secure with string under the rim but leave the paper and foil loose enough to puff up a bit. Make a string handle to lift up the pudding. Put the basin into a large saucepan and add enough boiling water to come half way up the sides. Cover the saucepan and simmer for about 2 hours, topping up with boiling water if necessary. Then lift out the basin, cut off the string, remove the paper and foil and serve the pudding straight from the basin.

SERVES 6

900g/2lb boneless skinless chicken

25g/1oz plain flour

2 tablespoons olive oil

1–2 fresh red chillies

5cm/2in piece fresh ginger

2 large cloves garlic

3 medium chicory

1 small red pepper

coarsely grated rind and juice of
1 lemon

salt

black pepper

For the crust:

175g/6oz self-raising flour

3 teaspoons paprika

2 level teaspoons ground mace

4–5 pinches cayenne pepper

100g/4oz white breadcrumbs

175g/6oz butter (grated from a
frozen packet of butter)

1 medium egg

Steamed Chicken and Chilli Pudding with a Spiced Crust

During the cold months we need so-called 'comfort food' for all sorts of reasons. To me, nothing brings more warmth and reassurance than an old-fashioned steamed pudding, either savoury – epitomized by steak and kidney pudding – or sweet, perhaps best exemplified by a jam sponge. However, it is possible to improve upon the classic recipes for these steaming old faithfuls while still retaining their joys.

This aromatic pudding has a gently exotic, lemony filling and a light, rich crust. It is equally suitable for Sunday lunch, a dinner party or just a homely supper, and needs only a crisp green vegetable such as broccoli or Savoy cabbage to accompany it, or simply a green salad.

Cut the chicken into largish chunks. Put the flour into a bowl and season with salt and black pepper. Add the chicken and turn it round to coat with the flour. Heat the olive oil in a large frying pan over a high heat, add the chicken pieces and fry just to brown them on all sides. Remove from the heat and leave to cool.

Meanwhile, make the crust. Put the self-raising flour in a bowl and mix in the paprika, mace, cayenne pepper and a sprinkling of salt. Stir in the breadcrumbs. Then, holding the block of frozen butter in a cloth at one end, coarsely grate three-quarters of it (175g/6oz) into the flour and breadcrumb mixture, mixing it in very lightly with your fingertips. Whisk the egg lightly in a measuring jug and make it up to 175ml/ 6fl oz with water. Gradually stir this liquid into the flour mixture, then bring together lightly with your hands and form a ball. Cut off a little over a quarter of the dough and set aside for the lid. Roll out the large piece of the dough fairly thinly on a floured board into a circle 33–35cm/13–14in across. Butter a 1.7 litre/3 pint pudding basin. Carefully lift the large piece of pastry and use to line the basin, pressing it together if it tears and leaving the excess hanging over the rim.

Put a large saucepan half full of water on to boil. Cut open the chillies lengthways under running water, discard the seeds and stems and chop the flesh finely. Peel the ginger and garlic and chop finely. Cut the chicory across into thick slices. Cut the red pepper in half, discard the seeds and stem and slice thinly. Mix the chillies, ginger, garlic, chicory, red pepper and grated lemon rind in a bowl with the browned chicken. Stir in the lemon juice and season with salt and black pepper.

Spoon the mixture into the pastry-lined basin, piling it up in a mound at the top. Fold the overlapping pastry over the filling and dampen the edges. Roll out the reserved dough into a circle big enough to make a lid. Place on top of the basin and press the edges lightly to seal them.

Butter a piece of greaseproof paper, make a pleat in the middle and put it over the top of the pudding. Put a piece of foil fairly loosely over the paper and tie it securely round the rim of the basin with string. Attach a piece of the string to make a handle. Lower the basin into the saucepan of boiling water. Cover the pan and boil gently for 3–3½ hours (or 1 hour in a pressure cooker), topping up the water now and then so it doesn't boil away. Serve the pudding in the basin, wrapped in a large white napkin.

900g/2lb stewing beef

2 medium to large onions

1 medium red pepper

6 large cloves garlic

100g/4oz piece rindless bacon

100g/4oz carrots

3 tablespoons olive oil

3 teaspoons oregano

150ml/¼ pint red wine

1 tablespoon balsamic vinegar

100g/4oz stoned black olives

salt

black pepper

For the pastry:

175g/6oz plain flour

1 teaspoon baking powder

¼ teaspoon salt

50g/2oz fresh white breadcrumbs

50g/2oz strong cheese, grated

100g/4oz vegetable suet

a little milk, to glaze

Beef and Olive Pie with a Cheese and Suet Crust

Suet pastry sounds very old-fashioned but it is delicious, and perfect for a winter dish. The inclusion of breadcrumbs and cheese in this variation makes the pastry both light and flavourful. In the slowly cooked beef filling, the vegetables blend into the juices, forming the body of the sauce.

Slice the beef into 2.5cm/1in cubes. Peel the onions and slice them in rings. Cut open the pepper, discard the seeds and stem, then chop the flesh up finely. Peel the garlic. Slice the bacon into small pieces. Top and tail the carrots and grate them finely.

Preheat the oven to 140°C/275°F/gas mark 1. Put 2 tablespoons of the olive oil into a large cast iron or other flameproof casserole over a fairly high heat. Add the beef and brown all over. Using a slotted spatula, transfer it to a plate on one side. Add the remaining oil to the casserole, then add the onions and fry until richly brown. Return the beef to the casserole. Add the whole garlic cloves, the red pepper, bacon, grated carrots and oregano. Pour in the wine and balsamic vinegar and stir to mix together, adding salt and black pepper. Cover the casserole and bring the mixture up to bubbling on top of the stove, then put it on a low shelf in the oven and cook for 3 hours. After this, slice the olives up roughly, add to the casserole and put back in the oven for another hour. Remove from the oven, add a little more salt and pepper if necessary, then spoon the mixture into a pie dish that it just about fills and leave until cool.

Preheat the oven to 200°C/400°F/gas mark 6. Meanwhile, make the pastry. Sift the flour, baking powder and salt into a bowl and stir in the breadcrumbs, cheese and suet. Stir in enough cold water to make a stiff dough. On a floured surface, roll out the pastry into a piece slightly larger than the pie dish. Moisten the edges of the dish and lay the pastry on top, pressing the edges down lightly. Cut 2 holes in the pastry to allow steam to escape and then trim the edges. Roll out the trimmings and cut out decorations. Moisten the underside of these and arrange on the pastry. Brush the pastry with milk and bake the pie in the centre of the oven for 25–35 minutes, until golden brown.

Lamb Casserole with Pumpkin and Ginger

SERVES 4

900g/2lb piece pumpkin

5cm/2in piece fresh ginger

4 cloves garlic

675g/1½lb lamb fillet

75g/3oz butter

2 teaspoons caraway seeds

150ml/¼ pint cider

1 rounded teaspoon dried green peppercorns

150ml/¼ pint double cream or crème fraîche

handful fresh coriander leaves

sea salt

black pepper

This is a mildly aromatic casserole with a delicious pale orange sauce; simply made but sophisticated. Serve with baked or new potatoes and a green vegetable.

Preheat the oven to 180°C/350°F/gas mark 4. Scrape out the seeds from the pumpkin, remove the peel and cut the flesh into small pieces. Peel the ginger and garlic and cut both into small, thin slices. Slice the lamb fillet crossways at roughly 4cm/1½in intervals. Melt the butter in a heatproof casserole over a medium heat, add the ginger, garlic and caraway seeds, stir around once and then add the pumpkin, lamb, cider, green peppercorns and a sprinkling of salt. Stir with a wooden spoon to mix, then cover the casserole.

Move the casserole into the oven and cook for 1¼ hours. Then stir with a wooden spoon to break up the pumpkin until it becomes a purée. Cover again and return to the oven for another half an hour. Taste the pumpkin and add salt and a little black pepper if needed. Just before serving, pour the cream over the top and sprinkle with very roughly chopped coriander leaves.

Wild Boar Casserole with Chicken Livers, Juniper and Ginger

SERVES · 8-10

1.1kg/2½lb wild boar

225g/8oz large flat or chestnut mushrooms

450g/1lb ripe tomatoes, the plum variety if available

1 rounded teaspoon juniper berries

2 good sprigs fresh rosemary

4 large cloves garlic

5cm/2in piece fresh ginger

1 tablespoon olive oil

25g/1oz butter

400g/14oz tin chopped tomatoes

finely grated rind and juice of 1 large orange

350g/12oz chicken livers

bunch fresh flat-leaf parsley

salt

black pepper

Many butchers now stock wild boar. Truly wild boar has been extinct in the British Isles for 400 years but it can still be found in other European countries. However, it is now farmed here, hence the availability.

If you cannot find boar you can easily substitute stewing pork or even lamb in this recipe. The addition of chicken livers for the last part of the cooking adds a soft richness to the flavourful sauce. I serve this with new potatoes tossed in olive oil and plenty of chopped spring onions and fresh dill.

Cut the meat into roughly 2.5cm/1in pieces. Chop the mushrooms up finely, including the stalks – you can do this in a food processor if you like. Put the fresh tomatoes in a bowl, pour boiling water over them and leave for about 2 minutes, then drain, peel and chop roughly. Crush the juniper berries in a pestle and mortar. Pull the rosemary spikes off their stems. Peel the garlic and ginger and cut up roughly, then chop the rosemary, garlic and ginger together finely.

Preheat the oven to 170°C/325°F/gas mark 3. Heat the olive oil and butter in a very large flameproof casserole over a medium heat. Add the mushrooms and stir around for a minute or so, then add the chopped fresh tomatoes, rosemary, garlic, ginger and juniper berries. Stir around over the heat for about 10 minutes, until the tomatoes are soft and mushy, then stir in the tinned tomatoes and the orange rind and juice. Season with salt and freshly ground black pepper, then stir in the wild boar and cover the casserole. Bring to boiling point, then put in the oven and cook for about 1½ hours, until the meat is tender. Remove from the oven and stir in the chicken livers. Bring back to simmering point on top of the stove, then transfer to the oven again and cook for another 30 minutes. Check for seasoning and add more salt and pepper if necessary.

If you like, you can keep the casserole warm at the lowest possible oven temperature for an hour or two before eating. Then roughly chop the parsley and stir it in just before serving.

Creamy Lamb Casserole with Fennel and White Beans

SERVES 4

25g/1oz butter

2 tablespoons olive oil

800–900g/1¾–2lb stewing lamb
cutlets

2 rounded teaspoons caster sugar

1 rounded tablespoon plain flour

450ml/¾ pint milk

150ml/¼ pint double cream

2–3 pinches cayenne pepper

2 bulbs fennel

4 large cloves garlic

1 teaspoon fennel seeds

small sprig fresh rosemary

425g/15oz tin white cannellini beans

1 rounded teaspoon paprika

salt

At least a cold, grim and seemingly endless winter can make you appreciate home life and its comforts. On dark, Victorian-seeming nights, what could be nicer than coming home, lighting a fire and smelling the rich aroma of a casserole emerging from the kitchen?

Although this dish uses inexpensive stewing lamb and is extremely simple to make, the result is sophisticated enough to serve at an informal dinner. Broccoli or greens and sautéed potatoes go well.

Preheat the oven to 240°C/475°F/gas mark 9. Melt the butter and olive oil in a large frying pan over a fairly high heat. Add the lamb and caster sugar and stir until the meat has browned and caramelized. Using a slotted spatula, transfer the lamb to a casserole. Put the flour in a jug with a little of the milk and stir until smooth. Stir in the remaining milk and the cream, season with the cayenne pepper and some salt and pour over the lamb.

Cut the base, top stalks and any marked outer parts off the fennel and slice each bulb into quarters lengthways. Bash the garlic cloves with the back of a heavy knife – the skin will come off easily – and slice into quarters lengthways. Arrange the fennel and garlic pieces amongst the lamb and add the fennel seeds and rosemary. Cover the dish and put in the oven for 20 minutes, until simmering. Turn the oven down to 150°C/300°F/gas mark 2 and cook for another 1½ hours or until the meat is tender. Mix in the drained beans, sprinkle the paprika in the centre – but don't mix in – and put back in the oven for about 15 minutes to heat the beans.

50g/2oz pitted prunes

2 tablespoons chunky marmalade

50g/2oz tin anchovy fillets

2 small onions

2–2.5kg/4½–5½lb shoulder of English lamb

1 tablespoon wine vinegar or cider vinegar

600ml/1 pint lager

a little olive oil

225g/8oz shallots

2 rounded teaspoons honey

25g/1oz cornflour

sea salt

black pepper

Sweet and Tender Lamb Cooked in Beer

This recipe is specially suitable for English or Welsh lamb and makes a refreshingly different main course for a winter Sunday lunch party. The beer serves as a marinade which becomes an excellent gravy.

Chop the prunes finely and put them into a bowl with the marmalade, then empty the anchovies with their oil into the bowl. Peel and finely chop the onions and stir them into the mixture. Season with salt and black pepper and mix thoroughly.

Using a sharp knife, cut 3 or 4 deep pockets in the underside of the lamb. Spoon the prune and anchovy mixture into them, then rub the meat with the vinegar and season with salt and pepper. Turn the lamb over and put it into a roasting pan – not too big. Pour the lager into the pan, cover with cling film and leave in the fridge to marinate for at least 24 hours.

Preheat the oven to 170°C/325°F/gas mark 3. Rub the top of the lamb with a little olive oil and sea salt and cook in the centre of the oven for 2¼–2½ hours. After it has been in the oven for 30 minutes, peel the shallots, leaving them whole, and add them to the juices in the roasting pan, stirring in the honey at the same time. At the end of the cooking, turn off the heat, open the oven door slightly and leave the meat to rest for about 20 minutes – this makes it easier to carve.

When the lamb is ready, transfer it to a carving board. Using a slotted spoon, scoop up the shallots and put them into a serving bowl. Mix the cornflour to a smooth paste with 2 tablespoons of water and stir it into the pan juices. Put the roasting pan on top of the stove and stir over a medium heat, letting the juices bubble for 2–3 minutes, until thickened. Pour this gravy into the bowl with the shallots to spoon over the carved lamb.

Since eating lamb was such a feature of my early childhood in the Middle East, it has always been one of my favourite meats. Although lamb could be eaten every day it was also a festive dish.

My mother remembers being a guest at a Bedouin feast in a finely carpeted long black tent in the middle of the Syrian desert. The most important moment of the feast came when my stepfather, as principle guest, was given the lamb's eye to eat. Being an exceptionally unsqueamish man he popped it into his mouth and chewed it up with genuine enthusiasm. At the same time, my mother, also as a token of esteem, was given the lamb's tail. Having enjoyed lamb's tail pie in Oxfordshire during the war, she was delighted.

Pigeons with Spiced Plums and Red Cabbage

SERVES 4

2 medium onions

675g/1½lb red cabbage

450g/1lb red plums

5cm/2in piece fresh ginger

4 large cloves garlic

50g/2oz butter, plus extra for baking

2 teaspoons caraway seeds

2 teaspoons ground cinnamon

4–5 cardamom pods

cayenne pepper

2 rounded tablespoons plain flour

3 teaspoons paprika

4 pigeons

3 tablespoons groundnut or
   sunflower oil

salt

The first dish I made without following someone else's recipe was a pigeon casserole. I was a music student living in a damp basement flat and I bought pigeons because they were cheap. However, the dish really impressed my friends and I have enjoyed these humble birds ever since. In this casserole their full flavour goes well with both the spices and the sharp sweetness of plums. Serve with mashed potato and a green vegetable or leaf salad.

Peel the onions and chop roughly. Discard any marked outer leaves from the red cabbage, cut out the thick stalk, then slice the leaves finely. Cut the plums in half and remove the stones. Peel the ginger and cut across into thin slices. Peel the garlic and cut each clove in half lengthways.

Now melt the butter in a large flameproof casserole over a medium heat, add the onions and cook until soft and just beginning to brown. Then stir in the ginger and garlic with the caraway seeds, cinnamon and cardamom pods, lightly crushing the cardamom pods just to open them a bit. Stir in the cabbage and plums, season with 3–5 pinches of cayenne pepper and some salt, then remove from the heat.

Preheat the oven to 170°C/325°F/gas mark 3. Put the flour and paprika into a bowl, season with salt and another few pinches of cayenne pepper and stir to mix. Coat each pigeon thoroughly with the seasoned flour. Put the oil into a large, heavy-based frying pan over a high heat and brown the pigeons on all sides. Arrange them breast-side upwards on top of the red cabbage and plums, top each bird with a blob of butter, then cover the casserole and cook in the centre of the oven for 1½–2 hours, until the pigeons feel tender when you stick a small knife into the flesh.

I spend too little time in my Devonian orchard to make full use of the fruits from trees I have planted there. My plum, apple, quince and medlar trees now produce fruit that can be made into delectable jams and scented jellies, but I also bring them back to my freezer to use during the winter.

Quinces, apples and plums can all be used in savoury dishes as well as sweet. They go well with game, poultry, lamb and pork.

Oxtail Cassoulet

350g/12oz dried cannellini or haricot beans

3 large onions

2 tablespoons olive oil

900g–1kg/2–2¼lb oxtail

450ml/¾ pint dry cider

coarsely grated rind and juice of 1 orange

100g/4oz pitted prunes

1 large red pepper

3–4 bay leaves

1 rounded teaspoon juniper berries

3 large cloves garlic

400g/14oz tin chopped tomatoes

salt

black pepper

As the evenings get darker and a kind of semi-hibernation in the warmth of the house begins, there is something particularly pleasurable about food that has been cooked long and slowly, filling the rooms with a comforting aroma.

Oxtail is not a traditional ingredient for a cassoulet but its rich flavour is absorbed beautifully by the beans and I find it one of the best winter treats. Serve with carrots, and a simple green salad if you like.

Soak the beans in plenty of cold water for several hours or overnight. Preheat the oven to 240°C/475°F/gas mark 9. Peel and slice the onions. Heat the olive oil in a large frying pan over a fairly high heat, then add the oxtail and cook, turning, just until browned all over. Remove from the pan with a slotted spatula and transfer to a large casserole dish. Add the onions to the pan and fry, stirring around often, until soft and browned. Put the onions in the casserole with the cider, orange rind and juice. Cut the pitted prunes in half. Slice the pepper in half lengthways, remove the seeds and stem and slice across thinly. Add the prunes, pepper, bay leaves and juniper berries to the ingredients in the casserole and stir to mix. Season with salt and black pepper. Cover the casserole and cook on the centre shelf of the oven for about 20 minutes, until the liquid is just bubbling. Then turn the oven temperature down to 140°C/275°F/gas mark 1 and cook for 1½ hours.

Meanwhile, drain the beans, put them in a large pan of unsalted water and boil for 40–60 minutes, until just soft but not yet breaking up. Peel the garlic and slice the cloves across thinly. After the oxtail has been cooking for 1½ hours, add the beans, sliced garlic and tinned tomatoes. Cover again and put back in the oven for another 2½–3 hours, until the meat is falling from the bones. Before serving, taste and add more salt and pepper if needed.

Garlic Casserole with Duck and Chicken Slivers

2 whole heads garlic

50g/2oz soft pitted prunes

3 medium tomatoes

100g/4oz rindless smoked streaky bacon

2 tablespoons olive oil

25g/1oz butter

1 level tablespoon plain flour

300ml/½ pint Guinness

2 tablespoons soy sauce

1 chicken breast fillet

2 duck breast fillets

3–4 sprigs fresh tarragon

2–3 tablespoons plain yoghurt

salt

black pepper

Slowly cooked garlic becomes not only sweet and mellow but mild too. This dish combines both slow and quick cooking, as the chicken and duck are only briefly introduced to the garlic mixture. It makes a lovely contrast of tastes and textures. Serve with a crisp green vegetable such as broccoli or sliced sprouts and new or baked potatoes or basmati rice.

Preheat the oven to 170°C/325°F/gas mark 3. Peel the cloves of garlic but leave whole. Chop up the pitted prunes fairly small. Chop up the tomatoes. Slice the bacon roughly into 2.5cm/1in pieces.

Heat 1 tablespoon of the olive oil in a cast-iron casserole over a fairly high heat, add the bacon and stir until beginning to brown. Remove from the heat, add the butter and the second tablespoon of olive oil and stir until the butter has melted. Then add the cloves of garlic and stir to coat them with the oil and butter. Stir in the flour, then stir in the Guinness with a wooden spoon, a little at a time at first, until the sauce is smooth. Stir in the soy sauce, followed by the prunes and tomatoes. Season with salt and plenty of black pepper. Bring to the boil, stirring all the time. Bubble for 2–3 minutes, still stirring, then cover the dish and cook in the centre of the oven for about 1½ hours.

Meanwhile, remove the skin from the chicken and duck fillets and, using a really sharp knife, slice them across very thinly. Remove the leaves from the tarragon and chop roughly.

When the casserole is ready, remove it from the oven and put it on top of the stove again. When you are ready to eat, bring the mixture to the boil over a fairly high heat, stirring once or twice. Then add the chicken slivers and bubble for about 3 minutes, still stirring. Add the duck slivers and the chopped tarragon and stir for another minute or two. The duck flesh should still be slightly pink. Spoon the yoghurt unevenly on top of the casserole and serve at once.

I was 19 and staying with a boyfriend in Scotland. We stood together at dusk behind a woven wicker hide by a large, dark lake, waiting for the ducks to come in for the night. The sky was clear, changing every second in darkening shades of bluey purple streaked with wisps of black cloud. Everything became silent and still, until an increasingly loud flapping was heard and birds could be seen stretched out across the half-lit sky, before an onslaught of gunfire shattered the romance.

However, sad as it seems, I cannot deny that I enjoy the clear, distinctive taste of wild game far more than the economical farmed kind.

Casseroled Pheasants with Aromatics

SERVES 8

25g/1oz dried mushrooms

150ml/¼ pint hot water

a little fat or oil for frying

2 pheasants, jointed

2 lemon grass stalks

1 fresh red chilli

5cm/2in piece fresh ginger

3 large cloves garlic

4 strips orange rind

175g/6oz fresh blueberries

juice of 3 oranges and 1 lemon

1 tablespoon arrowroot or cornflour

handful fresh coriander leaves

sea salt

Casseroling or pot-roasting are the best ways to ensure that your pheasants don't become too dry. This gently cooked dish, although easy to prepare, was received as a treat at a dinner party I gave. It can be prepared in advance and kept warm for at least an hour in the lowest oven. Serve with potatoes mashed with olive oil and black pepper and a green vegetable.

Put the dried mushrooms into a bowl, pour over the water and leave to soak for about 2 hours.

Preheat the oven to 170°C/325°F/gas mark 3. Heat a little fat or oil in a large frying pan over a fairly high heat and fry the pheasant joints in 2 batches just until browned on each side. Transfer the joints to a large casserole dish. Using a sharp knife, slice the lemon grass across very finely. Cut open the chilli lengthways under running water and discard the seeds and stem. Peel the ginger and the garlic. Then chop the chilli, ginger and garlic up together finely and scatter, together with the lemon grass, over the pheasant joints in the casserole dish. Add the orange rind, blueberries and orange and lemon juice. Strain the soaking water from the mushrooms into the dish and then press the mushrooms down between the pheasant joints. Season with salt and cover the casserole. Cook on the centre shelf of the oven for about 2 hours, then pour the juices into a saucepan. Cover the casserole to keep the pheasant joints warm, or put it in a low oven if leaving for long.

Mix the arrowroot or cornflour with a little water in a cup until smooth and stir into the cooking juices. Bring to the boil, stirring all the time, and bubble, still stirring, for about 2 minutes. Remove from the heat and cover the saucepan, if making in advance. Just before serving, reheat the sauce and roughly chop the coriander leaves. Then pour the sauce over the pheasant and scatter with the coriander leaves.

Even if you don't shoot pheasants or get given them, they are the most available of game birds and can be found in many supermarkets (though they only seem to have the plumper, more tender hen birds and I always wonder what happens to the cocks – into their game pies, perhaps?). People living in the country often say they have too many pheasants during the autumn and winter and tell me they don't know what to do except roast them.

It was in India that I first realized how well game goes with spices, and with many ingredients such as fruit and vegetables which will add moistness and flavour to what can be a rather dry and, if not properly hung, a dull bird. Pheasants can be as much a vehicle for flavours as chicken, but add more of their own personality to the dish.

puddings for pleasure and nicest ices

My family sometimes calls me the Queen of Puddings, as this is the name of one of my favourite nursery puddings I am flattered. I have always had a sweet tooth, indulging as a child in dry Horlicks, spoonfuls of Radio Malt and undiluted squares of fruit jelly. But when I began cooking I discovered the wicked thrill of pudding making. Puddings are always welcome as a real treat, with home-made ice creams perhaps the most popular of all.

Caramelized Filo Apple Pie with Cinnamon and Pine Kernels

SERVES 6-8

900g/2lb dessert apples

100g/4oz butter

50–75g/2–3oz pine kernels

3 teaspoons ground cinnamon

100g/4oz light muscovado sugar

finely grated rind and juice of 1 lemon

350g/12oz filo pastry

icing sugar for dusting

Crisp, paper-thin filo pastry and a mouthwatering filling make this a very special apple pie. Serve with crème fraîche, cream or yoghurt.

Peel the apples, cut them in half and then into thickish half-moon slices, cutting out the core. Melt half the butter in a large, deep frying pan over a medium heat. Add the apple slices and toss them in the butter. Cook, stirring repeatedly, until they are soft when you insert a small knife but not disintegrating. Then add the pine kernels and stir around for a minute or two. Stir in the cinnamon and, after a minute, the sugar, grated lemon rind and juice. Stir the bubbling mixture until the juices have evaporated, then remove from the heat and leave to cool.

Preheat the oven to 200°C/400°F/gas mark 6. Melt the remaining butter in a saucepan and remove from the heat. Brush a large baking sheet, ideally a round pizza tin, with a little of the melted butter. Lay 2 sheets of filo pastry just overlapping on the baking sheet, brush thinly with melted butter and then lay on another 2 sheets of filo across the other way. Continue for 3–4 more layers. Then spoon the cooled apple mixture on to the pastry in a circle, roughly 25–30cm/10–12in in diameter. Fold the overlapping pastry over the mixture. Brush another 2 sheets of filo with butter and lay them on top of the apple; cover with another 2 buttered sheets laid across the other way and repeat with all the remaining pastry, brushing the top sheets with butter too. Press the sides to seal in the apple mixture and bring up the filo pastry edges to make an attractive crinkly border.

Bake the pie just above the centre of the oven for 35–45 minutes, until the pastry is richly browned. Carefully edge the pie off the baking sheet and on to a serving dish. Just before serving hot or warm, sprinkle a little icing sugar through a fine sieve on to the centre of the pie.

Fine Prune Tart

SERVES 6

225g/8oz frozen puff pastry

15g/½oz good butter, at room temperature

2½ tablespoons caster sugar

100g/4oz soft pitted prunes

This crispy caramelized tart is exceptionally delicious as well as being easy to make. It is certainly grand enough for a dinner party. Serve with crème fraîche or a good vanilla ice cream. The frozen pastry will thaw at room temperature in one hour or less.

Cut the pastry in half and shape the halves into 2 balls. Roll them out very thinly on a floured surface into 2 roughly circular shapes, about 25–27.5cm/10–11in in diameter. Put one circle on a large, buttered flat tin plate or baking sheet, smear with the butter and sprinkle it evenly all over with 2 tablespoons of the caster sugar through a sieve.

Cut the prunes in half crossways and flatten them by pressing them between your palms. Arrange the flattened prunes on the butter and sugar, spaced apart. Leave a 5mm/¼in border of uncovered pastry around the edge. Lay the second circle of pastry on top of the prunes and roll the edges round to seal them. Rest the tart in the fridge for 30 minutes or longer.

Preheat the oven to 220°C/425°F/gas mark 7. Brush the top of the tart lightly with cold water and sprinkle the remaining caster sugar all over it through a sieve. Bake the tart towards the top of the oven for 15–20 minutes, until it is blackened and shiny on top. Remove from the oven and, using a wide spatula, carefully transfer the tart to a flat serving plate. Serve warm, if possible.

Banana, Passion Fruit and Cardamom Meringue Pie

SERVES 6

2 limes

8 cardamom pods

6 medium bananas

25g/1oz butter

75g/3oz light muscovado sugar

4–5 wrinkled passion fruit

whites of 2 large eggs

½ teaspoon salt

100g/4oz caster sugar, plus extra for sprinkling

For a Sunday lunch on a cold English day this hot pudding is a great reminder of warm sunshine. The exotic aroma of cardamom enhances both fruit and meringue in the most exquisite way. Serve with crème fraîche, cream or Greek-style yoghurt.

Squeeze the juice out of the limes and keep on one side. Extract the seeds from the cardamom pods and grind either with a pestle and mortar or in a coffee grinder. Peel the bananas, cut in half crossways and then cut each half in half again lengthways.

Melt the butter in a fairly large, deep frying pan over a medium heat, add half the ground cardamom and stir around for about 2 minutes. Now add the muscovado sugar and the lime juice and stir together thoroughly. Then lay the banana pieces in the mixture and cook fairly gently until the bananas are completely soft. Remove the pan from the heat and, using a slotted spatula, take the bananas from the sauce and lay them in a 23cm/9in earthenware or glass flan dish. Put the sauce back over a higher heat and bubble for a few minutes until it has thickened substantially. Remove from the heat.

Cut the passion fruit in half and, using a teaspoon, scrape out the insides evenly on to the bananas. Spoon the sugar, butter and lime sauce over them and leave to cool.

Preheat the oven to 170°C/325°F/gas mark 3. Put the egg whites into a bowl with the salt and whisk until they hold fluffy peaks. Now whisk in 2 tablespoons of the caster sugar until the meringue is smooth, glossy and stands in peaks. Using a metal spoon, fold in the remaining caster sugar and the remaining ground cardamom. Spoon the meringue on top of the bananas and passion fruit and sprinkle a little extra caster sugar on top. Cook towards the top of the oven for about 20 minutes or until the meringue is tinged pale brown. Serve hot or warm.

Crisp and Aromatic Apple Tart

SERVES 7-8

100g/4oz butter

about 4 tablespoons caster sugar

1.1kg/2½lb dessert apples

finely grated rind of 2 oranges

3 rounded teaspoons ground cinnamon

1 rounded teaspoon ground cloves

400g/14oz filo pastry

a little quince, apple or redcurrant jelly (optional)

I love upside-down tarts (excuse the suggestive description!) and cannot stop making different variations. This one is made with sugared and spiced filo pastry and the apples are cooked gently until they go a beautiful shade of pink. Serve with cream or crème fraîche. The tart can be made in advance up until the second cooking stage or cooked beforehand and reheated.

Preheat the oven to 150°C/300°F/gas mark 2. Smear the bottom of a 26–27.5cm/10½–11in round earthenware flan dish with 25g/1oz of the butter and sprinkle 3 tablespoons of the caster sugar evenly on top. Core the unpeeled apples and thinly slice them into half moons. Arrange a neat layer of overlapping apple slices on top of the caster sugar in the dish. Sprinkle with half the grated orange rind and then arrange the remaining apple slices on top, evenly but not so neatly this time. Sprinkle with the remaining orange rind and cover with foil. Bake on the centre shelf of the oven for 1½–2 hours, until the apples are tender, then carefully pour any apple juice into a saucepan and boil fiercely until syrupy. Pour back over the apples and leave until cold.

Gently melt the remaining butter in a saucepan and remove from the heat. Put a rounded tablespoon of caster sugar in a small bowl and stir in the ground spices. Lay a sheet of filo pastry on top of the apples, folding the edges in to fit the dish. Brush with melted butter and scatter lightly and evenly with a little of the sugar and spice mixture. Lay another sheet of filo pastry on top and repeat the butter, sugar and spice procedure. Continue until all the filo pastry is used up, just buttering the last piece and sprinkling it with sugar.

Preheat the oven to 190°C/375°F/gas mark 5 and put the tart on the centre shelf. Cook for 25 minutes, then turn down the heat to 170°C/325°F/gas mark 3 and cook for a further 20 minutes, until the pastry is a deep brown. Put a large, flat serving plate on top of the flan dish and turn them both upside down. Give a shake and turn the tart on to the serving plate, carefully lifting the dish off. For extra gloss, brush with a little melted quince, apple or redcurrant jelly. Serve hot or warm.

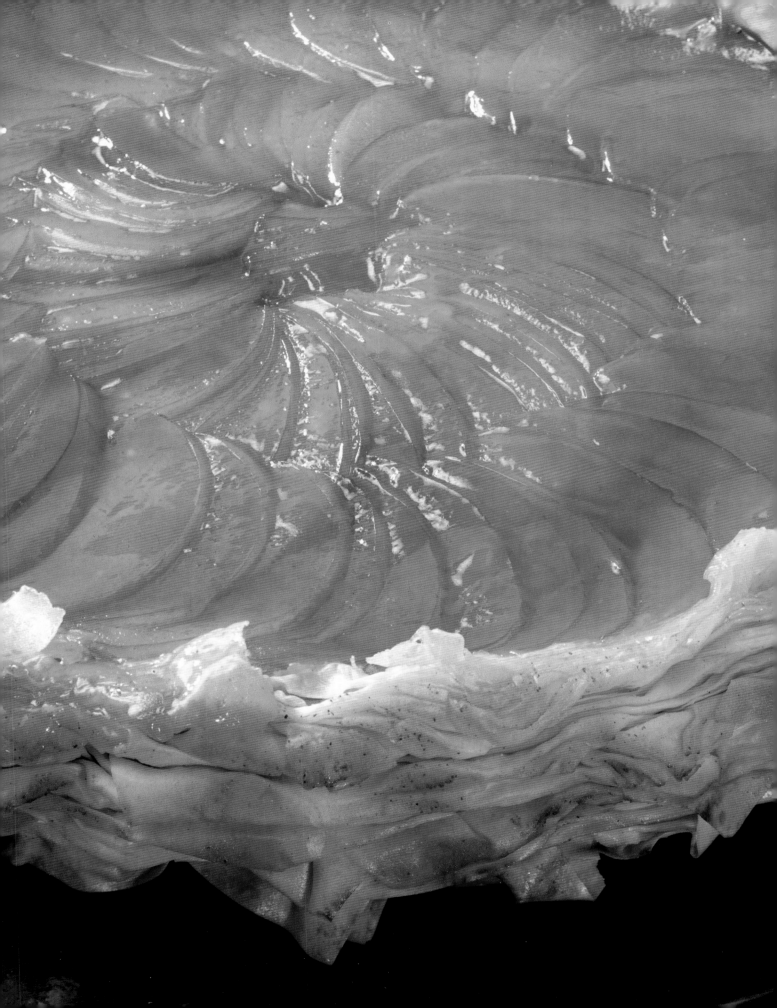

Chocolate and Lemon Meringue Tart

6 medium or large eggs

finely grated rind of 1 lemon

325g/11oz caster sugar

juice of 5 lemons

100g/4oz unsalted butter

¼ teaspoon salt

40–50g/1½–2oz plain chocolate, chopped into small pieces

For the pastry:

175g/6oz strong plain flour

2 heaped tablespoons cocoa powder

3 heaped tablespoons icing sugar

1 level teaspoon salt

100g/4oz butter

1 tablespoon water

Chocolate and lemon is a deservedly famous combination. Here, crisp dark chocolate pastry holds a sharp lemon curd filling topped with meringue, which is dotted with melted chocolate. A real treat for a special meal. Serve with cream if liked.

To make the pastry, sift the flour, cocoa powder, icing sugar and salt into a bowl. Gently melt the butter with the water and stir into the flour mixture with a wooden spoon to make a smooth dough. Press the warm dough evenly over the base and up the sides of a 26–27.5cm/10½–11in loose-based fluted flan tin and then chill while you prepare the filling.

Separate 4 of the eggs and put the egg yolks, the 2 whole eggs and the lemon rind into the top of a double boiler or a basin. Whisk together thoroughly with a fork. Then mix in 150g/5oz of the caster sugar. Put the lemon juice into a measuring jug and bring up to 300ml/½ pint with water. Stir into the egg yolk mixture. Put over gently simmering water and stir until the mixture thickens enough to coat the back of the spoon lightly. Now add the unsalted butter bit by bit and stir until melted. Remove from the heat and leave until cool.

Preheat the oven to 190°C/375°F/gas mark 5. Pour the cooled lemon curd into the chilled chocolate case and cook in the centre of the oven for 20–25 minutes. Remove from the oven and leave to cool for 10 minutes. Turn the oven down to 180°C/350°F/gas mark 4. When the tart has cooled slightly, put the egg whites into a large bowl, add the salt and whisk until the whites stand in soft peaks. Whisk in about half the remaining sugar, then fold in all the remaining sugar with a metal spoon. Spoon the meringue on top of the pudding and sprinkle with the chopped chocolate. Cook in the centre of the oven for 10–15 minutes, until the meringue is pale gold and the chocolate has melted. Remove from the oven and leave in the tin for about 10 minutes, then push the base up out of the rim and place on a serving plate. Serve warm or cold, but eat on the same day.

Mint-and Orange-glazed Grape Tart with a Crisp Orange Crust

SERVES 6

550–675g/1¼–1½lb seedless green grapes

225g/8oz orange jelly marmalade

1 tablespoon lemon juice

good handful fresh mint leaves

For the crust:

175g/6oz plain flour

2 tablespoons icing sugar

good pinch salt

finely grated rind and juice of 1 small orange

100g/4oz butter

A beautiful, shining end to a meal. Mint leaves go well with all sorts of fruit and the warm dough pastry for the crust is easy to make. Serve with crème fraîche or cream if liked.

To make the crust, sift the flour, icing sugar and salt into a bowl. Put the orange rind, juice and butter into a saucepan and heat gently until bubbling. Remove from the heat, leave to stand for a few minutes and then stir gradually into the flour mixture. Gather up the dough and press it into a fluted 24–25cm/9½–10in loose-based flan tin, spreading it evenly over the bottom and up the sides – the edge of the dough should come a little above that of the tin. Refrigerate for half an hour or more.

Preheat the oven to 200°C/400°F/gas mark 6. Put a piece of greaseproof paper on top of the dough and fill it with dried beans or rice. Bake blind on the centre shelf of the oven for 20–25 minutes, until cooked. Remove from the oven and lift off the paper and beans. Cool slightly, then put the flan tin on top of a jam jar or similar object and slip the loose sides of the tin down to expose the fluted crust. If you have a completely flat serving plate you can carefully ease the crust off the base with a spatula, but otherwise simply leave it on the base and put it on a serving plate.

When the crust is cool (don't refrigerate it), and not more than 6 hours before serving, wash and dry the grapes and arrange them in the crust. Put the orange jelly in a pan with the lemon juice and melt gently, stirring, until lump free. Slice the mint leaves across into very thin strips and stir them into the melted glaze. Remove from the heat, leave for 3–5 minutes, then spoon over the grapes. Serve at room temperature.

Honey and Lemon Tart

SERVES 6-8

225g/8oz plain flour

½ teaspoon salt

175g/6oz chilled butter

1 egg yolk

grated rind and juice of 2 lemons

5 rounded tablespoons honey

100g/4oz fresh white breadcrumbs

This is a luxurious version of treacle tart, made with honey instead of treacle. Make sure you use really good, unblended aromatic honey. I particularly like French lavender honey or, for a really strong taste, chestnut honey. Serve with cream, crème fraîche or yoghurt.

To make the pastry, sift the flour and salt into a mixing bowl. Add the butter, cut into small pieces, and crumble with your fingertips until evenly combined. Using a knife, mix in the egg yolk and the grated rind and juice of 1 lemon until the mixture just begins to stick together. Gather into a ball, wrap in cling film and chill for half an hour or more.

Preheat the oven to 200°C/400°F/gas mark 6. Roll out the pastry on a floured board to about 3mm/⅛in thick. Line a buttered 20cm/8in flan tin with the pastry and prick the base lightly with a fork.

Mix together the honey, breadcrumbs and the rind and juice of the second lemon. Pour into the pastry case. Roll out the pastry trimmings and cut strips to make a lattice pattern on top of the tart. Bake in the centre of the oven for 25–30 minutes. Serve warm or cold, not chilled.

SERVES 6

100g/4oz butter, at room temperature

150g/5oz fine demerara sugar or golden caster sugar

finely grated rind of 2 oranges

4 ripe passion fruit

100g/4oz ground almonds

3 large eggs, lightly whisked

icing sugar for dusting

For the sauce:

6 ripe passion fruit

juice of 2 oranges

2 tablespoons caster sugar

150ml/¼ pint double cream

Passion Fruit and Orange Puddings

Passion fruit and orange is a sublime mixture which makes these light and moist little almond cakes quite delectable. Ripe passion fruit are those with very wrinkled skins.

Butter 6 deep patty tins or individual dariole moulds and put a disc of baking parchment cut to fit in the bottom of each. Preheat the oven to 190°C/375°F/gas mark 5.

In a mixing bowl, beat the butter and sugar together until soft and fluffy, then beat in the grated orange rind. Cut the passion fruit in half and spoon the insides of 4 of the halves into the bowl with the butter and sugar. Strain the juice from the remaining passion fruit halves and add to the bowl, discarding the seeds. Whisk the mixture to break the flesh up and disperse the seeds, then whisk in the ground almonds and the eggs alternately, a little at a time. Spoon the mixture into the tins or moulds and bake in the centre of the oven for 25–35 minutes, until a small sharp knife inserted in the centre of a pudding comes out clean. Leave the puddings in the tins for at least 10 minutes, then pass a knife around the edges to loosen them and turn them out on to a wire rack, removing the discs of baking parchment. Leave to cool.

To make the sauce, cut the passion fruit in half and spoon the insides into a nylon sieve set over a bowl. Rub with a wooden spoon until as much juice as possible has gone through the sieve. Discard the mass of seeds. Strain the orange juice through a fine sieve into the bowl and add the caster sugar, stirring thoroughly so that it dissolves. Finally, stir in the double cream. Refrigerate the sauce until needed.

To serve, spoon the sauce on to 6 serving plates, place a pudding in the centre of each and generously sprinkle icing sugar over the puddings through a fine sieve.

My arrival in Peru at the age of 13, to join my parents in Lima, their new posting, was earthshattering in two ways. The first was literally so. In the middle of my first night I was woken by a sense of movement in the room. As it dawned on me that everything was rattling, shaking and trembling, my mother came in and told me not to worry, it was just an earth tremor and quite a usual thing. But in the morning the road outside was cracked deeply all down the centre.

However, what astonished me just as much that day was my introduction to grenadillas, or passion fruit. These wrinkled little fruit with their unprepossessing but ambrosial-tasting 'frog spawn' centre seemed a miracle to me, and have remained a true passion ever since.

Hot Lemon and Passion Fruit Soufflé

SERVES 6-8

4 wrinkled passion fruit

150ml/¼ pint fresh lemon juice

5 large eggs

100g/4oz caster sugar

finely grated rind of 2 lemons

½ level teaspoon salt

For this divine soufflé you can make the lemon and passion fruit base in advance, leaving only the egg whites to fold in when you cook the soufflé shortly before your meal. As an alternative to cream, try a purée of damsons, raspberries, blackberries or blackcurrants as a sauce.

Cut the passion fruit in half and scoop out the flesh, juice and seeds into a jug. Add the lemon juice and mix together with a fork.

Separate the eggs and put the yolks into the top of a double boiler or into a basin set over a saucepan of water, making sure the water is not touching the base of the bowl. Stir the sugar into the yolks and then add the lemon and passion fruit mixture a little at a time. Place the mixture over a low heat so the water in the bottom of the double boiler or the saucepan is gently simmering and stir until the mixture is thick enough to coat the back of a spoon. Stir in the grated lemon rind and leave until cold.

About an hour before you will be eating the soufflé, butter a 900ml/1½ pint soufflé dish or ovenproof glass dish. Preheat the oven to 150°C/ 300°F/gas mark 2. Put the egg whites in a large bowl with the salt and whisk until they hold soft peaks. Then, using a large metal spoon, lightly fold the cooled lemon and passion fruit curd into the egg whites. Spoon the mixture into the soufflé dish and cook just above the centre of the oven for 50–60 minutes, until the top of the soufflé is dark golden brown. Serve at once.

Apple Fudge Pudding Cake

SERVES 6-8

150g/5oz plain flour

1 teaspoon baking powder

¼ teaspoon salt

2 level tablespoons caster sugar

50g/2oz butter

1 large egg

½ teaspoon vanilla essence

a little full cream milk

For the topping:

550–675g/1¼–1½lb Bramley or other sharp-flavoured apples

75g/3oz butter

200g/7oz light muscovado sugar

2 teaspoons ground cinnamon

This gungy pudding cake is irresistible served warm, with cream, crème fraîche or Greek yoghurt.

Preheat the oven to 220°C/425°F/gas mark 7. Sift the flour, baking powder, salt and caster sugar into a bowl. Cut the butter into small pieces, add to the flour and crumble with your fingers, as though making pastry, until the mixture is like fine breadcrumbs. In a measuring jug, whisk the egg and vanilla essence together and add enough milk to make it up to 125ml/4fl oz. Add to the flour and butter mixture and stir thoroughly. Spoon the batter into a buttered rectangular dish measuring about 25 x 20cm/10 x 8in.

For the topping, peel and core the apples, then slice them thinly and arrange in closely overlapping rows on top of the cake mixture. Melt the butter in a pan, stir in the sugar and cinnamon and spoon evenly over the apples. Bake in the centre of the oven for 25 minutes, until risen and browned.

SERVES 5-6

550–800g/1¼–1¾lb Cox's Orange
Pippin apples

100g/4oz butter

1 heaped tablespoon light
muscovado sugar

100g/4oz caster sugar

3 large eggs

grated rind and juice of 2 small
oranges

1 heaped tablespoon self-raising
flour

a little over 150ml/¼pint milk

½ teaspoon cream of tartar

SERVES 6-8

2 tablespoons clear honey

about 225g/8oz kumquats

100g/4oz butter

150g/5oz light muscovado sugar

finely grated rind of 1 orange

3 medium or large eggs

50g/2oz ground almonds

50g/2oz self-raising flour

½ teaspoon salt

1 level teaspoon ground cinnamon

Apple and Orange Pudding

A three-layered pudding – caramelized apples underneath a top that separates into a fresh orange custard and the lightest possible sponge. Exactly the kind of pudding ingredients and flavours I like best.

Peel and core the apples, then cut them into thin slices. Melt half the butter in a frying pan and stir in the apples and muscovado sugar. Fry the apples over a high heat, stirring all the time, for about 2 minutes. Transfer them to an 18–20cm/7–8in soufflé dish – ovenproof glass looks good if you have it. Leave to cool while you make the topping.

Preheat the oven to 180°C/350°F/gas mark 4. Beat the remaining butter with the caster sugar until fluffy. Separate the eggs and beat the yolks into the butter and sugar mixture. Gradually beat in the orange rind and juice. Sift in the flour and then slowly add the milk, beating until smooth.

Whisk the egg whites with the cream of tartar until they stand in peaks. Gently fold into the orange mixture with a metal spoon. Pour this on top of the apples and bake in the centre of the oven for 40 minutes. Serve hot or cold, with or without cream.

Honeyed Kumquat Pudding

The most enchanting sight on a trip to Israel was the kumquat orchards – rows of perfect little trees laden with their small, sweet and sharp fruit, which looked from a distance like shining gold coins weighing down the delicate branches. It seemed like a scene from a children's fairy story in which we were giants walking among the trees, eating the magic fruit. On my return to England I made this upside-down pudding cake to remind me of that day. Serve with cream or crème fraîche.

Generously butter a 20cm/8in cake tin. Spread the honey over the bottom of the tin. Cut the kumquats in half lengthways and remove any pips you can see. Arrange the halves skin-side down in the tin, close together in a circular pattern so that they cover the bottom of the tin completely.

Preheat the oven to 180°C/350°F/gas mark 4. Cream the butter and sugar thoroughly together, then whisk in the orange rind. Whisk the eggs lightly in a bowl and then whisk in the butter and sugar mixture alternately with the ground almonds. Sift the flour, salt and cinnamon together and fold into the cake mixture with a metal spoon. Then spread evenly on top of the kumquats. Cook in the centre of the oven for 45–50 minutes, until a small knife inserted into the centre of the cake comes out clean. Remove from the oven and leave in the tin for a few minutes, then turn out on to a serving plate so that the kumquats are on top. Put the cake under a hot grill just to brown it slightly on top. Serve warm.

Country Weekend Pudding

SERVES 6-8

550–675g/1¼–1½lb cooking apples

1 teaspoon ground cinnamon

2 rounded tablespoons light
muscovado sugar

25g/1oz butter

grated rind and juice of 1 lemon

50g/2oz fresh breadcrumbs

50g/2oz caster sugar

300ml/½ pint soured cream

3 large eggs

¼ teaspoon cream of tartar

When I first published the recipe for this old-fashioned pudding it proved immensely popular. With its tangy, mousse-like top it certainly is delicious. Serve either hot or cold, with cream.

Butter a 1.5–1.7 litre/2½–3 pint ovenproof dish. Peel and core the apples and slice them thinly. Arrange the slices on the bottom of the dish and sprinkle with the cinnamon and muscovado sugar, then dot with the butter. Pour the lemon juice over the apples.

Preheat the oven to 190°C/375°F/gas mark 5. Put the breadcrumbs into a mixing bowl with the caster sugar, soured cream and lemon rind. Separate the eggs, putting the yolks into the bowl with the breadcrumbs and the whites in another bowl. Stir the breadcrumb mixture well to mix. Add the cream of tartar to the egg whites and whisk until they stand in soft peaks. Using a metal spoon, fold the whisked whites lightly into the breadcrumb mixture. Pour on top of the apples and cook in the centre of the oven for about 40 minutes, until well risen and brown.

Floating Apricots

SERVES 4-6

4 limes or small lemons

150–225ml/5–8fl oz unsweetened
orange juice

2 rounded tablespoons honey

40g/1½oz caster sugar, plus extra for
sprinkling

2 rounded teaspoons arrowroot

450g/1lb large fresh apricots

I always associate apricots with my childhood in Syria. They tasted wonderful eaten straight off the trees and we dried those we brought back on the flat, sun-baked roof of our house in Damascus.

Sadly, apricots for export must be picked before they have ripened on the tree, and this is why the apricots we buy in this country are not often worth eating uncooked. However, the slightest cooking miraculously brings out their true flavour, as in this lovely pudding. Serve with cream.

Squeeze the juice from the limes or lemons into a measuring jug, bring up to 300ml/½ pint with orange juice and pour into a saucepan. Add the honey and caster sugar and stir over a medium heat until dissolved. Remove from the heat.

In a cup, stir the arrowroot with a tablespoon of orange juice until smooth and then stir it into the juices in the saucepan. Put the pan back over the heat and bring to the boil, stirring all the time. Simmer for 2–3 minutes, until thickened. Pass the sauce through a fine sieve on to a large shallow dish or plate, spreading the sauce out all over it. Leave on one side to cool.

Preheat the oven to 240°C/475°F/gas mark 9. Halve the apricots and take out the stones. Lay the apricots, skin-side upwards, on a large baking sheet. Brush the apricot halves with enough water to moisten the skin and then sprinkle a teaspoon of caster sugar over each one. Put them at the very top of the oven for about 10 minutes, until they are soft. They will probably have a little undissolved caster sugar still on them. Leave to cool, then, using a slotted spatula, gently place them set apart on top of the cold sauce. Spoon any syrup from the apricots on top. Leave in a coolish place, but not the fridge, until needed.

Coconut Cream Pudding

SERVES 6

150ml/¼ pint double cream

300ml/½ pint full cream milk

75g/3oz coconut milk powder

1 teaspoon salt

3 large eggs

2 egg yolks

50g/2oz caster sugar

It was when I was travelling in Java that I first tasted all sorts of sweet things made with coconut milk. I noticed that very often a little salt was added to the sweetened milk, which really brings out the fresh coconut taste. This soothing pudding, which is like a baked coconut custard, is lovely accompanied by an exotic fruit salad.

Put a roasting pan three-quarters full of water on the centre shelf of the oven and preheat the oven to 170°C/325°F/gas mark 3. Put the cream and milk into a saucepan and bring barely up to bubbling. Add the coconut milk powder and salt, remove from the heat and stir until dissolved. Put the eggs, egg yolks and caster sugar into a bowl and whisk together thoroughly. Then whisk the hot coconut cream into the egg mixture a little at a time.

Pour the mixture into a 1.2 litre/2 pint ovenproof dish and stand it in the roasting pan of water in the oven. Cook for 1–1¼ hours, until the custard feels set to a very light touch but still wobbles slightly. Remove from the oven and leave until cold. Serve at room temperature.

Rum Punch Baked Apples

SERVES 4

100g/4oz dried apricots

finely grated rind and juice of 1 orange

2 teaspoons ground cinnamon

4 large cooking apples

½ nutmeg

1 large wine glass dark rum

juice of 1 lemon

4 rounded tablespoons dark muscovado sugar

about 25g/1oz butter

There are some old favourites one never tires of. These gleaming apples are stuffed with dried apricots and the rum makes a wonderful sauce. A sprinkling of Angostura bitters added with the rum is most effective. Serve with cream.

Preheat the oven to 190°C/375°F/gas mark 5. Chop the dried apricots finely and put them into a bowl, then stir in the grated orange rind and ground cinnamon. Put the orange juice into a fairly shallow ovenproof earthenware dish that is big enough to hold the apples. Make a shallow cut round the middle of each apple and remove the cores. Fill each apple with the chopped apricots and place in the dish. Grate the nutmeg over the apples and pour the rum and lemon juice around them. Finally, sprinkle the apples with the muscovado sugar, top each one with a good knob of the butter and bake on the centre shelf of the oven for 1–1¼ hours. Then drain the juices into a saucepan and boil fiercely until they become thick and syrupy. Pour the juices over the apples and serve immediately.

SERVES 4

500g/1lb 2oz thin-stalked
champagne rhubarb

1.25cm/½in piece fresh ginger

2–3 whole star anise

150ml/¼ pint water

juice of 2 limes

75g/3oz caster sugar

1 large or 2 small ripe mangoes

a few mint leaves, to decorate

Rhubarb and Mango à la Vong

This simple but utterly sublime combination was inspired by a fruit soup that I tasted at Vong, the French Thai restaurant in London. The appearance of deep yellow mango with clear pink rhubarb and the combination of their contrasting flavours is wonderful.

Preheat the oven to 170°C/325°F/gas mark 3. Slice the rhubarb across at 5cm/2in intervals – if the stalks are a bit thick, slice them in half lengthways, too. Peel the ginger, cut it in half and slice into small, very thin pieces. Put the rhubarb, ginger and star anise in a casserole dish. Put the water, lime juice and sugar into a saucepan and bring to the boil, stirring until the sugar has dissolved. Boil fiercely for 2 minutes, then pour on to the rhubarb, cover the casserole and put on the centre shelf of the oven for about 1½ hours, until the rhubarb is very soft. Remove from the oven, cool slightly, then spoon into a wide glass serving bowl or individual bowls.

Cut open the mangoes and cut the flesh off the stone, then skin them and slice into thin strips. Mix the mango strips with the rhubarb without breaking it up too much, then chill. Before serving, decorate with mint leaves and ensure that the star anise are visible near the top.

SERVES 4

350g/12oz strawberries

juice of 1 small orange

50–75g/2–3oz caster sugar, plus
extra for dusting

4–5 large, ripe white peaches

lemon juice

White Peaches with Strawberry and Orange Purée

White peaches (or white nectarines) are delectable, and at their best in this simple but ethereal dessert.

Halve the strawberries and put them into a food processor with the orange juice and caster sugar to taste. Whizz to a purée and then rub through a sieve into a bowl.

Shortly before eating, put the peaches into a bowl and pour boiling water over them. Leave for half a minute, then remove the peaches and peel off the skin. Slice them in thin half-moon slices, sprinkling the slices with lemon juice as you do so. Then spoon the strawberry and orange purée on to individual plates and arrange the peach slices in a neatly overlapping circle on top. Dust the peaches with a little caster sugar and serve.

RHUBARB AND MANGO
À LA VONG ▶

225g/8oz cream cheese

75g/3oz caster sugar

3 large eggs

25g/1oz cornflour

½ teaspoon salt

pinch cream of tartar

4 rounded tablespoons bramble or redcurrant jelly

225g/8oz fresh blackberries

icing sugar for dusting

Blackberry Cheesecake Roulade

During the late summer in Devon, some especially large and succulent blackberries clamber over an old apple tree in our orchard. I am always thinking of new ways to use them. This beautifully light cheesecake is rolled round a filling of blackberries. Serve with cream if liked.

Oil a 33 x 23cm/13 x 9in Swiss roll tin and line it with a piece of oiled baking parchment. Preheat the oven to 180°C/350°F/gas mark 4.

Whisk the cream cheese in a bowl to soften it, then whisk in the sugar. Separate the eggs and whisk the yolks into the cheese mixture one at a time. Finally, whisk in the cornflour and salt. Whisk the egg whites with the cream of tartar until they stand in soft peaks. Using a metal spoon, fold them gently into the cheese mixture. Pour into the Swiss roll tin and bake for 10–15 minutes, until light brown and springy to the touch. Leave to cool – it will sink slightly. When still just warm, loosen the edges with a knife and turn out on to a sheet of oiled baking parchment. Peel off the lining paper.

Gently melt the jelly in a pan, then turn it into a bowl and cool slightly. Stir in the blackberries and spread the mixture all over the cheesecake. Roll up like a Swiss roll with the help of the baking parchment – don't worry if it cracks a bit – and transfer to a serving plate. Before serving, sprinkle all over with icing sugar through a sieve.

675g/1½lb fresh apricots

150g/5oz demerara sugar

juice of 2 lemons

juice of 1 orange

3–4 elderflower heads, plus a few sprigs to decorate

350g/12oz fromage frais or ricotta cheese

75g/3oz icing sugar

225ml/8fl oz double cream

Apricots and Elderflowers on a Bed of White Cheese

Every year when the elderflowers are in bloom all over the countryside and even in the middle of the city, I marvel at the magical muscat flavour they impart to drinks, sorbets and ice creams. Gooseberry jam with elderflowers is a wonderful old-fashioned combination so I tried the flowers with apricots, both for stewing and for jam (see page 240); the effect is just as good, if not better.

Halve and stone the apricots. Put them in a pan with the demerara sugar and the strained lemon and orange juice. Cover and put over a low heat, stirring now and then, for a few minutes until the sugar has dissolved. Remove from the heat, shake in the flowers from the elderflower heads, then return to the heat and simmer in the open pan for 5 minutes or until the apricots are soft. The mixture should be thick; if it is at all liquid, boil fiercely for a minute or two to reduce the juices. Then leave to cool. Meanwhile, put the white cheese in a bowl, sift in the icing sugar and beat until soft. Whisk the cream until it stands in soft peaks and then fold it into the cheese. Pile the cheese mixture into the middle of a round serving plate and, using a spatula, press it out and smooth it into a wide circle about the height of a cheesecake. Chill it in the fridge for at least an hour. When the apricot mixture has cooled, keep that in the fridge too.

Shortly before serving, spoon the apricot mixture on top of the cheese and decorate with some fresh elderflower sprigs.

Cardamom Cheesecake with Ginger Crust

SERVES 6-8

150g/5oz ginger biscuits

50g/2oz butter

225g/8oz curd cheese

225g/8oz cream cheese

2 tablespoons full cream milk

1 level tablespoon cornflour

75g/3oz caster sugar

1 level teaspoon salt

2 large eggs

8 cardamom pods

icing sugar for dusting

Cardamom is wonderful in milky or creamy puddings, the way it is so often used in Indian sweetmeats. This is a particularly good, rich cheesecake.

Crush the biscuits in a food processor, then turn them into a bowl. Gently melt the butter in a small saucepan, pour on to the biscuits and stir in. Press the mixture evenly over the bottom of a well-buttered 22–23cm/8½–9in springform cake tin and then chill.

Preheat the oven to 170°C/325°F/gas mark 3. Put the 2 cheeses into a food processor with the milk, cornflour, caster sugar and salt. Separate the eggs, putting the yolks in the food processor and the whites in a large bowl. Extract the cardamom seeds from the pods, grind them in a pestle and mortar or a coffee grinder and add to the food processor. Whizz thoroughly and turn into a bowl.

Add a pinch of salt to the egg whites, then whisk them to soft peaks and fold gently into the cheese mixture. Pour on to the chilled base. Bake in the centre of the oven for 50–60 minutes, until just firm to a soft touch in the centre. Leave to cool completely, then gently release the sides of the tin and, using a palette knife, carefully transfer the cheesecake from the base on to a serving plate. Before serving, sprinkle with icing sugar through a sieve.

Chilled Rice Pudding with Caramelized Pine Kernels

SERVES 6

900ml/1½ pints water

200g/7oz pudding rice

150ml/¼ pint double cream

4 rounded tablespoons thick plain yoghurt

4 tablespoons caster sugar

finely grated rind of 1 orange and 1 lemon

50g/2oz pine kernels

Old-fashioned baked rice puddings are very comforting but a chilled rice pudding can be equally good and completely different. This mixture of cream, yoghurt and citrus rind is both opulent and refreshing, while the crisp, golden top transforms it into a pudding fit for any occasion.

Bring the water to the boil in a medium saucepan. Add the rice and simmer until it is just tender but still has a slightly nutty bite to it. Drain in a sieve and rinse through with cold water until completely cold. Put the cream into a large bowl and whisk until it holds soft peaks. Then fold in the yoghurt, half the caster sugar and the grated citrus rind. Add the cooked rice and gently but thoroughly stir it in. Turn into a large glass serving bowl or 6 individual ones and chill.

Meanwhile, put the pine kernels into a sieve, rinse through with water and turn into a bowl. Stir in the remaining caster sugar. Lay a large sheet of foil on a flat surface. Put a large, dry pan over a high heat. When hot, tip in the sugar-coated pine kernels and stir around constantly for a minute or two until browned. Turn them out on to the foil, spreading them around quickly to separate them as much as possible. Just before serving, spoon the pine kernels evenly on top of the chilled rice.

SERVES 6

600ml/1 pint freshly squeezed
orange juice

75ml/3fl oz elderflower cordial

150ml/¼ pint water

3 envelopes gelatine

6–7 wrinkled passion fruit

1–2 white- or yellow-fleshed
nectarines

Passion Fruit and Nectarine Jelly

This wonderful fresh fruit jelly has both magical looks and taste, and is easy to do. As it is refreshing, glamorous and can be made well ahead, it is perfect for a dinner party. You will need a 1.2 litre/2 pint ring mould. Serve with cream.

Pour the orange juice through a fine sieve into a fairly wide bowl. Mix the elderflower cordial with the water. Pour about a quarter of this liquid into a small saucepan and the rest of it into the bowl with the orange juice. Heat the liquid in the pan to boiling point, then remove from the heat, sprinkle in the gelatine and stir thoroughly until completely dissolved. Then pour into the orange juice mixture, stirring briskly all the time to disperse the gelatine. Put the bowl in the fridge and leave for an hour or more until the jelly is lightly set.

Meanwhile, cut open the passion fruit and, with a teaspoon, scrape out the insides into a small bowl. Stir to mix and break up the flesh, juice and seeds. When the jelly in the fridge is ready, take it out and whisk until smooth but still thick. Stir in the passion fruit flesh and seeds.

Now slice a nectarine into very thin half-moon slices and arrange them closely together pressed against the sides of 1.2 litre/2 pint ring mould – you may need part of a second nectarine. Finally, spoon or carefully pour in the jelly mixture. Put back in the fridge and leave to set for several hours or overnight.

To turn out, wipe the mould thoroughly with a very hot cloth or dip it extremely briefly in a bowl of hot water until it slips out when given a good shake against a flat serving plate. Keep in the fridge until needed.

SERVES 6-8

1 tin lychees (approximately
425g/15oz – sizes vary)

juice of 3 oranges

juice of 1 lemon

50g/2oz caster sugar

4 rounded teaspoons gelatine

300ml/½ pint soured cream or
creamed smatana

250g/9oz Greek-style yoghurt or
whole-milk yoghurt

Yoghurt and Lychee Jelly

Being opaque, this doesn't really look like a jelly at all. But its consistency makes it intriguing and the delicate, fresh taste is most welcome after a rich meal.

Drain the juices from the lychees into a saucepan. Add the orange and lemon juice and the caster sugar and heat the juices until the sugar has dissolved, then sprinkle in the gelatine and stir over a very gentle heat until completely dissolved. Pour into a mixing bowl and leave until just beginning to set. Stir around, then stir in the soured cream or smatana and the yoghurt. Lastly, add the lychees. Pour into a 1.2 litre/2 pint metal bombe or jelly mould and chill for several hours, until very firmly set. Then dip the mould momentarily in a sink of hot water and turn it out, with a good shake, on to a dark-coloured serving plate.

PASSION FRUIT AND
◀ NECTARINE JELLY

500g/1lb 2oz fresh apricots

125g/4½oz caster sugar

2 rounded teaspoons Sichuan peppercorns

1 teaspoon coriander seeds

juice of 2 lemons

450g/1lb fresh strawberries

300ml/½ pint double cream

350g/12oz raspberries

caster sugar for sprinkling

1 teaspoon icing sugar

For the pastry:

225g/8oz strong plain flour

½ teaspoon salt

grated rind and juice of 1 orange

175g/6oz butter from a 225g/8oz block frozen butter

3 tablespoons very cold water

Sichuan Peppered Fruit

Sichuan peppercorns, much used in Chinese cookery, can be bought in oriental food stores and some large supermarkets. Mild and wonderfully aromatic, they make this mixture of poached apricots (or you could use yellow plums) and fresh strawberries truly mouthwatering. The colours are very glamorous, too.

Preheat the oven to 170°C/325°F/gas mark 3. Slice the apricots in half and remove the stones. Place in a fairly large ovenproof dish and sprinkle with the caster sugar. Roughly crush the peppercorns and coriander seeds and scatter them amongst the apricots. Pour in the lemon juice and cover the dish with foil, then place on the middle shelf of the oven for 45 minutes–1 hour, until the apricots are soft. Remove the foil from the dish and leave to cool. Finally, slice the strawberries lengthways and mix with the apricots and syrup. Chill until ready to serve, with or without cream.

Raspberry Flake

This impressive-looking pudding is simply raspberries and cream sandwiched between two circles of orange-flavoured flaky pastry, which is easy to make. Alternatively you can use strawberries.

To make the pastry, sift the flour and salt into a bowl and add the orange rind. Put a grater into the bowl on top of the flour. Hold the frozen block of butter at one end in a cloth and grate off three-quarters (175g/6oz) of it on the coarsest blade. Using a knife, mix the butter roughly into the flour until crumbly. Then add the orange juice and cold water, mixing again with a knife. Gather up the dough in your hands and press into a ball. Wrap in cling film and refrigerate for at least an hour.

Preheat the oven to 220°C/425°F/gas mark 7. Butter two 22–23cm/8½–9in sandwich tins. Cut the pastry in half and shape each half into a ball. Roll out into 2 rather thick circles, big enough to fit tightly into the sandwich tins. If necessary, press in the edges to make them neater. Prick all over with a fork and bake just above the centre of the oven for 20–25 minutes, until risen and golden brown. Leave to cool in the tins.

Put one pastry circle on a serving plate. Whisk the cream until thick. Spread half the cream on the pastry circle, then pile on the raspberries sprinkled with a little caster sugar. Dollop the rest of the cream over them. Top with the second pastry circle and sprinkle the icing sugar through a fine sieve on top of this. Once assembled, serve as soon as possible.

SERVES 6 - 8

175g/6oz plain chocolate

50g/2oz butter

2 large eggs, separated

75g/3oz dark soft brown sugar

1 tablespoon plain flour

1 tablespoon cocoa powder

2 teaspoons ground cinnamon

good pinch of salt

1 red rose, to decorate

For the chocolate glaze:

175g/6oz plain chocolate

2 teaspoons vanilla essence

4 teaspoons plain yoghurt

Chocolate Heart Cake

If you make this dark and densely chocolatey cake in a heart-shaped tin it is particularly appropriate for Valentine's Day or any other occasion when you want to show that you have cooked with love. The cake is best made the day before but glazed with chocolate shortly before eating. Use chocolate that contains at least 50 per cent cocoa solids.

Butter a heart-shaped cake tin (approximately 20cm/8in across at its widest point), line the base with a piece of buttered baking parchment cut to shape and dust lightly with flour.

Break up the chocolate and put it with the butter into a bowl set over a pan of very hot but not boiling water, making sure the water is not touching the base of the bowl. Stir until melted and smooth, then remove from the heat. Put the egg yolks into a mixing bowl, whisk in the sugar and then very thoroughly whisk in the melted chocolate mixture. Sift the flour, cocoa powder and cinnamon on to the mixture and stir in evenly. Preheat the oven to 180°C/350°F/gas mark 4.

Whisk the egg whites with the salt until they hold soft peaks. Using a metal spoon, fold the whites into the chocolate mixture a little at a time. Then spoon the mixture into the prepared cake tin. Bake the cake in the centre of the oven for 25–30 minutes, until a small knife inserted in the centre of the wide part of the heart comes out just about clean – this cake should not be allowed to overcook.

Remove the cake from the oven and leave in the tin for a few minutes – it will sink slightly. Then loosen the edges carefully with a knife and turn the cake out on to a rack to cool, removing the baking parchment and turning the cake the right way up.

To make the glaze, break up the chocolate and put it with the vanilla essence into a bowl set over a pan of very hot water, making sure the water is not touching the base of the bowl. Stir until the chocolate has melted, then stir in the yoghurt.

Put the cold cake on a flat serving dish and place 4 strips of baking parchment just under the cake – one on each side of the cake to stop the glaze getting on to the plate. Pour the chocolate glaze on to the cake and spread it all over the top and sides with a palette knife.

Place one real red rose at the top of the heart to one side. When the chocolate has set, carefully pull out the strips of baking parchment from under the cake. Keep the cake at coolish room temperature but not in the fridge. Serve with crème fraîche or cream. A raspberry purée makes a lovely additional accompaniment.

40g/1½oz self-raising flour

15g/½oz cornflour

150g/5oz caster sugar

4 large egg whites

1 tablespoon cold water

½ teaspoon cream of tartar

½ teaspoon salt

For the filling:

5 large egg yolks

75g/3oz caster sugar, plus extra for sprinkling

finely grated rind of 2 lemons

125ml/4fl oz lemon juice

225–350g/8–12oz strawberries

Angel Cake Filled with Fresh Lemon Curd and Strawberries

An angel cake is an American fantasy. Ultra light and pure white, it can make a spectacular end to a special meal. As the cake is made with egg whites only, I use the yolks to make a fresh lemon curd, which combines beautifully with strawberries in the filling. Alternatively, make an orange curd using one large orange instead of the lemons.

Preheat the oven to 140°C/275°F/gas mark 1. Line the base of 2 ungreased 18.5–20cm/7½–8in straight-sided sandwich tins with discs of baking parchment. Sift the flour and cornflour together several times to make them extra fine.

Sift the caster sugar and add 1 heaped tablespoon of it to the flours. Whisk the egg whites in a large bowl with the water, cream of tartar and salt until they stand in soft peaks. Using a large metal spoon, gradually fold in the remaining sugar. Fold in the sifted flours, a little at a time, sifting them directly on to the egg whites. Pour into the tins and bake on the lowest shelf of the oven for about 1½ hours, until well risen and springy. Remove from the oven and leave in the tins until almost cool.

While the cakes are cooking, prepare the lemon curd. Put the egg yolks into a heatproof bowl set over a pan of simmering water, making sure the water does not touch the base of the bowl. Stir in the caster sugar, grated lemon rind and lemon juice. Cook, stirring, until the mixture is thick enough to coat the back of a wooden spoon, then leave until cold.

When the cakes are almost cool, loosen the sides carefully with a palette knife. Turn out and peel off the baking parchment, then place on a wire rack to cool completely.

Halve the strawberries if large. Put one cake on a large serving plate. Spread with the lemon curd, then arrange the strawberries evenly on the curd. Top with the second cake and sprinkle thickly with caster sugar. Eat within a day.

Chocolate Peppermint Cream Cake

SERVES 14

100g/4oz plain chocolate

2 tablespoons water

225g/8oz butter

225g/8oz caster sugar

4 large eggs

50g/2oz ground almonds

100g/4oz self-raising flour

50g/2oz cocoa powder

1 rounded teaspoon baking powder

For the filling:

150g/5oz unsalted butter

225g/8oz icing sugar

2 tablespoons single cream

1–2 teaspoons peppermint essence

For the icing:

75g/3oz granulated sugar

4 tablespoons water

150g/5oz plain chocolate, broken into small pieces

1–2 teaspoons peppermint essence

I invented this cake for my youngest daughter's birthday party. It was a great success, eaten as a finale to the festive meal. It is a large four-tiered cake which can easily be made the day before – in fact I think it tastes even better if it is. Use chocolate that contains at least 50 per cent cocoa solids.

Butter a deep 19–20cm/7½–8in round cake tin and line the base with a disc of buttered baking parchment. Preheat the oven to 170°C/325°F/gas mark 3.

Gently melt the chocolate with the water and then remove from the heat. Whisk the butter until soft, add the caster sugar and whisk until light and fluffy. Thoroughly whisk in the melted chocolate, then whisk in the eggs one at a time. Stir in the ground almonds. Sift the flour with the cocoa and baking powder. Sift again on to the cake mixture and fold in gently but thoroughly. Spoon into the prepared cake tin and smooth level. Bake in the centre of the oven for 60–70 minutes, until firm to the touch in the centre. Remove from the oven and leave in the tin for about 10–15 minutes, then loosen the edges with a knife and turn out on to a wire rack to cool.

To make the filling, whisk the unsalted butter until soft. Sift in the icing sugar and whisk until smooth, then whisk in the cream and the peppermint essence to taste.

When the cake is completely cold, cut it into 4 thin layers with a long sharp knife. Put the bottom layer on a serving plate and slip 4 strips of baking parchment under the edge in a square shape, thus protecting the plate from any icing which may spill down. Assemble the cake, spreading the filling evenly between the layers.

To make the icing, put the granulated sugar and water in a saucepan and stir over a gentle heat until dissolved. Then boil fiercely without stirring for 1 minute. Remove from the heat and, when the bubbles subside, stir in the broken chocolate until melted and smooth. Add the peppermint essence to taste. Immediately spoon the icing on top of the cake, letting it fall down the sides as evenly as possible and spreading it round the sides quickly with a palette knife. If you are putting candles or decorations on the cake do it now before the icing sets.

When the icing has set, remove the strips of baking parchment. If you like, write a birthday message on the top in white icing – I simply squeeze it through a tiny hole cut in the end of a small polythene bag.

Peppermint Cream Parfait

SERVES 6-8

whites of 2 large eggs

½ teaspoon salt

175g/6oz caster sugar

6 tablespoons water

½ teaspoon peppermint essence

300ml/½ pint whipping cream

100–150g/4–5oz box wafer-thin chocolate peppermint creams

fresh mint leaves, to decorate

A light and irresistible ice cream dotted with pieces of chocolate peppermint cream. It can be made at least a day in advance. If you have any, add a little crème de menthe with the peppermint essence.

Put the egg whites in a bowl with the salt and whisk until they stand in soft peaks. Dissolve the sugar in the water in a saucepan over a gentle heat, then increase the heat and boil fiercely, without stirring, for 3 minutes. Pour immediately on to the egg whites in a thin stream, whisking all the time with an electric whisk at high speed. Add the peppermint essence and continue whisking until the mixture is thick. In a separate bowl whisk the cream until softly thick and then gently but thoroughly fold it into the egg white mixture with a metal spoon. Using a sharp knife, cut the peppermint creams into thin pieces and fold them into the ice cream mixture. Then pour into a serving bowl – glass looks nice – and freeze for at least 5 hours.

You should be able to serve the parfait straight from the freezer but if it seems too hard, leave it in the main part of the fridge for half an hour or so before eating. Decorate with a cluster of mint leaves before serving.

Real Chocolate Ice Cream

SERVES 8-10

25g/1oz cocoa powder

1 teaspoon instant coffee

3 large eggs

pinch of salt

175g/6oz caster sugar

150ml/¼ pint water

75g/3oz plain chocolate, broken up, plus extra to decorate

300ml/½ pint whipping cream

A chocolate finale to a special meal invariably provokes the most appreciation; few things more so than a deeply chocolatey ice cream like this one.

Put the cocoa powder and instant coffee into a bowl, add 4 tablespoons of very hot water and stir until smooth. Leave on one side.

Whisk the eggs with the salt until pale and frothy. Dissolve the caster sugar in the water in a saucepan over a low heat, then bring to the boil and bubble fiercely for 3 minutes. Remove from the heat and immediately add the broken chocolate, stirring constantly until melted and smooth. Stir in the cocoa mixture. Pour this hot chocolate syrup on to the eggs, whisking all the time with an electric whisk at high speed. Continue whisking until cool. Then whisk the cream until thick and fold it gently but thoroughly into the chocolate mixture. Pour into a serving bowl and coarsely grate a little chocolate on top – or you can make chocolate curls or leaves, if you like. Freeze for at least 6 hours and serve straight from the freezer.

TOP LEFT: PEPPERMINT CREAM PARFAIT

RIGHT: REAL CHOCOLATE ICE CREAM

BELOW: LAYERED CRANBERRY AND SATSUMA PARFAIT WITH ORANGE CURAÇAO (PAGE 223)▶

Ginger and Chocolate Swirl Ice Cream

SERVES 6-8

100g/4oz darkest chocolate, broken into pieces

6 tablespoons ginger wine

2.5cm/1in piece fresh ginger

whites of 2 large eggs

½ teaspoon salt

150g/5oz demerara sugar

5 tablespoons water

75g/3oz ginger in syrup

300ml/½ pint whipping cream

A prize ice cream which is especially good served with a bowl of raspberries or strawberries or, early in the year, a compote of rhubarb.

Put the chocolate and 4 tablespoons of the ginger wine into a bowl set over a saucepan of hot but not bubbling water. Stir until melted and smooth, then remove the bowl from the hot water and leave on one side.

Peel the fresh ginger and chop finely. Put the egg whites and salt into a bowl and whisk to form soft peaks. Then put the chopped ginger, the demerara sugar and water in a saucepan over a lowish heat. Stir all the time until the sugar has dissolved, then increase the heat and bring to the boil. Boil fiercely, without stirring, for 3 minutes. Pour at once in a thin stream on to the egg whites, whisking all the time at high speed. Continue whisking until cool and thick, then whisk in the remaining ginger wine.

Chop the ginger in syrup into small pieces. Whisk the cream until thick and, using a metal spoon, fold it thoroughly into the egg white mixture with the chopped ginger in syrup. The melted chocolate should still be soft enough to drop from a spoon; if not, reheat slightly. Then drop spoonfuls of the chocolate on to the ice cream mixture but do not stir in. Finally pour the mixture into a serving bowl – glass looks best – and freeze for several hours or overnight.

Passion Fruit and Blood Orange Parfait

SERVES 8

whites of 3 large eggs

good pinch of salt

150ml/¼ pint blood orange juice

225g/8oz granulated sugar

4–5 wrinkled passion fruit

juice of 1 large lemon

300ml/½ pint whipping cream

This is a magical and easily made ice cream. Supermarkets often sell freshly squeezed blood orange juice (which they more delicately call ruby red) – or you can squeeze your own.

Put the egg whites into a bowl with the salt and whisk with an electric beater until they stand in soft peaks. Strain the blood orange juice through a sieve into a saucepan, add the sugar and stir over a low heat until dissolved. Then increase the heat and boil fiercely, without stirring, for 3 minutes. Pour immediately in a thin stream on to the egg whites, whisking all the time at high speed. Continue whisking until the mixture looks like uncooked meringue. Cut the passion fruit in half and scoop the insides out with a teaspoon on to the egg white mixture. Then whisk into the mixture, adding the lemon juice.

Whisk the cream in a separate bowl until thick but not stiff and fold it gently but thoroughly into the meringue mixture. Transfer to a serving bowl and freeze for at least 3 hours. The ice cream should be soft enough to serve straight from the freezer; if it seems at all hard, transfer it to the main part of the fridge for half an hour or so before eating.

Layered Cranberry and Satsuma Parfait with Orange Curaçao

SERVES 8

For the cranberry sorbet:

250g/9oz fresh cranberries

150g/5oz granulated sugar

125ml/4fl oz red wine

1 egg white

For the satsuma ice cream:

5–7 satsumas

finely grated rind of 1 orange

175g/6oz demerara sugar

2 egg whites

¼ teaspoon salt

150ml/¼ pint whipping cream

3 tablespoons orange curaçao

thin slivers of orange rind

A refreshing treat during the winter, this is both ice cream and sorbet, layered in stripes of creamy orange and brilliant scarlet – so freeze it in a glass bowl if possible. It is a perfect party dish as it can be made ahead and served straight from the freezer.

Put the cranberries, sugar and wine into a saucepan and bring gradually to the boil, stirring to dissolve the sugar. Then cover and simmer for about 8 minutes until the cranberries are mushy. Purée in a food processor and leave until cold. Whisk the egg white until it forms soft peaks and fold into the cranberry purée with a large metal spoon. Halve the satsumas and squeeze out as many as will provide 150ml/¼ pint of juice. Put the juice into a saucepan with the grated orange rind and demerara sugar. Put the egg whites and the salt into a bowl and, using an electric beater, whisk until they form soft peaks. Put the satsuma juice over the heat and stir until the sugar has dissolved, then bring to the boil and boil fiercely for 3 minutes. Pour the syrup immediately on to the whisked egg whites in a thin stream, whisking all the time. Continue whisking until the mixture is cool and thick.

In another bowl, whisk the cream until it holds soft peaks. Fold into the egg white and syrup mixture with a metal spoon. Add the curaçao a tablespoonful at a time and fold gently into the mixture.

To assemble the parfait, spoon a thin layer of cranberry sorbet mixture into a glass serving bowl, followed by a thicker layer of satsuma ice cream. Continue like this, ending with a layer of cranberry sorbet. Finally, arrange a few thin strips of orange rind in the centre and freeze for at least 6 hours.

Banana and Rum Ice Cream

SERVES 8

3 large eggs

½ teaspoon salt

175g/6oz raw cane demerara or light muscovado sugar

6 tablespoons water

4 medium to large bananas

juice of 1 lemon

4–5 tablespoons light rum

300ml/½ pint whipping cream

Bananas mashed with brown sugar and cream were one of my earliest passions – this rich ice cream captures the essence of that mixture.

Using an electric whisk, whisk the eggs and salt in a fairly large bowl until frothy. Dissolve the sugar in the water over a low heat, then bring to the boil and boil fiercely, without stirring, for 3 minutes. Pour immediately in a thin stream on to the eggs, whisking all the time at high speed. Continue whisking until the mixture thickens.

Put the bananas in a food processor with the lemon juice and rum and whizz until smooth. Then whisk into the egg and sugar mixture. In another bowl, whisk the cream until thick but not stiff and fold thoroughly into the mixture. Pour into a serving bowl and freeze for several hours or overnight.

tea time

I have always found tea the most irresistible of all meals. It is sad that it doesn't really fit into the modern pattern of life, but surely a long Sunday afternoon walk is perfected by the pleasure of eating warm scones, freshly made cake and biscuits, or simply toast and home-made jam at the end of it. It is certainly the home-made element that can make tea time a moment of ecstasy rather than just satisfying the hunger brought on by fresh air and exercise.

Almond and Orange Torte

SERVES 6-8

3 medium or large eggs

100g/4oz icing sugar, plus extra for dusting

3 tablespoons unsweetened orange juice

finely grated rind of 1 orange

good pinch of salt

100g/4oz ground almonds

This is a simple but delicious cake with a delicate texture. If you want to serve it as a pudding, accompany it with a bowl of fresh orange slices.

Butter the sides of deep 19–20cm/7½–8in cake tin and line the base with a disc of non-stick baking parchment. Preheat the oven to 180°C/ 350°F/ gas mark 4. Separate the eggs and whisk the yolks with 75g/3oz of the icing sugar until pale. Whisk in the orange juice, followed by the rind.

In a separate bowl, whisk the egg whites with the salt until they form soft peaks. Sift in the remaining icing sugar and whisk again. Fold the whisked egg whites and the ground almonds alternately into the egg yolk mixture. Pour into the prepared cake tin and cook in the centre of the oven for 30–35 minutes, until springy to a light touch in the centre. Remove from the oven and leave in the tin for about 10 minutes, then loosen the sides with a knife and turn out on to a wire rack to cool. Put the cake on a serving plate and dust with icing sugar through a sieve all over the top.

Hazelnut, Sultana and Lemon Cake

SERVES 8

finely grated rind and juice of 1 lemon

50g/2oz sultanas

100g/4oz butter

100g/4oz golden caster sugar, plus extra for sprinkling

3 large eggs

75g/3oz ground hazelnuts

50g/2oz plain flour

An easy cake to make for Sunday tea, this is also moist and light enough for a pudding, served with crème fraîche or Greek-style yoghurt. Ground hazelnuts are available from healthfood shops, or you can grind whole, unblanched ones in a food processor.

Put the lemon juice and sultanas into a saucepan and heat until the juice bubbles, then leave to cool. Butter a fairly deep 17.5cm/7in sandwich tin and put a disc of buttered baking parchment on the bottom. Lightly flour the tin. Preheat the oven to 180°C/350°F/gas mark 4.

Put the butter and sugar in a bowl and whisk until light and fluffy. Whisk in the eggs and ground hazelnuts alternately and thoroughly. Stir in the cooled lemon juice and sultanas together with the lemon rind. Then fold in the flour with a metal spoon. Turn the cake mixture into the prepared tin and smooth the top level. Bake the cake in the centre of the oven for 45–50 minutes, until springy to the touch in the centre. Leave to cool in the tin before loosening the sides with a knife and turning it out. Put the cake on to a serving plate and sprinkle the top evenly with golden caster sugar.

Better-than-ever Chocolate Brownies

MAKES 12

100g/4oz butter

40g/1½oz cocoa powder

50g/2oz plain chocolate, broken into small pieces

2 medium or large eggs

½ level teaspoon salt

225g/8oz light muscovado sugar

50g/2oz self-raising flour

75g/3oz pecan nuts, roughly chopped (optional)

The title of this recipe evolved because I tried several variations until I arrived at this version. These brownies are exactly as they should be: dark and gooey, yet chewy. Brownies keep well either in an airtight tin or in the freezer but these are so popular that they nearly always disappear before being stored away.

Preheat the oven to 180°C/350°F/gas mark 4. Butter a 17.5cm/7in square cake tin. Put the butter into a saucepan over a gentle heat and stir until melted. Stir in the cocoa powder until it is smoothly blended, then add the chocolate. Continue stirring until melted and then remove from the heat.

Put the eggs in a large bowl with the salt and sugar and whisk thoroughly until light and frothy. Then whisk in the butter and chocolate mixture. Sift the flour on to the mixture and fold in lightly with a large metal spoon. Stir in the chopped nuts, if using, and pour the mixture into the buttered pan. Bake in the centre of the oven for 30–40 minutes – it should still feel slightly undercooked. Cool in the tin, then cut into squares or oblongs and remove from the tin with a flexible spatula.

Chocolate and Walnut Thins

MAKES 15

100g/4oz butter

25g/1oz bitter chocolate

1 teaspoon instant coffee

75g/3oz dark muscovado sugar

½ teaspoon vanilla essence

1 large egg, lightly whisked

25g/1oz plain flour

½ teaspoon salt

50g/2oz walnuts, roughly chopped

These are irresistible, rather like thin, light brownies; the crisp top becomes slightly gooey underneath. For a more firmly crisp result, bake for a further 5 minutes. Use chocolate with at least 50 per cent cocoa solids.

Butter a Swiss roll tin, approximately 25 x 37cm/10 x 14in. Preheat the oven to 190°C/375°F/gas mark 5.

In a heavy saucepan, melt the butter and chocolate over the lowest possible heat; do not allow it to bubble. Stir with a wooden spoon until smooth, then add the instant coffee and stir to dissolve. Remove from the heat and stir in the sugar and vanilla essence. Add the whisked egg and mix thoroughly. Sift in the flour and salt and mix until smooth. Pour into the prepared tin and spread evenly. Sprinkle the chopped walnuts all over.

Bake below the centre of the oven for 15 minutes, turning the tin round half way through the cooking to ensure even browning. Remove from the oven and cut at once, carefully, with a sharp knife, into squares or oblongs. Then, using a metal spatula, remove the biscuits while still warm and cool on a wire rack.

Chocolate-topped Sharp Lemon Cake

SERVES 10

175g/6oz butter

175g/6oz caster sugar

3 medium or large eggs

finely grated rind and juice of 2 lemons

1 rounded teaspoon baking powder

pinch of salt

175g/6oz self-raising flour

3–4 tablespoons milk

50g/2oz granulated sugar

For the chocolate topping:

100g/4oz dark chocolate

25g/1oz unsalted butter

Lemon and dark chocolate are one of the great taste combinations. This is a moist cake infused with the sharpness of fresh lemon juice. The chocolate should be equally intense; choose the brand with the highest percentage of cocoa solids – some have as much as 70 per cent.

Preheat the oven to 180°C/350°F/gas mark 4. Butter a 19–20cm/7½–8in square cake tin and line the base with a piece of buttered baking parchment. Put the butter and caster sugar in a bowl and beat until fluffy. Beat in the eggs thoroughly, one at a time, and then the grated lemon rind. Sift the baking powder and salt with the flour and fold into the mixture with a metal spoon. Stir in enough milk to give a soft, dropping consistency. Spoon the mixture into the cake tin and bake in the centre of the oven for about 45 minutes, until springy to the touch in the centre.

Loosen the sides of the cake with a knife and turn it out on to a baking sheet or a flat plate, then turn it over so it is the right way up. Make holes all over the top of the cake with a skewer, piercing right through to the bottom. Put the granulated sugar and the strained lemon juice into a pan, bring to the boil, stirring to dissolve the sugar, then bubble fiercely for 30 seconds. Pour the hot syrup slowly all over the top of the cake, letting it seep into the holes. Smear the last bit of syrup roughly along the sides of the cake. Press a long, wide strip of baking parchment all round the sides, coming at least 2.5cm/1in above the top of the cake. Leave until cold.

To make the topping, break up the chocolate and put it with 2 teaspoons of water in a bowl set over a pan of hot but not boiling water, making sure the water is not touching the base of the bowl. Stir until melted and smooth and then stir in the butter until also melted. Cool briefly, until slightly less liquid, then pour or spoon all over the top of the cake – the baking parchment should contain the chocolate. When the chocolate has cooled and set, carefully remove the paper and cut the cake into small squares with a sharp knife.

TOP: BETTER-THAN-EVER CHOCOLATE BROWNIES (PAGE 227)

BELOW: CHOCOLATE-TOPPED SHARP LEMON CAKE

4–5 cardamom pods

7.5cm/3in piece cinnamon stick

100g/4oz darkest chocolate (containing at least 50% cocoa solids)

2 tablespoons water

4 large eggs

100g/4oz light muscovado sugar

1 level teaspoon salt

1 rounded tablespoon cocoa powder

2 rounded tablespoons Greek yoghurt

50g/2oz stale white bread, made into breadcrumbs

icing sugar for dusting

Aromatic Chocolate Cake

The smell of spices as you cut into this intense, squidgy cake is, to me, incredibly exciting. The cake is better if made at least a day in advance. It uses breadcrumbs instead of flour, which give it a moist, crumbly texture.

Butter a 15cm/6in cake tin (or a small loaf tin), put a disc of buttered baking parchment on the bottom and dust with flour. Extract the seeds from the cardamom pods and break up the cinnamon roughly. Put the spices into a coffee grinder and whizz until finely ground. Put a bowl over a pan of simmering water, making sure the water does not touch the base of the bowl. Put the ground spices into the bowl and leave them for 2–3 minutes, stirring once or twice to release their aroma. Break up the chocolate and add it with the water to the bowl. Turn the heat right down, or off, and stir constantly until the chocolate is melted and smooth. Remove from the heat.

Preheat the oven to 180°C/350°F/gas mark 4. Separate the eggs into 2 bowls, a larger one for the whites. Whisk half the sugar with the egg yolks until pale and very thick, then stir in the melted chocolate, salt, cocoa powder, yoghurt and breadcrumbs. Whisk the egg whites until stiff and then gradually fold in the remaining sugar before folding into the chocolate mixture. The mixture should almost be a dropping consistency. If it is very stiff, stir in a tablespoon of water.

Spoon the mixture into the cake tin and cook in the centre of the oven for 30–40 minutes, until it feels firm to a light touch in the centre. Remove from the oven and leave in the tin for 5–10 minutes. Then loosen the edges with a knife and turn out, right-side up, on to a rack to cool. Remove the disc of baking parchment. When cold, wrap in cling film and keep in a cool place until needed. Before serving, lightly sprinkle icing sugar through a sieve on top of the cake.

Chocolate is certainly one of the most consuming passions of my life; it consumes me, I consume it. I don't think of myself as an addictive person – if chocolate is unavailable (as it often is when travelling abroad) I can do without it with no pangs at all, but if I see chocolate I buy it and if I have chocolate in the house I eat it – all of it, fast.

I don't think I am alone in my overindulgence. I have noticed over the years that recipes for chocolate cakes and puddings provoke more response from my readers than any others. For birthdays in our family there is never any question but that the cake must be chocolate: it is more of a treat, more of an orgy, more of a kick, more wicked and more beautiful than any other cake.

Mountaineers sometimes survive for days on chocolate; it is known to be nutritious and sustaining. I once met a trim, rosy-cheeked woman called Joy who ran a chocolate house in the north of England. She looked the epitome of health and happiness. Her secret, she said cheerfully, was that she lived entirely on 2lb of good chocolate a day, plus a few tomatoes for extra vitamins. I almost believed her.

SERVES 6-8

100g/4oz self-raising flour

1 teaspoon salt

175g/6oz caster sugar

4 tablespoons sunflower oil

5 tablespoons water

1 teaspoon vanilla essence

3 large eggs, separated

225g/8oz carrots, finely grated

1 level teaspoon cream of tartar

For the candied carrot top:

225g/8oz carrots

1 lemon

225g/8oz granulated sugar

4 tablespoons water

Light Carrot Cake with a Candied Carrot Top

Carrots are good for you in all sorts of ways – or so they say. In any case they are a sweet and versatile vegetable and I particularly like them in cakes. The texture of this one, made with oil, is lighter than usual, and the brilliant orange candied carrot topping makes it a conversation-stopping cake.

Preheat the oven to 170°C/325°F/gas mark 3. Line an oiled 17.5–20cm/ 7–8in round cake tin with oiled greaseproof paper. Sift the flour, salt and caster sugar into a bowl. Add the oil, water, vanilla essence and egg yolks and beat or whip thoroughly to make a smooth batter. Stir in the grated carrots. In a large bowl, whisk the egg whites with the cream of tartar until they stand in soft peaks. Fold into the batter gently with a metal spoon. Transfer to the prepared cake tin and bake in the centre of the oven for 1½ hours. Insert a sharp knife in the centre; if the knife comes out clean, take the cake from the oven and leave it in the tin for about 10 minutes. Then loosen the edges with a knife and turn on to a wire rack to cool.

While the cake is cooking, make the topping. Peel the carrots and, using a food processor, slice across as finely as possible. Coarsely grate the lemon rind and squeeze out the juice. Put the sliced carrots, lemon rind and juice, sugar and water into a saucepan and boil fiercely for 6–10 minutes until a blob of the syrup dropped on a cold plate sets. Leave in the saucepan to cool.

When the cake is cold, put it on a serving plate and spread the candied carrots over the top. If the syrup has become too stiff, add a tablespoon of water and reheat a little to make it spreadable. Serve the cake with cream.

Carrots are sweet, carrots are cheap, carrots are healthy. They are also surprisingly versatile and their vibrant colour adds greatly to the appearance of any dish they are used in.

For centuries carrots have been reputed to have properties supposedly promoting good sight, curly hair, good digestion and a lively libido. Nowadays, because they know carrots are a prime source of vitamin A, some very health-conscious people go over the top, eating so many that their skin begins to turn orange. However, eaten more moderately the carrot is a wonderful vegetable, available at any time of year. Large old carrots still make excellent purées and soups, main-crop ones have the most concentrated flavour, and there are few things as delicious as tiny new carrots, briefly cooked.

SERVES 6-8

150ml/¼ pint milk

2 generous pinches saffron strands

225g/8oz plain flour

150g/5oz self-raising flour

175g/6oz butter

175g/6oz golden caster sugar

1 level teaspoon salt

3 large eggs

3–4 sprigs fresh thyme

Saffron and Thyme Madeira Cake

To me, there is something compulsive about the texture and buttery taste of Madeira cake; once I start, I can never stop eating it. I also serve this as a pudding, accompanied by a fresh blood orange jelly or a fruit compote.

Put the milk and saffron in a saucepan, bring to the boil and remove at once from the heat. Leave on one side to cool. Butter a deep 16–17.5cm/6½–7in round cake tin and line with a disc of buttered greaseproof paper. Dust lightly with flour. Preheat the oven to 180°C/350°F/gas mark 4.

Sift the 2 flours together into a bowl. In another bowl, whisk the butter with the sugar and salt until pale and fluffy. Whisk the eggs in a small bowl with a fork and add to the butter and sugar mixture a little at a time, whisking after each addition. Then, using a large metal spoon, fold the sifted flours into the mixture. Strip the thyme sprigs and put the little leaves into the saucepan of cooled saffron milk – it need not be completely cold.

Using a metal spoon again, mix the saffron milk into the cake mixture. Spoon the mixture into the prepared cake tin, smooth the top level and bake on the centre shelf of the oven for 1–1¼ hours, until a small sharp knife inserted in the centre comes out clean. Leave the cake in the tin for a few minutes, then turn out on to a wire rack to cool.

SERVES 8

175g/6oz caster sugar

2 rounded tablespoons clear honey

225ml/8fl oz sunflower oil

3 large eggs

1 teaspoon ground cardamom or mace

½ teaspoon salt

175g/6oz self-raising wholemeal flour

275g/10oz carrots, grated

100g/4oz unsweetened desiccated coconut

100g/4oz walnuts, roughly chopped

Carrot and Coconut Cake

Although I used to abhor desiccated coconut on the luridly coloured little cakes we had for tea at school, I later discovered that its use in baking need not always be scorned.
The tropical island of Bali is the last place you would expect to find carrot cake, but in a little tea house in the hills I ate a memorable one, made with coconut. When I tried to reproduce it I developed the best carrot cake I have made to date.

Butter a 19–20cm/7½–8in cake tin (not one with a loose base) and line it with a disc of greaseproof paper. Preheat the oven to 180°C/350°F/gas mark 4.

Put the caster sugar and honey into a bowl, add the sunflower oil and whisk until well mixed. Whisk in the eggs one at a time until amalgamated. Continue whisking until the mixture is pale and frothy. Mix the spice and salt into the flour and then whisk the flour into the egg mixture a little at a time until thoroughly mixed. Stir in the carrots, coconut and chopped walnuts and pour the mixture into the prepared tin. Cook in the centre of the oven for 1½–1¾ hours, until a small, sharp knife stuck into the centre comes out clean. If the top of the cake begins to look too brown, lay a piece of greaseproof paper or foil loosely over the top. Turn out on to a wire rack to cool.

Moist Apricot, Prune and Cherry Cake

SERVES 8

100g/4oz dried apricots

100g/4oz pitted prunes

100g/4oz glacé cherries

175g/6oz butter

175g/6oz light muscovado sugar

300ml/½ pint unsweetened orange juice

50g/2oz candied peel

225g/8oz plain flour

1 teaspoon bicarbonate of soda

2 large eggs

The old-fashioned boiled fruit method is easiest for fruit cakes. It also produces a particularly moist cake which stays fresh for weeks or months in an airtight tin, so you can always have some cake ready for tea.

Vary the ingredients as you like; I often add nuts as well as different dried fruits. Nowadays tropical fruits such as mango, papaya and pineapple are available dried, which gives you great scope.

Roughly chop the apricots and prunes and halve the cherries. Put the butter, sugar and orange juice into a saucepan over a medium heat and stir until the butter has melted and the sugar has dissolved. Then add the prepared fruit and the candied peel. Bring to the boil, cover the pan and simmer gently for 10–15 minutes. Leave to cool.

Preheat the oven to 180°C/350°F/gas mark 4. Butter a 19cm/7½in cake tin, put a disc of buttered baking parchment on the bottom and dust lightly with flour. Sift the flour and bicarbonate of soda into a mixing bowl. Add the cooled fruit mixture and stir with a wooden spoon to mix in the flour evenly. Whisk the eggs lightly in a small bowl and then stir them thoroughly into the cake mixture. Pour the mixture into the tin and bake in the centre of the oven for 1–1½ hours, until firm to a light touch in the centre. Leave in the tin for 10 minutes, then loosen the sides of the cake with a knife and turn out carefully on to a wire rack to cool.

Mango Biscuits

MAKES 28

100g/4oz dried mango slices

175g/6oz butter

50g/2oz golden caster sugar

225g/8oz self-raising flour

1 teaspoon salt

Dried mango has a lovely intense flavour. It is now easily available in supermarkets and oriental grocer's, and is especially good for these easily made butter biscuits. Alternatively you could use crystallized ginger.

Preheat the oven to 190°C/375°F/gas mark 5. Chop the mango slices into small pieces. Put the butter in a food processor with the caster sugar and whizz until soft and fluffy. Sift in the flour and salt and whizz until mixed to a dough. Then add the chopped mango and whizz briefly. Flour your hands and gather the dough into a ball. Roll it out on a floured board about 3–5mm/⅛–¼in thick. Using a biscuit cutter, cut into shapes, rerolling the dough as necessary.

Lay the rounds on lightly buttered baking sheets and bake in the centre of the oven for 8–12 minutes, until pale golden brown. Let the biscuits cool on the baking sheets.

Saffron and Currant Biscuits

MAKES 35

2 tablespoons cream or milk

generous pinch saffron strands

175g/6oz butter

50g/2oz icing sugar

175g/6oz self-raising flour

50g/2oz fine semolina

100g/4oz currants

You can easily whip up these light and crunchy biscuits shortly before tea.

Preheat the oven to 190°C/375°F/gas mark 5. Put the cream or milk and the saffron into a small saucepan, bring just to bubbling point and then leave to cool, stirring once or twice so that the saffron infuses well. Beat the butter and icing sugar together until soft, then beat in the saffron cream – make sure no saffron strands are left on the beater or spoon. Stir the flour, semolina and currants into the mixture with a wooden spoon. Using floured hands, gather the dough into a ball. Roll out on a floured board until it is 5mm/¼in thick and cut into rounds with a pastry cutter. Place on lightly buttered baking sheets and bake for 8–10 minutes, until pale brown. Leave to cool on the baking sheets.

TOP: **MANGO BISCUITS**

CENTRE: **LEMON AND CARDAMOM DROPS (PAGE 239)**

BELOW: **SAFFRON AND CURRANT BISCUITS** ▶

Sophie's Scones

MAKES 8

225g/8oz plain flour

3 teaspoons baking powder

1 level teaspoon salt

25g/1oz caster sugar

50g/2oz butter

1 small egg

125ml/4fl oz buttermilk or yoghurt

Sophie lives on the island of Lewis in the Outer Hebrides. Her Gaelic lilt is so gentle that it is almost lost in the sound of the gale, but she suggests that the less the dough is handled the lighter the scones will be. Buttermilk or yoghurt lightens them still further and the dough should be patted out thickly as thin scones can become hard.

In Scotland these were served spread with whipped cream and then jam. In Devon I would use clotted cream – and it makes all the difference if the jam is home-made.

Preheat the oven to 230°C/450°F/gas mark 8. Sift the flour, baking powder, salt and caster sugar twice through a fine sieve into a bowl. Cut the butter into small pieces and rub it in with your fingertips until the mixture looks like fine breadcrumbs.

Whisk the egg into the buttermilk or yoghurt with a fork. Make a well in the flour mixture, add the liquid and stir with a fork to form a soft dough. Butter a large baking sheet very lightly indeed and place it on a shelf towards the top of the oven. With well-floured hands, gather the dough together and knead very lightly just until smooth. On a floured surface, press the dough out lightly with the palm of your hand, not less than 1.25cm/½in thick.

Using a 5cm/2in cutter, cut out the scones firmly. Gather up the scraps, knead them together lightly and cut out more scones. Using a spatula, transfer the scones gently to the heated baking sheet and sprinkle with a little flour. Then put them in the oven for 10–12 minutes, until risen and pale golden brown.

1 large egg

100g/4oz icing sugar, plus extra for coating

½ teaspoon baking powder

50g/2oz ground almonds

100g/4oz ground rice

1 teaspoon ground cardamom

finely grated rind of 1 large lemon

MAKES ABOUT
1.75–2.5KG/4–5LB

1.2 litres/2 pints water

about 675g/1½lb scented red or pink rose petals

juice of 2 lemons

900g/2lb granulated sugar

Lemon and Cardamom Drops

These lovely aromatic drops, which I developed from an old American recipe, are half biscuit, half little cake. They are easy to make and irresistible.

Preheat the oven to 180°C/350°F/gas mark 4. Whisk the egg with the icing sugar until very pale. Stir in the baking powder, ground almonds, ground rice, cardamom and grated lemon rind. Mix together thoroughly.

Grease a large baking sheet and put some icing sugar in a small bowl. Wet your hands with water, take up a little of the mixture and form into a ball the size of a large marble. Dip one side of the ball in the icing sugar and place it sugar-side up on the baking sheet. Continue like this, placing the balls well spaced out on the baking sheet as they spread quite a bit – you will probably have to cook them in 2 batches.

Bake in the centre of the oven for 10–12 minutes, until palest brown. Carefully ease the biscuits off the baking sheet with a palette knife and leave to cool on a wire rack.

Rose Petal Jam

It was on a trip to Turkey as a young girl that I first tasted rose petal jam. The jar captivated me: it bore a romantic, old-fashioned label showing a flopping damask rose and contained a clear pink, syrupy jam, dotted with translucent petals. I have returned to Turkey frequently since then and every time I look forward to a breakfast of thick yoghurt into which I stir a generous dollop of the scented, runny jam. Here at home I love it on toasted white bread or muffins and I use it as a topping for creamy puddings and tarts.

It is hard to believe that roses can have such a definite taste. They are not sickly scented; instead they have real flavour and a unique texture, too. It is important to use petals from the most scented roses you can find – old-fashioned varieties are usually best. Don't expect this to be a really set jam; it is more like a thick syrup, the same consistency as runny honey.

Wash 4–5 jam jars, arrange on a large baking sheet and put into a low oven to dry. Put the water into a fairly large saucepan and bring to the boil. Add the rose petals, cover the pan and simmer for about half an hour. Then strain the liquid through a sieve into another large saucepan, pressing the rose petals to extract all the liquid. Reserve the rose petals. Strain the lemon juice into the liquid, then add the sugar and stir over a low heat to dissolve. Boil until the syrup reaches 105°C/220°F on a sugar thermometer. Stir in the rose petals and remove from the heat. Stir thoroughly and leave for about 5 minutes before putting into the heated jam jars. Cover immediately with waxed paper discs and screwtop lids.

Apricot and Elderflower Jam

MAKES ABOUT
3-3.5KG/7-8LB

1.75kg/4lb large (dark-orange-
coloured but firm) fresh apricots

300ml/½ pint freshly squeezed
orange juice

juice of 2 lemons

1.75kg/4lb sugar with pectin

15g/½oz unsalted butter

8–10 elderflower heads

3–5 teaspoons apricot brandy
(optional)

Although the excellent combination of gooseberries and elderflowers in jam is fairly well known, fresh apricots are just as successful; in fact I think more so. The large, deep-orange, rose-tinged apricots available nowadays have more juice and flavour than the small, hard, pale ones that for years were the only kind available in this country.

Almost too good for toast, this jam makes a lovely topping for tarts and creamy puddings and is wonderful spooned into Greek-style yoghurt.

Wash 7–8 jam jars, arrange on a large baking sheet and put into a low oven to dry. Slice the apricots in half and remove the stones. Using a nutcracker, pestle or small hammer, crack about half or more of the stones and remove the kernels. Put them into a small saucepan of boiling water, boil for 1 minute, then drain. Now put the kernels and apricot halves into a preserving pan.

Put the orange and lemon juice in a jug and make up to 450ml/¾ pint with water. Add to the apricots. Bring to the boil and simmer for 10–15 minutes, until the apricots are soft but not mushy. Remove from the heat and add the sugar, stirring until it dissolves. Then stir in the butter. Shake and pull the elderflowers off into the apricot mixture and stir in. Return to the heat and boil vigorously for 4–5 minutes. Stir in the brandy if using. Skim off any scum and spoon the jam into the heated jars. Cover immediately with waxed paper discs and screwtop lids.

Greengage and Passion Fruit Jam

MAKES ABOUT
2.75-3KG/6-7LB

1.75kg/4lb greengages

finely grated rind and juice of
2 lemons

8 passion fruit

1.75kg/4lb sugar with pectin

This lovely jam is also excellent made with yellow or orange plums. You could also stir in a little plum liqueur or Calvados before potting the jam .

Wash 6–7 jam jars, arrange on a large baking sheet and put into a low oven to dry. Halve and stone the greengages. Put into a preserving pan with the lemon juice and cook over a low heat, stirring, until the juices run and the fruit is very soft. Remove from the heat. Cut the passion fruit in half and spoon the insides of 4 of them into a sieve. Hold the sieve over the preserving pan and rub the passion fruit juices and membranes through, leaving just the black seeds. Spoon out the remaining 4 passion fruit, including seeds, into the pan and stir to mix. Add the sugar and lemon rind and bring slowly to the boil, stirring to dissolve the sugar. Boil rapidly for 4–5 minutes. Skim off any scum and spoon the jam into the heated jars. Cover immediately with waxed paper discs and lids.

TOP: APRICOT AND ELDERFLOWER JAM

CENTRE: GREENGAGE AND PASSION FRUIT JAM

BELOW: ROSE PETAL JAM (PAGE 239)▶

special
occasions

Cooking for special occasions can be immensely satisfying. It is an expression of friendship to your guests and they are bound to appreciate your efforts. This chapter contains dishes I have served at small dinner parties, larger gatherings and drinks parties. Nothing too formal or elaborate but with the emphasis very much on special flavour and appearance to suit the mood.

450–675g/1–1½lb young vegetables, such as courgettes, small carrots, celery, fennel and cauliflower

50g/2oz walnut pieces

25g/1oz crustless bread

a little milk

1–2 cloves garlic

2 teaspoons green peppercorns in brine

2 tablespoons white wine vinegar

60ml/2fl oz walnut oil

75ml/3fl oz groundnut oil

3 tablespoons Greek-style yoghurt

sea salt

black pepper

225g/8oz wholemeal flour

4 level teaspoons baking powder

3 teaspoons paprika

½ teaspoon cayenne pepper

2 teaspoons caraway seeds

350g/12oz strong-flavoured cheese, grated

225g/8oz butter

4 egg yolks

Raw Vegetables with a Walnut Dip

This is useful for a drinks party, or you can serve it as a first course. Vary the vegetables according to what is really fresh in the shops – as long as they are firm enough to hold the sauce.

Wash the vegetables thoroughly and cut them into 5–6cm/2–2½in sticks or pieces. Leave to one side. Put the walnut pieces into a food processor and whizz until finely ground.

Dip the bread into a small bowl of milk and then squeeze dry. Peel the garlic and chop roughly. Put the squeezed-out bread, garlic, green peppercorns and vinegar into the food processor with the walnuts and whizz to a thick mush. With the motor running, gradually add the oils and whizz until you have a fairly smooth mixture. Then whizz in the yoghurt and season to taste with crushed sea salt – if you want it more peppery, add a little black pepper. Spoon the mixture into a bowl, put it in the centre of a large plate and arrange the prepared vegetables round the bowl.

Light Wholemeal Cheese Straws

Cheese straws are universally popular at a party and these are an especially good version. You can vary them by substituting 2 teaspoons of curry powder for the paprika. Conveniently, the straws can also be made several days ahead.

Sift the flour and baking powder into a bowl, add the paprika, cayenne pepper and caraway seeds and mix all evenly together. Then stir in the grated cheese. Cut the butter into small pieces and rub it into the flour and cheese mixture with your fingertips. Add the egg yolks and mix with a wooden spoon to a stiff dough.

Preheat the oven to 220°C/425°F/gas mark 7. Gather the dough into a ball and press out with your hands on a floured surface. Then roll out with a floured rolling pin to about 1.25cm/½in thick. Cut into rectangular strips about 7.5 x 1.25cm/3 x ½in and lay them slightly apart on ungreased baking sheets. Bake towards the top of the oven for 8–12 minutes or until a light golden brown.

Cool and then keep in an airtight container until needed. They are even nicer if reheated slightly before eating.

RAW VEGETABLES WITH A WALNUT DIP▶

Cheese and Anchovy Biscuits

MAKES 45-60

225g/8oz plain flour

2 teaspoons baking powder

4–5 pinches cayenne pepper

2 teaspoons caster sugar

175g/6oz unsalted butter

2 x 50g/2oz tins anchovy fillets

100g/4oz strong Cheddar cheese, grated

freshly grated Parmesan cheese, for sprinkling

People really appreciate freshly made nibbles to eat with drinks. For these light and thin savoury biscuits you can make the dough as far in advance as you like and keep it in a long roll in the freezer, ready to be quickly made into biscuits.

Sift the flour, baking powder, cayenne pepper and sugar into a bowl. Cut the butter into small pieces and rub into the flour until crumbly. Drain the oil from the anchovies into the mixture, slice the anchovy fillets into very small pieces and stir them into the mixture with the grated Cheddar. Using floured hands, gather up the dough into 2 balls and form each ball into a long roll, either round- or oval-shaped, about 4cm/1½in in diameter. Wrap each roll in cling film and place carefully on a flat surface in the freezer.

To bake the biscuits, preheat the oven to 180°C/350°F/gas mark 4. Take a frozen roll from the freezer and, using a very sharp knife, slice off pieces of dough as thinly as possible. Place fairly close together on a large baking sheet. Wrap the remaining part of the roll up again and put it back in the freezer. Sprinkle the biscuits with a little grated Parmesan and bake in the centre of the oven for 7–8 minutes, until pale brown. Ease the biscuits off the baking sheet with a palette knife while still warm. Cool on a wire rack.

Cheeseballs with Pink Peppercorns

MAKES 30

450g/1lb curd cheese

4 tablespoons double cream

275g/10oz blue cheese

2 heaped teaspoons pink peppercorns in brine, roughly crushed

a little olive oil

very large bunch fresh parsley

salt

black pepper

TOP: CHEESEBALLS WITH PINK PEPPERCORNS

CENTRE: LIGHT WHOLEMEAL CHEESE STRAWS (PAGE 244)

BELOW: CHEESE AND ANCHOVY BISCUITS

It is useful if nibbles for a party can be made well ahead. If you feel you can afford it, Roquefort cheese has the best flavour of all for this recipe. But otherwise a strong Gorgonzola or even good old Danish blue does well for these pretty little green and white balls, which are best eaten off toothpicks. Bottled pink peppercorns are sold in most supermarkets.

Put the curd cheese into a bowl and stir in the cream with a wooden spoon. Crumble in the blue cheese and work in thoroughly. Stir the crushed pink peppercorns into the mixture. Season to taste with salt, if necessary, and pepper.

Lightly oil your hands with olive oil and take up enough of the mixture to roll into a marble-sized ball. Continue like this, re-oiling your hands when necessary.

Chop the parsley very finely and spread it out on a flat surface. Then take up the balls and roll them one by one, first in the parsley and then lightly in your hands again so the parsley sticks on. Place the balls separately on baking sheets or large plates and chill, or freeze if you are making them in advance. When frozen, put together in a plastic bag. To thaw, arrange the frozen balls on serving dishes and thaw in the refrigerator. Serve straight from the fridge.

Barbary Duck Breasts with Blackberry Sauce

SERVES 4

3 tablespoons oyster sauce

1 teaspoon cayenne pepper

4 Barbary duck breast fillets

1 bunch spring onions

450g/1lb blackberries

25g/1oz caster sugar

300ml/½ pint unsweetened apple juice

2 tablespoons sherry vinegar

3 teaspoons arrowroot or cornflour

sea salt

black pepper

The French Barbary duck is killed when it is older than a normal Aylesbury-type duck and has darker, more gamey-flavoured flesh. Autumn fruits such as apples, quince and, as in this recipe, blackberries go especially well with duck. Make sure your grill is really hot so that the duck flesh remains pink and tender while the outside browns darkly.

Put the oyster sauce into a shallow dish and stir in the cayenne pepper. Then add the duck breast fillets, smear thoroughly with the oyster sauce and leave on one side.

Next make the sauce. Trim the spring onions and slice them across finely, using as much of the green part as possible. Put the blackberries into a saucepan with the caster sugar and apple juice. Bring up to bubbling and simmer in the open pan for 5 minutes until the blackberries are soft and the juices running. Stir in the sherry vinegar and remove from the heat. Put 1 tablespoon of water in a cup, add the arrowroot or cornflour, stir until smooth and then mix into the blackberries. Return to the heat, bring to the boil, and stir for about 2 minutes, until the sauce has thickened, adding the sliced spring onions about half way through. Remove from the heat and season with salt and black pepper. Keep in a warm place while you grill the duck breasts.

Heat the grill to its highest and grill the breasts on the flesh side for 4–5 minutes. Then turn and grill for another 3–5 minutes, until the skin is very dark brown. Put the fillets on a board and, using a very sharp knife, slice them thinly lengthways. Arrange the slices on heated serving plates and spoon the sauce next to them.

Poussins with Asparagus and Vermouth Sauce

SERVES 4

225g/8oz thin asparagus

4 poussins

12–16 thin rashers rindless smoked streaky bacon

750ml/1¼ pints dry vermouth

300ml/½ pint double cream

4 tablespoons milk

2 teaspoons sherry vinegar

sea salt

black pepper

Poussins are good for a small dinner party as fewer people always seem to eat more, and a whole bird makes a generous portion. They look like a special treat and the flesh is fine textured and moist. You only need the lightest first course, such as a clear soup.

Serve with new potatoes and a salad of halved cherry tomatoes with chopped fresh mint.

Preheat the oven to 190°C/375°F/gas mark 5. Remove any tough lower part of the stalk from the asparagus and then cut the tips off and put on one side. Steam or boil the stems until really soft and put them aside too. Then steam or boil the tips for a few minutes, until just tender but still bright green. Rinse with cold water to cool quickly and set aside.

Put the poussins in a roasting pan and place the bacon rashers closely together over the breasts and thighs of the birds, cutting the bacon to fit. Cook the birds in the centre of the oven for 40–45 minutes, pouring the vermouth into the roasting pan about 15 minutes before the end of cooking. At this stage put the cooked asparagus stems into a food processor with the cream and milk and whizz to a purée. Then rub this purée through a sieve into a bowl.

When the poussins are cooked, transfer them to a warm serving dish or individual plates (emptying any juices from their body cavities back into the roasting pan). Add the sherry vinegar to the pan juices and bring up to bubbling on top of the stove, then stir in the puréed asparagus mixture and bubble again, stirring all the time, for about 1 minute. Finally, stir in the reserved asparagus tips, remove from the heat, season to taste with salt and black pepper and pour into a bowl to serve with the poussins. If the birds are on individual plates, spoon the sauce on to each plate around them.

Pasta Stuffed with Veal and Fennel with Gorgonzola Sauce

SERVES 4

1 large red or orange pepper

1 large bulb fennel

2 large cloves garlic

2 teaspoons coriander seeds

3 tablespoons olive oil

450g/1lb lean minced veal

8 sheets fresh or no-need-to-precook lasagne

salt

black pepper

For the sauce:

25g/1oz butter

25g/1oz plain flour

600ml/1 pint milk

75g/3oz Gorgonzola cheese

Pasta is often impractical for entertaining as it needs cooking at the last minute. However, this flavourful dish is more suitable as you can even make it the day before if you like. Accompany it with a green leaf or frisée salad.

Cut the pepper in half, discard the seeds and stem and chop the flesh finely. Cut the base and tough stalks off the fennel and discard any scarred outer parts, reserving any green feathery bits to use as garnish later. Chop the fennel finely. Peel the garlic and chop finely. Roughly crush the coriander seeds.

Put the olive oil into a large, deep frying pan, add the chopped pepper, fennel and crushed coriander seeds and stir for a moment or two. Then cover and leave to cook, stirring occasionally, for about 10 minutes. When the vegetables are soft, add the garlic to the pan and stir for another minute or two, then increase the heat and stir in the minced veal. Stir around with a wooden spoon until the meat has separated, then cook for about 5 minutes. Season well and then turn the mixture into a bowl to cool slightly. Spoon some on to the centre of each sheet of lasagne, roll the pasta loosely round the filling and place each piece carefully in an oiled rectangular ovenproof dish, join-side down.

To make the sauce, gently melt the butter in a saucepan. Remove from the heat and, using a wooden spoon, stir in the flour until smooth. Gradually stir in the milk, then return to the heat and bring to the boil, stirring all the time until thickened. Remove from the heat again and crumble in the Gorgonzola. Stir until the cheese has melted, then season with black pepper, adding salt only if necessary. Gradually pour the sauce over the stuffed pasta, letting it sink down to the bottom of the dish as well.

You can either cook the dish now and then reheat it or you can cook it later. To cook, preheat the oven to 190°C/375°F/gas mark 5 and bake just above the centre for 35–40 minutes, until speckled brown.

Glossy Duck with Kumquats and Almonds

SERVES 4

4 duck joints

1 tablespoon groundnut or
   sunflower oil

2 large cloves garlic

2 teaspoons paprika

2 teaspoons ground cinnamon

3–4 pinches cayenne pepper

50g/2oz whole almonds, unskinned

150ml/¼ pint freshly squeezed
   orange juice

juice of 1 lemon

2 tablespoons honey mixed with
   150ml/¼ pint warm water

100g/4oz kumquats

small handful fresh coriander leaves

salt

The glowing colour of kumquats intensifies with cooking. Their skin is not bitter and the refreshing orange flavour goes well with rich ingredients such as duck and with warm spices such as these. Serve with basmati rice, or boiled potatoes and a green vegetable.

Prick the skin of the duck joints all over with a fork. Put the oil into a large frying pan and tip to coat the base thinly. Place over a high heat and fry the duck joints skin-side downwards until they are browned, then fry briefly on the other side. Transfer the joints to a large saucepan.

Peel the garlic, slice across finely and scatter over the duck, together with the paprika, cinnamon, cayenne pepper and almonds. Pour in the orange and lemon juice and the honey water. Bring to the boil, then cover and simmer gently.

Meanwhile, slice the kumquats lengthways and remove any pips. After the duck has been simmering for 20 minutes, add the kumquats, cover and simmer for another 20–30 minutes, until the duck is cooked through and tender. Using a slotted spoon, remove the duck joints, almonds and kumquats from the pan and arrange in a serving dish. Keep warm in a low oven while you boil the pan juices fiercely until they are much reduced, thickened and glossy. Remove from the heat and add salt to taste. Spoon the sauce over the duck just before serving and scatter with the coriander leaves.

The name kumquat means golden orange, although it is not strictly a member of the citrus family, just a distant relation. The kumquat has a thin, aromatic and edible skin which is sweet rather than bitter, combining the scented flavour of its pure white blossom with the sharp, citrussy taste of the flesh.

If you want to make an exceptional Seville orange marmalade, add slices of kumquat to it, or even whole kumquats, which look beautiful in the jar amongst the peel and the clear orange syrup. Kumquats, pricked and cooked in a sugar syrup and then put in a jar with an equal amount of brandy or vodka, can be stored indefinitely to provide a wonderful accompaniment to ice creams or creamy puddings.

Guinea Fowl with an Anchovy and Rosemary Sauce

SERVES 6-8

1.1–1.35kg/2½–3lb leeks

1.1–1.35kg/2½–3lb small potatoes

5–6 tablespoons extra virgin olive oil

3 tablespoons sherry vinegar

2 guinea fowl

50g/2oz tin anchovy fillets

4 large cloves garlic

300ml/½ pint double cream

300ml/½ pint full cream milk

2 good sprigs fresh rosemary

salt

black pepper

Guinea fowl have a fine texture but can taste bland. Here they are enhanced by the wonderful combination of rosemary and anchovies.
Anchovies are one of my favourite flavourings; they add not only salt but much more, and dissolved in a creamy sauce in this way no fishiness at all.

Preheat the oven to 200°C/400°F/gas mark 6. Wash and peel the leeks, cut them across in roughly 5cm/2in pieces and put in a large, deep roasting pan. Peel the potatoes and cut them across in fairly thick slices. Arrange the potato slices among the leeks and sprinkle with salt and black pepper. Drizzle the olive oil and sherry vinegar over the top, then lay the guinea fowl on the mixture, smearing the birds with a little more olive oil and sprinkling them with salt and pepper. Now cover the roasting pan with 2 layers of foil, pressing it securely around the edges. Put the roasting pan on the centre shelf of the oven for 1¾ hours, taking the foil off for the last 15 minutes.

While the guinea fowl are cooking, empty the anchovies and their oil into a small saucepan and stir constantly over a gentle heat until the anchovies disintegrate completely to a purée. Remove from the heat.

Now peel the garlic and put the cloves into the saucepan with the cream and milk. Stir together and add the rosemary and a sprinkling of salt and black pepper. Put the pan back over the heat, bring just up to the boil, then lower the heat and simmer as gently as possible for about 25 minutes, stirring often, until the garlic cloves are very soft and the creamy mixture is the thickness of a pouring sauce. When the sauce is ready, pour it through a sieve into another saucepan, rubbing it with a spoon to press the garlic and anchovies through and discarding the rosemary. Stir and keep on one side.

Just before you are ready to eat, reheat the sauce and pour it into a serving jug. Put the guinea fowl on a carving board. Remove the leeks and potatoes from the roasting pan with a slotted spatula and put them in a serving bowl. Put the roasting pan over a high heat and boil up the juices for 2–3 minutes, until reduced by about half, then pour them over the vegetables. As you carve the guinea fowl on to individual plates, pour some of the cream sauce over the slices.

Saddle of Lamb with Sweet Garlic and Saffron Sauce

SERVES 10

about 2kg/4½lb saddle of lamb

about 2 tablespoons fresh rosemary leaves

50g/2oz tin anchovy fillets

3 teaspoons bottled green peppercorns

juice of 2 lemons

4 tablespoons sherry

6 tablespoons olive oil

300ml/½ pint double cream

generous pinch saffron strands

8–10 large cloves garlic

2 teaspoons caster sugar

3 tablespoons Greek-style yoghurt

sea salt

black pepper

A saddle of lamb is a fine sight. I made this for Easter one year, hence the saffron sauce, as saffron is traditionally associated with the spring feast. The garlic for the creamy sauce is blanched and then roasted underneath the meat so it becomes mild and sweet. Prepare the saddle for cooking the day before. It should be carved in long thin strips down the length of the joint.

Using a sharp knife, make incisions in the lamb on the underside of the joint. Put the rosemary leaves, anchovy fillets and their oil, green peppercorns, lemon juice, sherry and 5 tablespoons of the olive oil into a food processor and whizz until as smooth as possible. Put the lamb into a large roasting pan and rub the puréed mixture all over the underside of the joint, pressing it firmly into the incisions. Leave the lamb underside-upwards, covered with a cloth, in a cold place until the next day, basting occasionally with any juices that seep on to the bottom of the pan.

Before you cook the lamb, put the cream into a saucepan with the saffron and bring to the boil, then remove from the heat and leave on one side to infuse. Peel the garlic and cut each clove lengthways into quarters or halves, depending on size. Bring a small pan of water to the boil, drop in the garlic and simmer for 2 minutes, then drain. Preheat the oven to 230°C/450°F/gas mark 8.

Turn the saddle of lamb over in the pan and smear the skin all over with the remaining olive oil and some crushed sea salt. Put on the centre shelf of the oven and, after 10 minutes, turn the oven down to 180°C/350°F/gas mark 4. Remove the roasting pan from the oven, put the blanched garlic underneath the meat and return to the oven. Roast for 20 minutes per 450g/1lb for lamb which will be pale pink and juicy in the centre. Then turn off the heat, open the oven door slightly and leave the meat for about 20 minutes. Remove the saddle of lamb from the roasting pan and put on a carving board on top of the stove.

Now make the sauce. Pour the excess fat from the roasting pan, leaving the juices and garlic in the pan. Stir in the caster sugar. Pour the saffron cream into the pan and bring to bubbling on top of the stove, stirring all the time. Bubble, still stirring, for about 2 minutes, then remove from the heat, season to taste with salt and black pepper, stir in the yoghurt and pour into a heated sauce bowl to serve with the carved lamb.

1.75–2kg/4–4½lb shoulder of lamb, boned

juice of 1 lemon

1 tablespoon olive oil

1 glass fresh orange juice

300ml/½ pint double cream

salt

black pepper

For the stuffing:

1 medium-sized mango, not too ripe

50g/2oz plain cashew nuts

2 large cloves garlic

1–2 fresh red chillies

finely grated rind of 1 lemon

1 egg, lightly whisked

Mango-stuffed Lamb for Easter

A boned and stuffed joint of meat makes for easier carving and a more complex flavour. This unusual stuffing also adds moisture. Ask your butcher to bone the shoulder of lamb but not to roll it up.

Well beforehand, lay the boned lamb out and, if it has not got deep pockets to hold the stuffing, make 2 or 3 with a sharp knife. Then smear the flesh all over with the lemon juice and olive oil and leave, covered, in the fridge for several hours or overnight. Then take the lamb from the fridge and let it stand at room temperature for at least an hour before cooking; this will bring out the flavour.

To prepare the stuffing, cut the mango up as well as you can, cutting off the skin and chopping the flesh up fairly small. Chop the cashew nuts roughly. Peel the garlic and chop finely. Cut open the chilli lengthways under running water, discard the seeds and stem and chop the flesh finely. Put all the chopped ingredients into a bowl, add the grated lemon rind, egg and a sprinkling of salt and mix all together.

Preheat the oven to 170°C/325°F/gas mark 3. Spoon the stuffing into the pockets of the lamb. Roll up the meat loosely to enclose the stuffing and either tie it up with string or secure with skewers, pushing back any stuffing that has fallen out during the rolling or handling. Rub the joint with oil and salt.

Put the lamb in a roasting pan and cook just above the centre of the oven for about 1½–1¾ hours for fairly pink meat. Turn off the oven and leave the lamb in it to rest with the door slightly open for 20–25 minutes before carving.

To make a delicious gravy, remove the lamb from the roasting pan and place on a carving board. Pour the excess fat from the roasting pan and then add the orange juice and double cream to the pan juices. Season with salt and black pepper and bubble in the pan, stirring for about a minute. Pour the gravy into a sauceboat and serve with the lamb.

Plum Duck with Kirsch Sauce

juice of 4 oranges

300ml/½ pint water

5–6 blades mace

8 breast and wing joints of duck

1.1kg/2½lb firm red plums

a little olive oil

600ml/1 pint double cream

3–5 tablespoons kirsch

thin slices of lemon, to garnish

salt

black pepper

This is a good dish for an autumn dinner party when there is a glut of red plums. Butchers and supermarkets now sell duck joints; otherwise ask for 2 small to medium ducks to be cut in quarters.

Put the orange juice, water and mace into a large, heavy-based saucepan, season with salt and pepper and bring to the boil. Put in the joints of duck, cover the pan and simmer gently for 15–20 minutes. Then remove the duck and pat dry with absorbent paper. Strain the liquid into another saucepan and keep on one side.

Preheat the oven to 240°C/475°F/gas mark 9. Cut the plums in half and remove the stones. Spread the plums, cut-side down, over the bottom of a large roasting pan and lay the duck on top. Smear the duck joints generously with olive oil and season well with salt and pepper. Cook towards the top of the oven for 20–25 minutes, until a rich golden brown. Then put the duck in a serving dish. Take the plums from the pan with a slotted spoon and arrange around the duck. Keep warm in a low oven while you make the sauce.

Pour off any excess fat from the roasting pan and pour the remaining juices into the saucepan containing the reserved cooking liquid. Boil up fiercely for about 8 minutes, until reduced and thickened, then stir in the cream and bring up to the boil for 1 minute. Remove from the heat and stir in the kirsch, salt and pepper to taste. Pour the sauce into a sauce boat. Garnish the duck with lemon slices and serve with the sauce.

Pork Fillets Rolled with Sage, Rosemary and Gruyère Cheese

SERVES 6 - 8

2 pork fillets, weighing about 350g/12oz each

¼ nutmeg

good handful fresh sage leaves

3–4 good sprigs fresh rosemary

225g/8oz Gruyère cheese

50g/2oz butter

300ml/½ pint soured cream

freshly grated Parmesan cheese, to serve

salt

black pepper

This dish looks as if you have made a real effort for your dinner party but it is very easy to do. Serve with small cubed potatoes smeared with olive oil, seasoned and cooked in a shallow pan in the top of the oven while you cook the pork underneath – and a green vegetable or salad.

Preheat the oven to 170°C/325°F/gas mark 3. Put the pork fillets, spaced apart, between 2 large sheets of greaseproof paper or cling film that have been smeared with oil. Then beat with a rolling pin until the meat has spread out thinly – it should be about 3mm/⅛in thick. Remove the paper, lay the fillets out and grate the nutmeg all over them. Finely chop the sage and rosemary and sprinkle evenly over the fillets, followed by salt and black pepper. Slice the cheese as thinly as possible and lay it evenly on top of the herbs. Roll each fillet up from the shortest end, folding over the edges of the meat to enclose the cheese.

Carefully put the rolls into a roasting pan, dot with butter, cover the pan with foil and cook for 1–1½ hours, until the cheese has just begun to ooze out and the juices run clear when a skewer is inserted in the meat. Transfer the rolls to a serving plate. Spoon the soured cream over them, sprinkling generously with Parmesan. To serve, cut the rolls across in round slices, using a sharp knife.

450g/1lb skinless streaky pork

450g/1lb pie veal

350g/12oz skinless chicken breast fillets

1 heaped tablespoon honey

finely grated rind of 1 lemon

1 teaspoon coriander seeds

1 teaspoon bottled green peppercorns

2 tablespoons tomato purée

225g/8oz rindless thin rashers streaky bacon

1 egg, beaten, to glaze

salt

black pepper

For the pastry:

350g/12oz plain flour

½ teaspoon salt

200g/7oz butter

4 tablespoons water

Political Pie

The general election was once described by H. G. Wells as 'Democracy's ceremonial, its feast, its great function'. Nowadays election night has become like a national party, with people all over the country gathering together to eat and drink and pass the night away while the results filter through.

I created this pork, veal and chicken pie for an election party in 1983 to keep friends going through the main rush of results in the early hours of the morning. It has remained a favourite.

To make the pastry, sift the flour and salt into a bowl. In a saucepan gently melt the butter in the water over a low heat and pour into the flour, stirring with a wooden spoon until you have a dough. Form into a ball, wrap in cling film and leave to cool. Grease a deep 17.5–20cm/7–8in loose-based cake tin.

Using a sharp knife, cut the pork and veal into small pieces and the chicken into slightly larger ones. Put the 3 different meats into separate bowls and season them all very well with salt and pepper. Then stir the honey into the pork, the lemon rind and coriander seeds into the chicken and the green peppercorns and tomato purée into the veal.

Preheat the oven to 170°C/325°F/gas mark 3. Cut off three-quarters of the cold pastry, shape into a ball and roll out on a floured surface into a circle large enough to line the cake tin and overlap the edges. Fit into the tin, pressing the pastry against the sides. Pack in the prepared meats in 3 layers, with bacon rashers in between: veal first, then chicken and finally the pork. Press the filling compactly down and fold the overlapping pastry edges over it.

Roll out the remaining pastry into a circle big enough to form a lid. Place on top of the cake tin and press the rolling pin around the edges to cut off the excess pastry. Moisten the underside edges of the pastry lid with water and press down lightly. Roll out the trimmings and cut out decorations or appropriate wording. Arrange them on top of the pie. Pierce 2 holes in the top and glaze with the beaten egg.

Cook the pie just below the centre of the oven for 2¼–2½ hours, until a rich golden brown, then leave in the tin until cool. Press the pie up out of the tin and transfer it carefully to a serving plate. Serve cold, but not chilled, and cut with a very sharp knife.

Poulet Vallée d'Auge, Devon style

SERVES 6

6 free range or cornfed chicken breast joints

600ml/1 pint dry cider

350g/12oz shallots

3 dessert apples

25g/1oz butter

150ml/¼ pint Calvados

300ml/½ pint double cream

sea salt

black pepper

On holiday in Devon a friend boasted that I would appreciate his cooking skills if he made a famous Normandy chicken dish from the Vallée d'Auge, which incorporates cream, cider, apples and Calvados, the apple brandy. Devon, with its bounty of cream, cider and apples, seemed the perfect place to recreate it. But my friend couldn't remember the exact recipe, so we cooked it together and I added some shallots for the wonderful sweetness they impart. It may not have been quite a classic dish but it was truly delicious. Plain steamed potatoes and a green vegetable or carrots go best with the creamy sauce.

Pierce the skin of the chicken joints in several places to allow the cider marinade to penetrate the flesh. Lay the chicken in a roasting pan, pour the cider over it, cover the pan with cling film and leave to marinate in a cool place for at least 3 hours, turning the chicken every now and then.

Meanwhile, peel the shallots but keep them whole. When ready to cook the chicken, preheat the oven to 220°C/425°F/gas mark 7. Remove the cling film from the roasting pan but leave the chicken in the marinade. Make sure the pieces are skin-side upwards. Place the peeled shallots amongst the chicken and sprinkle all over with salt and black pepper. Cook towards the top of the oven for about 1 hour, until the chicken has browned and the shallots feel soft when you insert a small sharp knife in the centre.

While the chicken is cooking, core the unpeeled apples and slice across in rings about 5mm/¼in thick. Melt the butter in a frying pan over a gentle heat and fry the apple rings on both sides until soft and pale gold. Leave in the pan on top of the stove.

When the chicken is cooked, remove it from the roasting pan with the shallots and place in a single layer in a warmed shallow dish. Pour the Calvados into a saucepan, bring to the boil, hold a lighted match over the pan until the liquid bursts into flame and then pour it all over the chicken. Keep warm in a very low oven while you make the sauce.

Pour the cider marinade and chicken juices (carefully pouring off excess fat first) into a largish saucepan and boil up fiercely over a high heat for 6–12 minutes, until well reduced to about a quarter of the original amount. Then stir in the cream and boil up again for about 5 minutes, until slightly thickened. Taste, add salt and pepper if needed and pour all over the chicken and shallots. Garnish with the fried apple slices and serve at once.

Roast Rib of Beef Stuffed with Smoked Oysters, with Chilled Cucumber Sauce

SERVES 10

1 tin smoked oysters

large bunch fresh parsley

1 small onion, red-skinned if possible

2.25kg/5lb rib of beef on the bone

a little olive oil

sea salt

black pepper

For the sauce:

1 cucumber

3 tablespoons plain yoghurt

2 teaspoons lemon juice

2–3 pinches cayenne pepper

600ml/1 pint double cream

Although I eat less meat than I used to, a large piece of rare roast beef remains one of my favourite treats. I particularly like this way of roasting it, as the oysters add a mild and irresistible smoky flavour to the meat. It is a simple idea which I thought up years ago but which, combined with the refreshing sauce, I find hard to improve upon.

Put the oysters in a bowl. Chop the parsley finely. Peel the onion, chop as small as possible and stir into the oysters with the parsley. Season with plenty of black pepper. Make several deep incisions in the joint with a knife and press the oyster mixture right into them. Rub the joint with olive oil and rub the outside fat with sea salt.

Put the meat into a roasting pan and leave for 3–4 hours at room temperature before cooking. Then preheat the oven to 220°C/425°F/ gas mark 7. Cook the beef towards the top of the oven, basting once or twice, for 10–12 minutes per pound to give rare meat. Then turn off the heat, open the oven door a little and leave the meat to rest for about 20 minutes before carving.

Make the sauce while the beef is cooking. Peel the cucumber, chop finely and put it into a bowl. Add the yoghurt and lemon juice and season with the cayenne pepper and a little salt. Whisk the cream until thick and fold gently into the cucumber mixture. Transfer to a serving bowl. Sprinkle with a pinch more cayenne pepper and keep in the fridge until ready to serve with the beef.

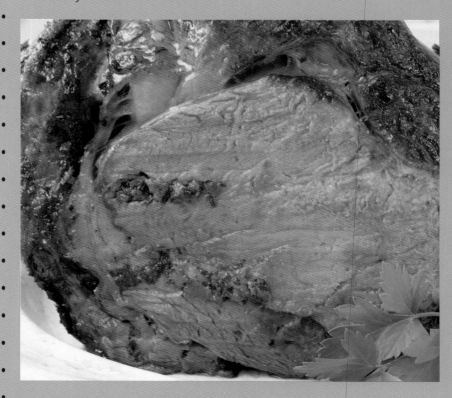

Pumpkin and Goat's Cheese Lasagne with Yoghurt and Cardamom

SERVES 6

900g/2lb piece pumpkin

2 small to medium onions

2 tablespoons olive oil

4–5 cardamom pods

2 teaspoons dried green peppercorns

1 teaspoon caster sugar

225g/8oz goat's cheese log

150–175g/5–6oz fresh lasagne sheets

2 rounded tablespoons cornflour

2 tablespoons milk

425g/15oz plain yoghurt

2 heaped tablespoons coarsely grated Parmesan cheese

salt

black pepper

I come back to this recipe again and again because it is the best variation of lasagne I have ever thought up. The yoghurt sauce is lighter in consistency than the usual béchamel and has a far more interesting flavour, which complements the sweet, golden pumpkin. I use sheep's milk yoghurt but you can also use full-cream cow's milk yoghurt. Melted goat's cheese is irresistible, so all in all it is a wonderful mixture. Lasagne is perfect for a party as it can be prepared well in advance and then cooked when you need it, or kept warm for some time. Serve with a mixed green salad.

Remove any seeds or stringy parts from the pumpkin. Cut off the skin and slice the flesh into 5–7.5cm/2–3in pieces. Steam or boil until soft, then drain, put in a bowl and mash roughly with a fork. Meanwhile, peel and chop the onions. Heat a tablespoon of the olive oil in a large frying pan and fry the onions over a gentle heat, stirring frequently, until soft. Extract the seeds from the cardamom pods and grind in a coffee grinder or pestle and mortar, then add the green peppercorns and grind roughly. Stir the ground cardamom and peppercorns into the pumpkin with the caster sugar and season to taste with salt. Then stir in the fried onions. Spread the remaining olive oil over the bottom of a large rectangular ovenproof dish about 1.2–1.7 litres/2–3 pints in capacity. Slice the goat's cheese across in thin slices without cutting off the rind. Arrange a layer of lasagne sheets over the bottom of the oiled dish. Then spoon a third of the pumpkin and onion mixture evenly over the pasta. Arrange a third of the goat's cheese slices on top of the pumpkin, followed by another layer of lasagne sheets, and so on, ending with a layer of pasta.

Preheat the oven to 200°C/400°F/gas mark 6. Put the cornflour into a saucepan, add the milk and stir until smooth. Stir in the yoghurt, then put on the heat and bring to the boil, stirring in one direction only. Lower the heat and allow barely to simmer, still stirring in one direction, for 8–10 minutes. Then season sparingly with salt and a little black pepper and spoon the sauce evenly over the lasagne. Lastly, sprinkle with the Parmesan. Cook the lasagne on the centre shelf of the oven for about 35 minutes, until it is speckled brown on top.

When I was a child I had no idea that pumpkins were edible. To me they were simply grown to hollow out and carve into leering, candlelit faces for Hallowe'en. Later on in America I discovered pumpkin pie, but its sickly richness discouraged me from thinking of pumpkin as a possible ingredient.

Now, every autumn, supermarket shelves groan under the weight of glowing pumpkins. This means that not only do children have fun with them but their valuable culinary qualities are becoming recognised at last.

12 large skinless chicken breast fillets

juice of 2 lemons

3 teaspoons ground cinnamon

2 teaspoons ground coriander

3 medium yellow or orange peppers

350g/12oz chestnut mushrooms

2–3 fresh red chillies

3 large cloves garlic

5–7.5cm/2–3in piece fresh ginger

2 medium eggs

400g/14oz fresh spinach

salad leaves and fresh coriander
    leaves, to garnish

salt

freshly ground black pepper

Spicy Chicken Catherine Wheels

These decorative tricoloured spirals can be prepared at least two days in advance and kept in the fridge. The only attention they need, shortly before the party, is to slice them and arrange neatly on a serving dish. Free range or cornfed chicken breast fillets are best.

Lay the chicken breast fillets on a large sheet of cling film, well spaced out. Lay another piece of cling film on top and bang with a rolling pin until the chicken has flattened out. Put the lemon juice in a bowl and stir in the spices and a little freshly ground black pepper. Lift off the top layer of cling film and spread the spiced lemon juice over the chicken. Lay the cling film loosely over the top again and leave for half an hour. Meanwhile, cut the peppers in half, discard the seeds and stem and put the halves, skin-side up, under a hot grill until blackened all over. Wrap in a plastic bag or tin foil until cool, then peel off the skin, slice the peppers across very thinly and put into a mixing bowl.

Put the mushrooms in a food processor, whizz to chop finely, then add them to the peppers. Cut the chillies open lengthways under running water, discard the seeds and stems and chop finely. Peel the garlic and ginger and chop finely. Add these ingredients to the bowl and season with salt. Whisk the eggs lightly and stir into the mixture.

Preheat the oven to 190°C/375°F/gas mark 5. Remove the stalks from the spinach and chop the leaves as finely as possible. Spread the chopped spinach evenly on top of each chicken breast fillet, patting it down. Then spread the pepper and mushroom mixture on top of the spinach. Roll up each chicken fillet, enclosing the stuffing. Don't worry if they fall apart a bit; just press together. Wrap each fillet in a fairly large piece of oiled foil to enclose completely, then wrap in a second piece of foil.

Put the bundles in a roasting pan and cook in the oven for 40–45 minutes. Leave to cool and then chill in the fridge, still wrapped up. To serve, unwrap the chilled bundles and cut across into slices 1.25cm/½in thick. Arrange salad leaves on large serving plates with the chicken slices on top and scatter with coriander leaves.

Spiced Pigeon and Spinach Pie with Apricots

SERVES 6-8

6 wood pigeons

3 large cloves garlic

5cm/2in piece fresh ginger

350g/12oz red onions

100g/4oz dried apricots

1 tablespoon groundnut oil

65g/2½oz butter

2 teaspoons ground cumin

2 teaspoons ground cinnamon

1 rounded teaspoon paprika

450g/1lb fresh spinach

1 heaped tablespoon thick-cut marmalade

cayenne pepper

400–450g/14–16oz filo pastry

salt

The best pigeons I have ever tasted were cooked simply in a little restaurant on the straight road that leads out of Cairo to the Pyramids. Although they are cheaper than any other game birds, pigeons can still seem a treat. They have a full flavour which goes specially well with spices, ginger and garlic, as in this rather exotic pie.

The plump breasts of the pigeon are more or less the only part you can eat. You can put the carcasses in a large saucepan of water with root vegetables and boil up a delicious game stock to use for a risotto or soup later.

This pie is practical for a dinner party as it can either be kept warm in a low oven or made ahead and reheated. Serve simply with a salad and new potatoes and a bowl of whole-milk yoghurt as a sauce.

Using a very sharp knife, slice the breasts off the pigeons and remove the skin. Cut the flesh into thin slices. Peel the garlic and ginger and chop finely. Peel the onions and chop them fairly small. Chop the apricots roughly.

Heat the oil and 15g/½oz of the butter in a large, deep frying pan over a medium heat and stir in the chopped garlic and ginger and the spices. Add the sliced pigeon, stir around for a minute to seal and then stir in the onions and apricots. Cover the pan tightly with foil and leave just bubbling over a low heat for 45 minutes–1 hour, until the pigeon is tender to the bite. Stir the mixture now and then, especially towards the end when the juices evaporate – if all the liquid hasn't evaporated by the time the pigeon is tender, remove the foil and bubble strongly. Meanwhile, wash the spinach and take off the stalks. Bring a large pan of salted water to the boil and plunge in the spinach leaves for just a minute or so. Drain well, pressing out all the liquid, then chop up small.

When the pigeon is done, remove from the heat and stir in the marmalade and spinach. Season to taste with cayenne pepper and salt and leave until cold.

Preheat the oven to 180°C/350°F/gas mark 4. Gently melt the remaining butter in a saucepan. Brush a deep 17.5–18.5cm/7–7½in loose-based cake tin thinly with butter. Lay in a whole sheet of the filo pastry, press it down in the tin and let the ends hang over the sides. Brush the pastry in the tin lightly with butter. Now lay another sheet of pastry across the other way so the tin is completely lined. Continue like this in layers, buttering each sheet and letting the pastry hang out all round the edges of the tin. Spoon in the cold pigeon mixture, then bring the overlapping pastry loosely over the top, sheet by sheet, buttering each piece. The top 2 or 3 layers should be crumpled, sticking up towards the centre.

Cook the pie in the centre of the oven for about 30 minutes, until browned. Then put the tin on a narrower round object and push the pie carefully up and out. Using a wide spatula, lever it carefully off the tin base on to an ovenproof serving plate and put it back in the oven for 20–30 minutes.

Lemon and Orange Salmon Cooked with Bay Leaves

3.25–3.75kg/7½–8½lb whole salmon, gutted, with the head left on

finely grated rind and juice of 3 lemons and 2 oranges

cayenne pepper

at least 20 bay leaves, fresh if possible

a little sunflower oil

900ml/1½ pints creamed smatana

salt

If your budget is limited, farmed salmon remains an ideal, affordable way of feeding people generously at a large party. But it can taste bland so you must pay attention to added flavour. The combination of bay leaves (which go surprisingly well with fish) and citrus rind and juice is most effective, and makes a delicious sauce with creamy smatana. Creamed smatana is a cultured milk product, similar to rich whole-milk yoghurt. It is available at supermarkets and always makes a good alternative to double cream, with the bonus of being about a third of the price.

Using a sharp knife, make deep, slanting cuts across the salmon, about 2.5cm/1in apart, on both sides of the fish. Put the grated lemon and orange rind into a bowl, add 1 teaspoon of cayenne pepper, a sprinkling of salt and the juice of 2 of the lemons. Stir around to mix well. Press this mixture right into the cuts in the salmon and then insert a bay leaf into each cut. Put a few more bay leaves in the body cavity of the salmon. Lay a very large piece of foil on a flat surface and smear all over with sunflower oil. Lay the salmon in the middle of the foil, bring up the sides all round and pour the rest of the lemon and orange juice over the fish. Wrap the fish up securely in the foil, then in 2 more layers of foil to ensure the juices don't escape while cooking.

Preheat the oven to 140°C/275°F/gas mark 1. Put the wrapped fish on the centre shelf and cook for 8 minutes per 450g/1lb – this should produce lightly cooked moist flesh; overcooking will ruin the texture. When the salmon is cooked, remove from the oven and leave it wrapped in the foil for about 20 minutes. Then open one end of the foil and very carefully tip all the juices out into a saucepan. Open out the rest of the foil and slit the skin below the head of the fish and at the back of the tail before peeling it off on one side. Remove the bay leaves and discard. Then carefully turn over the fish to do the same on the other side. Finally, wrap the fish up again and leave to cool.

Meanwhile, make the smatana sauce. Bring the fish cooking juices to the boil in the saucepan and boil fiercely for a few minutes until reduced by about a third. Cool slightly, then put the creamed smatana into a bowl, gradually stir in the cooking juices and season to taste with salt and cayenne pepper. Cover and leave in the fridge.

To serve, open the foil again and carefully transfer the fish to a large serving dish. Garnish with a border of pretty salad leaves, if liked – you can also garnish the centre of the salmon with thin slices of lemon. Pour the smatana sauce into serving jugs.

christmas creations

I have cooked the Christmas meal for 29 years and written countless articles and three books of festive recipes, so you might think I have had just about enough of Christmas cooking. However, each Christmas presents a challenge which I enjoy: to create a new seasonal dish and, of course, to think up yet another way of using the leftover turkey.

Poached Brussels Sprouts on a Spiced Parsnip Bed

SERVES 8-10

1.75 kg/4lb parsnips

6–8 cardamom pods

2 rounded teaspoons coriander seeds

200g/7oz butter

1.35kg/3lb Brussels sprouts

2 large cloves garlic

300ml/½ pint vegetable or chicken stock

freshly grated nutmeg

sea salt

black pepper

Here's a much more interesting way of serving your sprouts for the Christmas meal. Any vegetarian guests will also be pleased as it makes a proper main-course dish for them. The parsnip purée can be prepared in advance and reheated but the sprouts must be cooked at the last minute.

Peel the parsnips, cut them up roughly and steam or boil until soft. Extract the seeds from the cardamom pods, then grind finely in a coffee grinder with the coriander seeds. Put a dry frying pan over a fairly low heat, add the ground spices and stir for a minute, then add half the butter. Stir until melted and then remove from the heat. Purée the parsnips in a food processor with the spiced melted butter and a generous seasoning of salt and pepper. Spread the parsnip purée in a large, round shallow serving dish, bringing it up slightly round the sides. Loosely cover with foil and keep warm in a low oven.

Trim the sprouts, then slice across thinly lengthways. Peel the garlic and slice finely across. Heat the remaining butter and the stock in a pan over a medium heat. When the mixture is bubbling, add the sprouts and garlic. Cover and simmer for 3–4 minutes, until the sprouts are bright green and just soft. Remove the lid and stir the sprouts around over a higher heat until all the liquid has evaporated. Remove from the heat, taste and add salt and pepper if needed. Spoon the sprouts on to the parsnip purée, leaving the purée showing round the sides. Grate a little nutmeg on to the sprouts and serve at once.

Sautéed Spiced Parsnips and Mushrooms

SERVES 6-8

675g/1½lb small parsnips

225g/8oz chestnut mushrooms

2–3 large cloves garlic

5cm/2in piece fresh ginger

1 fresh red chilli

50g/2oz butter

2 tablespoons groundnut oil

2 teaspoons ground cumin

1 teaspoon ground cinnamon

3 teaspoons fennel seeds

generous handful fresh coriander leaves

salt

I prefer to serve this with the turkey instead of rather dried-up roast parsnips. Both parsnips and mushrooms go wonderfully well with spices and garlic and will liven up the slightly bland taste of the bird.

Top and tail the parsnips, then peel them and cut into 1.25cm/½in pieces. Slice the mushrooms across thinly. Peel the garlic and ginger and chop together finely. Cut open the chilli under running water and discard the seeds and stem, then slice across as thinly as possible.

Melt the butter with the oil in a large, deep sauté pan over a medium heat. Add the ground spices and the fennel seeds and stir for 1 minute. Next add the parsnips and stir for 5–8 minutes, until just beginning to soften. Then add the mushrooms, garlic, ginger and chilli and stir for another 5 minutes or until the mushrooms are cooked. Remove from the heat and add salt to taste. Roughly chop the coriander leaves. Just before serving, stir them into the mixture and turn into a heated serving dish.

POACHED BRUSSELS SPROUTS ON A SPICED PARSNIP BED ▶

Chestnut, Parsnip, Apricot and Leek Stuffing

**MAKES ENOUGH FOR A
4.5–6.3KG/10–14LB BIRD**

350g/12oz parsnips

275g/10oz leeks

5cm/2in piece fresh ginger

4 large cloves garlic

75g/3oz dried apricots

75g/3oz butter

2 teaspoons ground cardamom

400g/14oz vacuum-packed chestnuts

1 rounded tablespoon tomato purée

salt

black pepper

This particularly light and moist mixture is for stuffing the body cavity of a turkey or goose. If you like, you can add the finely chopped heart and liver of the bird at the same time as the leeks.

Peel the parsnips and chop them into small pieces. Trim and wash the leeks, slice them in thin rings and then cut the rings in half, using as much of the green part of the leek as possible. Peel the ginger and garlic and chop finely. Chop the apricots up small.

Melt 50g/2oz of the butter over a medium heat in a large, deep frying pan. Add the chopped parsnips and stir around for about 8 minutes until they are almost, but not quite, soft. Using a slotted spatula, transfer the parsnips to a mixing bowl and add the remaining butter to the frying pan. When melted, add the leeks and stir around for 8–10 minutes, until softened, then stir in the ginger, garlic, apricots and ground cardamom. Stir around for another 2 minutes and then turn the contents of the pan into the mixing bowl. Chop up the chestnuts roughly and add them to the cooked ingredients. Using a wooden spoon, gently mix the ingredients together, stirring in the tomato purée and seasoning with salt and pepper. Leave to cool.

Goat's Cheese, Spinach and Walnut Stuffing

100g/4oz soft white goat's cheese

1 large egg, lightly whisked

100g/4oz fresh spinach

75g/3oz walnuts

finely grated rind of 1 lemon and 1 orange

2 teaspoons bottled green peppercorns, crushed

roughly crushed sea salt

You can use this delicious moist stuffing either for the neck cavity of a large turkey or as the main stuffing for a smaller one.

Put the goat's cheese in a bowl and, using a wooden spoon, slowly work in the whisked egg a little at a time. Wash and dry the spinach – this should be done very thoroughly – then chop it up into extremely fine pieces. Lastly, chop up the walnuts as finely as you can. Add the spinach, walnuts, grated lemon and orange rind and crushed peppercorns to the cheese and egg mixture and mix together very well. Season with salt and use to stuff the bird.

Oven-baked Bread Sauce

SERVES 12

1 large onion

150g/5oz brown or white bread

75g/3oz butter

6 cloves

¼ nutmeg, grated

750ml/1¼ pints milk

750ml/1¼ pints double cream

salt

black pepper

An Aga cooker is ideal for this best-of-all bread sauce but it can also be made successfully in a conventional oven set at a very low heat. It is much simpler to prepare than other bread sauces. Some kinds of bread absorb more milk than others, so you will have to check from time to time and add more if necessary. I much prefer it made with brown bread; never use sliced steam-baked bread.

Bread sauce can be made a day or two in advance and kept, covered, in the fridge. This recipe makes a large amount because I find that people eat so much and it's good with ham and cold turkey afterwards. However, halve the quantities if your numbers are small.

Peel the onion and chop it up small. Tear the bread into smallish pieces and put in an ovenproof dish with the onion. Dot with the butter and cloves and sprinkle with the nutmeg, a little salt and black pepper. Mix the milk with the cream and pour over.

Put the uncovered dish into the low oven of the Aga or into an ordinary oven preheated to 120°C/250°F/gas mark ½ for 1½–2 hours, until the milk has been absorbed and you have a fairly thick and creamy sauce. (You can either stir the sauce occasionally while cooking or leave it to form a crust on the top.)

Brussels Sprout Gratinée with Stilton Crust

SERVES 5-6

about 675g/1½lb cooked Brussels sprouts

150ml/¼ pint double cream

1 egg

¼ nutmeg, grated

75g/3oz Stilton cheese

75g/3oz fresh breadcrumbs

½ level teaspoon cayenne pepper

salt

black pepper

Personally, I prefer puréed to whole Brussels sprouts. This useful light lunch or supper dish goes extremely well with cold turkey and ham and is ideal for using up leftover sprouts.

Preheat the oven to 180°C/350°F/gas mark 4. Put the cooked Brussels sprouts into a food processor with the cream, egg and nutmeg and whizz until as smooth as possible. Season with salt and plenty of black pepper and turn into an ovenproof dish.

Crumble the Stilton into a bowl, add the breadcrumbs and cayenne pepper and mix together. Spoon the mixture on top of the sprout purée and spread level. Put on a high shelf in the oven for 25–35 minutes, until the crust is well browned.

Glazed Goose with Special Stuffing

1 x 4.5–6.3kg/10–14lb goose

2 tablespoons caster sugar

2 tablespoons soy sauce

juice of 1 orange

300ml/½ pint apple juice

juice of 1 lemon

salt

black pepper

For the stuffing:

75g/3oz dried apricots

the goose liver

3 cloves garlic

5cm/2in piece fresh ginger

2 dessert apples

50g/2oz butter

2 teaspoons ground coriander

finely grated rind of 1 orange

3–4 pinches cayenne pepper

50g/2oz fresh breadcrumbs

1 large egg, lightly whisked

I have spent many Christmases over the years in deepest South Devon. We often used to have goose instead of turkey because a lady at a nearby farm would fatten one up for us. A goose seems more traditional and old-fashioned than turkey and it usually has a stronger flavour. It's a good change, anyway.

Just as with turkey, an interesting stuffing makes all the difference to the festive bird. If you have already decided to have turkey for Christmas, this stuffing would also do well for it. Remember to stuff the bird and get it ready for roasting the night before. Bread sauce, made with brown bread and added cream, is as good with goose as it is with turkey. To work out how many people a goose will feed, allow 350–450g/12oz–1lb per person. Remember to keep the goose fat for roasting potatoes on a future occasion, if not used on Christmas Day.

To make the stuffing, first cut the apricots up roughly and soak them in water for an hour or two. Remove the giblets and lumps of fat from the inside of the goose. Then chop the goose liver up into small pieces. Peel the garlic and ginger and chop together finely. Peel and core the apples and chop them fairly small. Melt the butter in a large frying pan over a medium heat. Add the chopped garlic, ginger and ground coriander and stir around for a minute or so. Add the chopped liver and toss around for 2–3 minutes. Then add the chopped apples and well-drained apricots and stir around for 3–5 minutes, until the apples are just soft but not broken up. Stir in the grated orange rind, season with cayenne pepper and salt to taste and remove from the heat. Turn the mixture into a bowl and leave to cool.

When cool, stir in the breadcrumbs and the whisked egg. Spoon the stuffing into the neck cavity of the goose. Skewer the neck skin to the back of the bird to enclose it. If there is any stuffing left over, spoon it into the body cavity or into a small covered casserole dish. Now you can leave the goose in a cold place until you are ready to cook it.

Preheat the oven to 180°C/350°F/gas mark 4. Before roasting the goose, rub the skin all over with salt and put the bird, breast-side down, on a rack in a large roasting pan. Place any pieces of goose fat on top of the goose and cover the pan with foil, then roast for 20 minutes per 450g/1lb.

About 45 minutes before the goose has finished cooking, pour as much fat as possible from the pan, leaving any juices behind. (You can pour this fat into another roasting pan now and roast some fully boiled potatoes, cut up rather small, in it at the very top of the oven above the goose.) Turn the goose over so it is breast-side up.

Stir the caster sugar into the soy sauce and brush this mixture all over the goose. Pour the orange juice, apple juice and lemon juice into the roasting pan with the goose and put it back into the oven without any foil for 15–20 minutes, until the bird is richly browned. Transfer the goose to a carving board, bubble the juices in the pan fiercely for 1–3 minutes until slightly reduced and then pour into a gravy jug to serve with the bird.

Holy Land Turkey Pie

SERVES 6-8

675g/1½lb tomatoes

2 medium onions

900–1kg/2–2¼lb skinless boneless cooked turkey

75g/3oz stoned black olives

3 large cloves garlic

1 tablespoon sunflower oil

90g/3½oz butter

2 rounded teaspoons ground coriander

2 rounded teaspoons ground cinnamon

2 level teaspoons cumin seeds

finely grated rind and juice of 1 lemon

1 dessertspoon honey

450g/1lb filo pastry

salt

black pepper

There is always the problem of how to use up leftover turkey. Made with spices, olives and honey, all of which are common in the Holy Land, this pie is thoroughly appropriate for the Christmas season. It can be made in advance up to the uncooked pastry stage, or cooked and kept warm for at least an hour. Serve with a green salad.

Put the tomatoes into a bowl, pour boiling water over them and leave for a minute or two, then drain, peel and cut up roughly. Peel the onions, cut in half and then slice them thinly across. Cut the turkey meat into smallish pieces. Chop the olives roughly. Peel the garlic and chop finely.

Put the oil and 15g/½oz of the butter into a large, deep frying pan over a medium heat, add the sliced onions and stir around until completely soft and browned. Then add the garlic and spices and stir around for a minute or two. Next stir in the chopped tomatoes, lemon rind and juice and the olives and cook, stirring often, until the tomatoes have become a thick mush. Remove the pan from the heat and season to taste with salt and plenty of black pepper. Stir in the honey until dissolved, then transfer the mixture to a large bowl. Mix the turkey meat into the thick tomato sauce and leave to cool.

Preheat the oven to 180°C/350°F/gas mark 4. Gently melt the remaining butter in a saucepan. Brush a deep 17.5–18.5cm/7–7½in loose-based cake tin thinly with butter. Lay a sheet of filo pastry in the tin so that it comes up and over the sides. Brush the pastry thinly with butter and lay another sheet across the other way so the whole tin is lined. Continue like this in layers, buttering each sheet and letting the pastry hang out all round the edge of the tin. Then spoon in the cold turkey and tomato mixture and bring in the overlapping pastry, sheet by sheet loosely over the top, lightly buttering each piece. The top 2 or 3 layers should be especially crumpled.

Cook the pie on the centre shelf of the oven for about 30 minutes, until the top is well browned. Then put the tin on a narrower round object and push the pie carefully up and out of the sides. Using a wide spatula, lever the pie carefully off the base on to an ovenproof serving plate and put back in the oven for 20–30 minutes.

I remember the Christmas when my children stopped believing in Father Christmas. Both my husband and I found it increasingly nerve-racking to creep in and place the stockings noiselessly at the foot of their beds. So one year my six-foot four-inch brother said he would dress up as Father Christmas. At 1.30am, dressed in scarlet sailing oilskins and blinded by a large white sheepskin rug thrown over his head, he stumbled into my children's bedroom carrying their bulging stockings. The children lay quite still during his stormy entrance, apparently asleep, but no one could have slept through the crackle of that stiff plastic suit. As the monstrous Father Christmas left the room, my youngest daughter was heard saying to my son in an urgent whisper, 'Henry, wake up, I've seen him.' But in the morning she told me confidently that she didn't believe in Father Christmas any longer. 'I know', she said, fixing my brother with a meaningful look.

Poultryman's Pie

SERVES 6

900g/2lb potatoes

150ml/¼ pint double cream

75g/3oz Cheddar cheese, grated

¼ nutmeg, grated

2 eggs

2 large onions

900g/2lb skinless boneless cooked
    turkey

450g/1lb tomatoes

75g/3oz butter

2 teaspoons ground cinnamon

handful fresh sage leaves

salt

black pepper

This is really just a Christmas-season shepherd's pie but made with leftover turkey instead of lamb. A nice, homely dish after all the more elaborate feasting.

Peel the potatoes and boil until tender, then drain and mash them with the cream, 50g/2oz of the cheese and the grated nutmeg. Whisk the eggs until frothy and mix them with the mashed potatoes. Season well with salt and plenty of black pepper.

Preheat the oven to 180°C/350°F/gas mark 4. Peel the onions and chop up fairly small. Cut up the turkey into small pieces, either briefly in a food processor or by hand. Put the tomatoes into a bowl, pour boiling water over them and leave for a minute or two, then drain, peel and chop up roughly.

Melt 50g/2oz of the butter in a large, deep frying pan, add the onions and stir over a fairly high heat until they begin to brown. Stir in the cinnamon and remove from the heat. Turn the onions and butter into a large bowl. Roughly chop the sage leaves and mix in, together with the turkey and tomatoes. Season with salt and black pepper. Transfer to a large, fairly shallow ovenproof dish. Spread the mashed potatoes over the top, dot all over with the remaining butter and sprinkle with the remaining grated cheese. Cook in the centre of the oven for 50–60 minutes, until richly browned.

Gratinée of Turkey with Stilton and Almonds

SERVES 6

900–1.1kg/2–2½lb skinless boneless
    cooked turkey

75g/3oz butter, plus a little extra for
    dotting

100g/4oz blanched almonds

2 heaped tablespoons plain flour

750ml/1¼ pints milk

½ small glass brandy or sherry

175g/6oz Stilton cheese, crumbled

2 large cloves garlic, finely chopped

a little freshly grated Parmesan
    cheese

salt

black pepper

A simple and ever-popular way of using up leftover turkey. My children used to love this, especially when they knew it had some brandy in it.

Preheat the oven to 170°C/325°F/gas mark 3. Cut the turkey into pieces and arrange in a large, fairly shallow ovenproof dish. Melt 25g/1oz of the butter in a frying pan and toss the almonds in it for a minute or two until golden brown. Sprinkle them in among the turkey pieces.

Melt the remaining butter in a fairly large saucepan, then remove from the heat and stir in the flour with a wooden spoon. Gradually stir in the milk and then return to the heat and bring to the boil, stirring all the time, until the sauce is thick and smooth. Let it simmer, still stirring, for 2–3 minutes, then add the brandy or sherry, Stilton and garlic. Stir until the cheese has melted, then add salt and black pepper to taste.

Pour the sauce over the turkey and almonds, dot with a little butter and sprinkle with grated Parmesan. Cook in the centre of the oven for 35–40 minutes, until golden brown.

450g/1lb trimmed leeks

1 large onion

5cm/2in piece fresh ginger

50g/2oz butter

1 rounded teaspoon caraway seeds

350–400g/12–14oz vacuum-packed chestnuts

4 teaspoons whole grain mustard

1 egg yolk, beaten

sea salt

black pepper

For the pastry:

350g/12oz plain flour

3 rounded teaspoons paprika

3–4 pinches cayenne pepper

½ teaspoon salt

100g/4oz Stilton cheese

175g/6oz chilled butter

1 egg yolk

3 tablespoons chilled water

Chestnut and Leek Pie with Stilton Pastry

This shiny, star-shaped pie is delicious, whether you are a vegetarian or not. For convenience, you can make it a day or two ahead up to the uncooked pastry stage so that it is ready just to pop in the oven. I find the vacuum-packed chestnuts by far the best.

To make the pastry, sift the flour, paprika, cayenne pepper and salt into a bowl. Crumble in the Stilton and stir in with a knife. Cut the butter into small pieces, add to the bowl and rub in with your fingertips until the mixture resembles breadcrumbs. Using a fork, lightly whisk the egg yolk with the chilled water, then pour it gradually into the flour mixture, mixing with the fork until the pastry begins to stick together. Lightly press the pastry into a ball, wrap it in cling film and chill while you make the filling.

Cut the leeks across into 2.5cm/1in pieces, discarding the base and top. Peel the onion and chop into small pieces. Peel the ginger and chop very finely. Melt the butter in a large, heavy-based frying pan. Add the leeks, onion and caraway seeds and fry over a gentle heat, stirring frequently, until the leeks and onion are soft. Stir in the ginger and fry for another 1–2 minutes. Gently stir in the whole chestnuts and the mustard. Season with sea salt and black pepper and set aside to cool.

Butter a large, flat ovenproof circular plate or pizza tin. Take the pastry from the fridge, cut in half, knead briefly and form into 2 balls. Roll out one ball on a lightly floured surface into a rough circle about 23–25 cm/ 9–10in in diameter. Turn over the edges a little to make a more exact circle and place it on the buttered plate or pizza tin. Spoon the cool leek and chestnut mixture to within 2.5cm/1in of the pastry's edge.

Roll out the second half of the pastry into a similar-sized circle. Then, using a sharp knife, cut all round the outside to make a fairly deep, pointed zigzag pattern like a child's drawing of a many-pointed star. Lay this second piece of pastry on top of the filling and press gently to seal it to the bottom circle of pastry – there should be gaps between the inner parts of the star to allow steam to escape.

Squeeze the pastry trimmings together, then roll them out and cut out 2 or 3 stars to decorate the top of the pie. Moisten the underside of these stars with a little water and press them firmly on top of the pie. Refrigerate the pie for at least 30 minutes, or until you are ready to cook it.

Preheat the oven to 220°C/425°F/gas mark 7. Brush the pastry all over with the beaten egg yolk. Bake the pie in the centre of the oven for 30–35 minutes, until golden brown. If you want to reheat a precooked pie later, it will take 20–25 minutes at 170°C/325°F/gas mark 3.

3 cloves garlic

200g/7oz vacuum-packed chestnuts

3 medium tomatoes, the plum
variety if available

2 tablespoons groundnut oil, plus
extra for brushing

3–5 pinches cayenne pepper

2 teaspoons ground cinnamon

½ teaspoon ground cloves

1 rounded teaspoon caraway seeds

350g/12oz lean minced lamb

50g/2oz tin anchovy fillets

450g/1lb puff pastry

salt

Little Lamb Pies with Chestnuts and Spices

These excellent little spiced pies are useful at Christmas because they can be made ahead and frozen. They are then ready if you have friends round at short notice over the busy Christmas period.

Peel the garlic and chop finely. Cut the chestnuts into pieces. Put the tomatoes into a bowl, pour boiling water over them and leave for 2 minutes, then drain, peel and cut into small pieces. Put the oil in a large frying pan over a medium heat, add the garlic and spices and stir for half a minute. Then add the chopped tomatoes and stir around for 2 minutes. Turn up the heat, add the minced lamb and stir for 8–10 minutes, until the meat is browned and the juices have evaporated. Then stir in the chestnuts and remove from the heat. Cut the anchovies into small pieces and stir into the mixture. Check for seasoning and add salt to taste and more cayenne pepper if wanted. Leave to cool.

Preheat the oven to 220°C/425°F/gas mark 7. Roll out the puff pastry until it is 3–5mm/⅛–¼in thick. Brush either one or two trays of patty tins with oil – you will probably have to make these pies in relays. Use a 7.5cm/3in fluted pastry cutter to cut out enough rounds to line your patty tins. Spoon the cooled filling up to the top of each one. Then, using a 6cm/2½in cutter, cut out the tops. Moisten the edges of the smaller rounds and place on top of the mixture, pressing down slightly round the edges to seal. Brush the pies with a little oil and cut a small hole in the centre of each. Cook on the centre shelf of the oven for about 15 minutes, until well risen and golden brown.

Turn the pies out on to a wire rack and leave until cold, then pack carefully in a plastic container and freeze. When you want to eat them, thaw for an hour or two in the fridge, then put on a baking tray and reheat in a moderate oven for about 15 minutes.

As a result of a diplomatic upbringing spent mostly abroad, I have experienced some very odd Christmases indeed. They took place on a beach and in an Arab garden in the Middle East, and in the high Andes and jungles of South America. But even in Damascus my parents tried to be traditional at Christmas. The turkey we ate ran round our formal garden for weeks beforehand, being fattened up on leftover Embassy meals.

Official visitors were slightly surprised by what they thought was not very Ambassadorial behaviour, and even more so when, on their way up the main stairs for their appointment, I used to pull them into a pitch-dark room on the half landing which I had made into a ghost house. Fake cobwebs brushed against their faces and in the far corner sat my eccentric governess, Miss Ross, dressed up as a witch and playing 'O come, all ye faithful' on her violin.

Christmas Plum Pudding with Fresh Orange, Walnuts, Ginger and Cloves

SERVES 8-10

350g/12oz pitted prunes

100g/4oz crystallized ginger

40g/1½oz walnuts

225g/8oz raisins

coarsely grated rind and juice of 2 oranges

125g/4½oz fresh brown breadcrumbs

125g/4½oz shredded vegetable suet

1 teaspoon ground cloves

3 large eggs

2–3 tablespoons brandy

The original Christmas plum pudding, like mince pies, contained a substantial amount of meat. The meat was combined with prunes (the dried plums that gave the pudding its name), raisins, currants, spices and brown bread. The flour was a much later addition and I find that breadcrumbs and the absence of sugar make a far lighter pudding which is even popular with children (the fruit makes it sweet enough). Serve with brandy butter and cream or crème fraîche. If you want to make a round pudding you can buy special moulds, or I use a foil-lined Chinese rice steamer.

Generously butter a 1.7 litre/3 pint pudding basin. Cut the prunes into fairly small pieces and roughly chop the ginger and walnuts. Put the prunes, ginger and walnuts into a large bowl with the raisins, grated orange rind, breadcrumbs, suet and ground cloves. Stir to mix. In another bowl whisk the eggs until frothy and thickened and stir into the dry ingredients. Lastly stir in the orange juice and brandy (and silver charms if liked). Spoon the mixture into the buttered pudding basin and smooth the top. Cover with a double layer of buttered foil and tie tightly with string, making a handle to lift the basin. Put a metal biscuit cutter or inverted saucer in a large saucepan and stand the pudding basin on top. Pour in enough boiling water to come three-quarters of the way up the sides of the basin. Cover the pan and steam gently for about 6 hours, checking now and then to see if the water needs topping up.

When the pudding is cold, put away in a cool place until Christmas Day. Then replace the foil with clean buttered layers of foil and steam for another hour or so before serving. To serve, turn out on to a warmed serving plate, stick a sprig of holly on top, pour bubbling brandy or brandy mixed with sherry round the pudding and set alight.

Rum Butter with Orange Rind

SERVES 10

225g/8oz unsalted butter

150–175g/5–6oz light muscovado sugar

finely grated rind of 1 orange

4–5 tablespoons dark rum

I love both brandy and rum butter but this one, with its flavour of muscovado sugar and orange rind, is a special favourite.

Cream the butter with an electric whisk until soft. Thoroughly whisk in the sugar, followed by the orange rind, then whisk in the rum a little at a time. (If you use a food processor, simply whizz the first 3 ingredients together until smooth and then add the rum gradually.) Keep in the fridge, but take out and bring to room temperature well before you start the meal. Serve with the Christmas pudding.

Brandy Ice Cream

SERVES 10

2 large egg whites

good pinch of salt

175g/6oz demerara sugar

6 tablespoons water

4–6 tablespoons brandy

450ml/¾ pint whipping cream

This wonderful ice cream can be served with the Christmas pudding or mince pies, or on its own at another meal. You can also make it into Christmas pudding ice cream after the festive meal by crumbling leftover pudding into the mixture before freezing. It's a convenient ice cream as it can be made days ahead and served straight from the freezer.

Whisk the egg whites in a large bowl with the salt until they stand in soft peaks. Add the sugar to the water in a saucepan and dissolve over a low heat, then increase the heat and boil fiercely for 3 minutes without stirring. Pour immediately on to the egg whites in a thin stream, whisking all the time with an electric whisk at high speed. Then very gradually whisk in the brandy to taste. Continue whisking until it is really thick and looks like a very smooth meringue mixture.

In a separate bowl, whisk the cream until thick but not too stiff and then gently but thoroughly fold it into the egg white mixture with a metal spoon. Pour the mixture into a large serving bowl and freeze overnight (or for several days if more convenient) before serving.

Dark Chocolate Pudding with Brandied Fruits

SERVES 6-8

4–6 tablespoons peaches, apricots or other fruits in brandy

150g/5oz best bitter chocolate

150g/5oz unsalted butter

150ml/¼ pint warm water

100g/4oz caster sugar

4 large eggs

25g/1oz self-raising flour

½ teaspoon cream of tartar

icing sugar for dusting (optional)

So often the pretty jars of fruits in brandy that one is given at Christmas sit on a shelf for years unopened. Here is something wonderful to do with them. The pudding has a light spongy top and a gooey underneath which blends exquisitely with the fruits. It can be served warm or cold.

Butter a 1.7 litre/3 pint ovenproof dish – a glass one looks best. Slice any large fruits in halves or quarters and spoon the fruit and brandy syrup into the bottom of the prepared dish. Preheat the oven to 200°C/400°F/gas mark 6 and put a roasting pan half full of water on the centre shelf.

Put the chocolate and butter into the top of a double saucepan or a bowl set over a pan of very hot water, making sure the water is not touching the base of the bowl. Stir until melted and smooth. Add the warm water and sugar and stir again until smooth. Pour this mixture into a bigger mixing bowl. Separate the eggs, add the yolks to the bowl and stir with a wooden spoon. Then add the flour and whisk until the mixture is smooth and free of lumps.

Add the cream of tartar to the egg whites and whisk until they stand in soft peaks. Fold them lightly into the chocolate mixture with a metal spoon. Spoon the mixture gradually into the prepared dish on top of the fruits, put the dish into the roasting pan of water and cook for 10 minutes, then lower the oven temperature to 170°C/325°F/gas mark 3 and cook for 30 minutes longer. If you want to serve the pudding cold, sift some icing sugar on to it after it has cooled.

Dome of Cranberry and Chocolate with a Surprise

SERVES 7-8

250g/9oz fresh cranberries

5 tablespoons water

150g/5oz caster sugar

2 tablespoons dark rum

1 lemon

300ml/½ pint double cream

50g/2oz icing sugar, sifted

150g/5oz plain chocolate

Gone are the days when cranberries were used only for cranberry sauce. Their brilliant colour and tart taste make them a bonus for both sweet and savoury dishes.

Here is an exciting end to the festive meal. The surprise in this layered dome is a centre of lemon syllabub. The dome should not be made more than 24 hours in advance, and although it looks elaborate and takes time to chill, the actual preparation is quick.

Put all but 4 or 5 cranberries into a saucepan with 3 tablespoons of the water and the caster sugar. Stir over a medium heat until the sugar has completely dissolved, then cover the pan and simmer gently for 6–8 minutes, until all the berries have popped and the consistency is mushy and very thick. Remove from the heat, stir in the rum and leave to cool completely. Then spoon the mixture into a 1.2 litre/2 pint pudding basin and spread it up the sides to line the basin thickly and as evenly as possible.

Next grate the lemon rind and squeeze the juice of half the lemon. Whisk the cream until it starts to thicken, then whisk in the sifted icing sugar and continue whisking until the cream holds soft but not stiff peaks. Very gradually stir in the lemon juice with a metal spoon, followed by the grated rind. Spoon the syllabub into the cranberry-lined basin and refrigerate for at least 6 hours.

Break the chocolate into small pieces. Put it with the remaining 2 tablespoons of water in a bowl set over a saucepan of very hot, but not boiling, water; make sure the water is not touching the base of the bowl. Stir the chocolate now and then until it has melted smoothly, then remove from the heat and leave to cool for 10–15 minutes. Remove the pudding basin from the fridge, dip it into a sink of very hot water for just a minute or two, and turn out on to a flat serving plate, giving it a firm shake. Then slowly spoon the melted choolate over the cranberry dome as evenly as you can, though it doesn't matter if little bits of cranberry show through towards the bottom. Top the dome with the reserved cranberries and refrigerate again until your 'surprise' is ready to serve.

index